Analyzing Japanese Syntax

JN062467

Analyzing Japanese Syntax

A Generative Perspective

Hideki Kishimoto

HITUZI
SYOBO

Hituzi Syobo Publishing

Yamato bldg. 2f, 2-1-2 Sengoku
    Bunkyo-ku Tokyo, Japan 112-0011
Telephone: +81-3-5319-4916
Facsimile: +81-3-5319-4917
e-mail: toiawase@hituzi.co.jp
http://www.hituzi.co.jp/
postal transfer: 00120-8-142852

ISBN978-4-89476-988-5
Printed in Japan

Contents

PART V
Grammatical Constructions

Preface

This textbook is an introduction to Japanese syntax. It illustrates the core notions entertained in recent treatments of syntax (in generative grammar) and explains how they can be applied in analyzing various grammatical constructions, mainly in Japanese. This textbook aims to explain the basic notions in an accessible way to facilitate the understanding of novices and to show how such notions are relevant for the analysis of Japanese syntax. Most data come from Japanese, but occasionally, a comparison between Japanese and English is made for better understanding of the notions introduced. No background in syntactic analysis is assumed, but general linguistic knowledge at the level of introductory linguistics is desirable. Since many hypotheses on language structures advanced in generative grammar are considered to be universal, it is expected that the particular analysis applied to Japanese (as well as to English) will be extendable, often with some modification, to other languages.

   This textbook consists of 21 chapters, each of which elucidates some core notions in syntactic analysis. Each chapter has a different emphasis, depending on its goal. Accordingly, the chapters are categorized into five groups. The letters A-E, added after each chapter title, indicate the categories, which are classified according to the following criteria:

[A] ...Theoretical and philosophical backgrounds
[B] ...Elementary level
[C] ...Intermediate level
[D] ...Advanced level
[E] ...Analyses of specific grammatical constructions

The level indications allow readers to approach the chapters selectively. Readers who are interested in gaining basic knowledge of generative grammar may be most interested in the chapters marked [A] to [D]. If readers are interested in learning more about linguistic facts, they can start at the [B] level and read up to the [C] level. Readers who would like to know more about recent developments in generative grammar may find the chapters from the [B] level to the [E] level rewarding.

   A remark on the theory introduced here is in order. This textbook introduces the basic ideas and notions of one version of generative grammar theory, but in actuality, many different versions of the proposals are available in the generative literature. This might be a natural consequence of the fact that there has been a long history of rigorous research in generative linguistics, and the availability of alternative analyses may be one of the main reasons why many different theoretical frameworks have branched off from generative grammar. Even within generative grammar, which has a history of over sixty years by now, various important proposals are continuously being advanced. It is not possible to cover all of them, and thus the topics covered are not exhaustive. Instead, some prominent proposals, in particular those advanced in the Government and Binding framework (the Principles and Parameters Approach), and also those in the early Minimalist Program, are elucidated in a concise manner.

Readers interested in the latest developments may need to investigate updated versions of the notions presented here. Nevertheless, many of the notions introduced in the textbook are useful in the analysis of empirical data from individual languages. Theories change and are renovated as new insights are presented in the literature, but once we have a good grip of how the core notions are motivated and introduced in the theory, we can evaluate new proposals without being overwhelmed by them, and it should not be so difficult to keep abreast of shifts and changes in theory.

Japanese is one of the more well-studied languages, with numerous studies having been conducted. Nevertheless, there are many questions that are still open, both theoretically and empirically. There are many aspects of linguistic phenomena in Japanese that merit further exploration. Because of these facts, Japanese continues to be an inspiring object of investigation. It is my sincere hope that more researchers will start researching on Japanese syntax.

Notes on "For Further Research" and Exercises

The "For Further Research" unit at the end of each chapter provides additional materials and information which may be useful for investigating Japanese syntax. In the main texts, important terms and notions are introduced often without their precise formal definitions, but as further information, some formal definitions, which may be useful for those who would like to know their precise details are given in Section (A) of this unit. Additional notes on theoretical analyses, as well as some issues on Japanese syntax that might be worth further exploring, are provided in this section as well. Some related topics for further investigations and prospective research questions, which are intended to provide motivation for further syntactic research, are briefly addressed in Section (B).

In addition, a set of exercises for checking the reader's understanding, as well as answer keys for them, are available on the web page of the NINJAL project on parsed corpora (http://npcmj.ninjal.ac.jp/explorer/syntax_exercises/). These exercises are divided into basic/elementary, intermediate, and advanced levels, and may be used as materials for classroom instruction, as well as for self-teaching. Advanced exercises are provided for readers who wish to think about the syntactic analysis of naturally occurring data in Japanese corpora, which are searchable using the search engines available at the project webpage.

Acknowledgments

This textbook was developed in collaboration with the NPCMJ corpus project at NINJAL(http://npcmj.ninjal.ac.jp/?lang=en). The primary aim of this project is to promote research in Japanese syntax through providing an annotated corpus of written and spoken Japanese. Another important task of the project is to develop education materials. As a main collaborator of this section of the project, I engaged in writing this textbook, which is intended as a study guide (in generative grammar) for those who would like to start research on Japanese syntax.

In the course of writing this book, I have benefitted from discussions with many people. In particular, I would like to express my thanks to the following people (many of whom are involved in the textbook project directly or indirectly): Prashant Pardeshi, Yusuke Kubota, Stephan Horn, Caroline Heycock, Yasuhito Kido, Takaya Yamaguchi, Akitoshi Maeda, Yoichiro Tanaka, Mina Funakura, Kazushige Moriyama, Naohiro Otani, Koharu Morimoto, Satoshi Yatsunami, Shingo Okubo, Daiki Endo, Jun Nakai, Yomogi Ura and other NPCMJ project members. I am also grateful to John Haig for providing numerous suggestions, hints, and comments, all of which were extremely helpful for improving the style and the contents of the present book.

This work was supported by the NINJAL project "Development of and Research with a Parsed Corpus of Japanese" and also by JSPS Kakenhi Grants JP16K02628 and JP20K00605.

List of Abbreviations

1	first person	PP	postpositional phrase/
2	second person		prepositional phrase
A	adjective	PRT	particle
ABL	ablative	PRS	present/non-past
ACC	accusative	PST	past
ADV	adverb	Q	question marker
AUX	auxiliary	RECP	reciprocal
C	complementizer	RelC	relative clause
CAUS	causative	S	sentence/subject
CL	classifier	SP	secondary predicate
COP	copula	SUBJ	subject
COND	conditional	T	tense
CONJ	conjunctive/conjunction	TOP	topic
CP	complementizer phrase	TP	tense phrase
D	determiner	UG	universal grammar
DAT	dative	V	verb
DP	determiner phrase	VN	verbal noun
ECM	exceptional case marking	vP	little verb phrase
FL	faculty of language	VP	verb phrase
GEN	genitive		
GER	gerundive		
HON	honorific		
INS	instrumental		
LF	logical form		
LOC	locative		
NP	noun phrase		
NEG	negative		
NOM	nominative		
NOMLZ	nominalizer		
O	object		
OBJ	object		
OBL	oblique		
P	postposition/preposition		
PASS	passive		
PF	phonetic form/		
	phonological form		
PL	plural		
POTEN	potential		

PART I

Theoretical Foundations

CHAPTER 1

Scientific Approach to Language [A]

1.1 What Is Language?

Anyone interested in the study of language or in learning about languages (including Japanese) might ask the following question: "What is language?" Although it is not easy to give a ready answer to this question, it is worthwhile to think about it for a moment. Language is often said to be a vehicle of thought since we can express any kind of idea or thought verbally. Superficially, **human language** looks similar to the animal communication systems displayed by some animals (like chimpanzees, dolphins, or bees). Animal communication systems make use of a variety of signs, including vocal sounds and bodily movements. Nevertheless, animal communication lacks a key feature of human language: it cannot create new signs in response to newly encountered circumstances. In this respect, human language substantially differs from animal communication, and thus it is plausible to say that only humans use language. In effect, the possession of language is the most prominent attribute of human beings, and it is often claimed that language is what makes us human.

For the purpose of identifying the quintessential properties of language, it may be instructive to observe first how language is used in our community. One commonly discussed view is that language is a means (or tool) of communication. It is easy for us to communicate with each other if we are the members of a community where everyone speaks the same language. On the other hand, we often confront great difficulty in conveying messages when we travel and visit a place where people speak a language we are not familiar with. In terms of its function, language primarily serves as a medium of communication, i.e. a mode of conveying messages between us. Although it is beyond doubt that this is one prominent aspect of language, this function alone cannot provide an answer to the question why we can exchange novel ideas or thoughts via language. To find a real answer to the question, it is necessary to uncover the precise mechanism of how language works, and the real challenge is to account for what makes it possible at all for us to transmit and exchange ideas and thoughts in such an unbelievably precise manner through the mediation of human language.

To get closer to the true nature of language, let us consider what underlies language that guarantees this amazingly accurate transmission of information. At first sight, this would appear to be a difficult philosophical question, but actually the answer is rather straightforward. Human language has a highly sophisticated and elaborated system, which is called **grammar**. This system allows us to express our ideas or thoughts in the form of linguistic expressions, no matter how complex they may be. The term "grammar" here refers to the rules regulating how expressions (or sentences) are constructed by combining words. To exchange complex ideas using a particular language, we need to know the rules of the language in a precise manner. Importantly, every single member of the community needs to share exactly the same knowledge about the rules of the language; otherwise, we would never expect to be able to communicate with each other (accurately) using the language.

In the following discussions, we will delineate a hypothesis about the grammar of human language—**knowledge of language**. Before embarking on this enterprise, however, we need to be a bit more precise about what is meant by "grammar" because this term is used in a variety of different ways. The term "grammar" is sometimes used to refer to not only our linguistic knowledge but also operational systems (or programs) necessary for running computers, i.e. "artificial" languages. Needless to say, at least for the purposes of this textbook, the term "grammar" is intended to refer to the rule system of **natural language** (or human language) wired in our brain, and not artificial languages.

Note also that the grammar of language we are talking about differs substantially from so-called "prescriptive grammars," e.g. the English grammar or Japanese grammar taught for educational purposes in schools. Our investigation aims at uncovering the tacit knowledge of language in our mind. It is important to observe that prescriptive grammars do not necessarily match our linguistic knowledge. Prescriptive grammars often provide norms or standards that we are told we should follow to produce linguistic expressions in a correct and proper manner, which, in actuality, does not necessarily reflect the knowledge of language in our mind.

Arguably, what allows us to speak a language comes from the functions of our brain, and only human beings have the ability to manipulate languages. The human cognitive system that makes up this unique linguistic ability is called **Faculty of Language (FL)**. The ultimate research goal of **generative grammar** is to explain why we have linguistic intuitions as we do; i.e. generative grammar seeks to find an answer to the question of what the Faculty of Language is like, and to account for how and why only humans are endowed with the ability to acquire (and use) a language.

1.2 Linguistic Data: What We Need to Look at

As noted above, the ultimate goal of our linguistic research is to uncover the system of human language. How can we accomplish this? If the grammar of human language is wired in our brains as we have remarked above, one might think that one handy way to check how language works would be by observing our brain tissues directly, which may be possible if a piece of the skull were removed from our head by surgery. Nevertheless, there is little hope of finding out about the internal system of human language with this kind of method; it is not possible to learn precisely how language works by just observing our brain tissues. Even if such observations of brain tissues were possible, it would be unethical to remove human skull bones for the purpose of linguistic research, although a qualified surgeon might be able to perform this kind of operation in treatment of brain damage. Recently, fMRIs (functional magnetic resonance imaging), which can visualize how brains react to various stimuli, have been used in the study of language, but still, this does not enable us to directly look into the internal system of human language, and we can only infer how language works from the reactions of our brains to stimuli.

The rule system (or the grammar) of human language has properties analogous to those found in computer programs in that inputs are changed to linguistic expressions or signs through certain specified algorithms, i.e. when we say something, our thought (the input) is converted to a sequence of words according to grammatical rules, and then the string of words is pronounced as its output. Grammar is an abstract system, which constitutes a black box. Accordingly, just as it is not possible to tell what kind of program is installed in a computer merely by checking the hardware (or its parts), so too we cannot tell what kind of rule system, i.e. grammar, we have in our brain by directly observing human brain tissues. (Of course, no one knows who invented human language; even if we can identify the inventor, we cannot directly ask him about what it is like and how it works.)

Owing to the limitations on research methods, all that we can do is observe the outputs the grammar of human language produces together with its assumed inputs. Then we can analyze and reconstruct the grammar based on its products, so as to know what kind of rule system is available in our brain. There is a huge variety of linguistic expressions that can be used for this purpose, including poems, literary works, news reports, talks over the phone, or chats that people have on the street. As a matter of fact, we have an essentially unlimited number of speech samples to choose from. In theory, we can use any type of data (or speech) to investigate the grammatical system of human language, but it is also true that not all linguistic data are equally useful for our investigation.

Let us discuss a little more how linguistic data can be analyzed. First of all, a sentence is defined as a group of words that are combined to form a meaning, that is, as the minimal linguistic unit expressing a complete thought. Accordingly, sentences are generally used as primary data for syntactic analyses. Of course, this does not exclude the option of using other kinds of data, such as longer texts or shorter non-sentential elements, for the purposes of our research. We can in principle pick out whatever range of data we desire, as long as it serves our purpose of investigating the nature of language.

The term "language" has been used in different senses even when referring to human language; in particular, it is claimed in generative grammar that language can be either **I-language** or **E-language**. (I-language and E-language are the abbreviations of 'Internalized language' and 'Externalized language,' respectively.) Essentially, I-language refers to the knowledge or the internal system of language in our mind. E-language refers to the linguistic phenomena observed in the external world, which could be actual linguistic expressions that we routinely come across, for instance. The question that immediately arises is which type of language will be the object of our inquiry. Given the ultimate goal of research in the paradigm of generative grammar, the target of our investigation is, of course, I-language.

Despite the conceptual distinction between I-language and E-language, it is not easy in practice to draw a clear line between the two, owing to their close affinity. It is true, however, that E-language is, at least in part, a product of I-language. Then, by virtue of this fact, we are entitled to look into E-language to discover the nature of I-language. Nevertheless, E-language is not always a faithful reflection of the output of I-language, i.e. observable speech acts are not necessarily genuine products of I-language. Utterances we produce, which represent E-language, are often incomplete and/or contain errors; in fact, we often encounter speech fragments, resulting from inattentiveness, or a sudden change of mind in the middle of a conversation. Even worse, when serious errors are included, our utterances could be far from what one would expect as products of I-language. A lot of distracting factors are involved in our daily speech, which would be an obstacle for research on I-language, and we cannot solely rely on such speech products (i.e. E-language) for our research. To investigate the rule system of language (i.e. I-language), the distracting factors ("noise") need to be removed from raw speech data in order to discover the nature of I-language. This process of creating ideal cases for scientific research is called **idealization**. Although it might sound like a difficult task, it is one of the routine procedures that we go through when running scientific experiments, i.e. this kind of experimental method, which makes use of carefully designed/controlled data, is fairly common in scientific research.

Linguistics is often claimed to be an **empirical science** (as opposed to a formal science), in the sense that it seeks to find a principled account for phenomena that we can perceive directly. In particular, generative grammar, which is seen as a branch of cognitive science, places a particular emphasis on conducting research with the scientific method. Succinctly put, any research can be scientific if conducted in accordance with the procedure outlined in (1).

(1)   observation   →   hypothesis   --›   prediction   →   verification
                              ↑_____|

The scientific method in (1) involves the following steps: (A) observing data, (B) forming a hypothesis (or a generalization) based on the observations, (C) making predictions based on the hypothesis, and (D) verifying the hypothesis by checking whether its predictions are correct. If the original hypothesis turns out not to be appropriate, the hypothesis will be modified; it is also possible to replace it with an entirely new hypothesis. In syntax, the procedures concern constructing a hypothesis or a model concerning sentence structure.

The routine procedure depicted in (1) tells us nothing about the instruments that might be used in scientific research. One might imagine that, just as a high-resolution telescope is used for observing the cosmos (in astronomy), and an electric microscope for watching atoms (in atomic physics), so high-tech devices are necessary for scientific inquiry in linguistics. This is not true, at least in the study of syntax, because we can conduct our research by observing the linguistic phenomena around us, which are the products of I-language. In many cases, we only need a sheet of paper and a pencil to record/document the data for analysis.

One fairly common method for data collection in generative grammar is to resort to the native speaker's **intuition** (also called 'introspection'). Introspective data are obtained via the native speaker's judging whether sentences are acceptable or not by comparing them with the internalized grammar of his/her language. For example, a native speaker of Japanese can tell that while (2a) is a good sentence in Japanese, (2b) is a bad sentence (and in fact, is an unintelligible mishmash).

(2)   a. Kore-wa   wakariyasuku   kak-are-ta   hon   da.
         this-TOP   lucidly   write-PASS-PST   book   COP
         'This is a book that was written lucidly.'
      b. *Kore-wa   kak-are-ta   wakariyasuku   hon   da.
         this-TOP   write-PASS-PST   lucidly   book   COP

(The asterisk (*) placed at the front of the sentence in (2b) is the conventional sign used in works on syntax to indicate that the sentence is judged unacceptable (or **ungrammatical**). On the other hand, the example in (2a) without the asterisk is a good or grammatical sentence by convention.) The surface difference between the two sentences in (2) lies solely in the position of *wakari-yasuku* 'lucidly' and *kak-are-ta* 'was written'. In light of this fact, we can put forth a hypothesis; for instance, we could claim that the deviance of (2b) is simply caused by the reversal of the order of the two phrases. However, this hypothesis cannot be correct. A glance at the examples in (3) shows that Japanese does not have a general ban on the switching of word order.

(3) a. Ano   hito-ga   hon-o   yon-da.
         that   man-NOM   book-ACC   read-PST
         'That man read the book.'
     b. Hon-o   ano   hito-ga   yon-da.
         book-ACC   that   man-NOM   read-PST
         'The book, that man read.'

Japanese has SOV as its basic word order (i.e. the subject (S) marked with nominative case is followed by an object (O) marked with accusative case and the verb (V) in linear order). Accordingly, it can be postulated that (3a) is a basic clause, and that (3b) is derived from (3a) by reversing the order of *ano hito-ga* and *hon-o*. This kind of word order change is frequently observed because Japanese has a grammatical rule permuting arguments, which is often called "scrambling".

By comparing the data in (2) and (3), it should be apparent that (2b) is not excluded as unacceptable on the grounds that Japanese has a rule blocking a change in word order. Thus, we need to come up with a new hypothesis (or modify the old one) to account for the facts. When we start working on this task, we will follow the procedure for revision outlined in (1); first we observe some further data, and then devise an improved or a new hypothesis on the basis of the observations. After that, we check or verify the adequacy of the proposed hypothesis. If it turns out that this revised hypothesis does not work or if further revision is required, we will begin another round of the procedure for an even better hypothesis to account for the facts, as depicted in (1).

In conducting scientific research, it is important to formulate a hypothesis that can be verified, i.e. a hypothesis that can be proven to be correct or incorrect. Since hypotheses are verified by running additional experiments that specifically test for the predictions based on them, we need to formulate hypotheses that make a number of clear predictions. It is also necessary that the results of the experiments be consistent; the experiments are not reliable unless the same results are obtained every time we conduct the same experiments. A good hypothesis is **falsifiable**, which means that the hypothesis must be sufficiently clear, so that we can determine whether it is correct or not. A thumb of the rule here is that the higher the degree of **falsifiability**, the better the hypothesis is. The impetus behind this is the idea that we are highly unlikely to have a perfect hypothesis initially, so we need to refine the quality of the hypothesis through its examination and, if necessary, revision in a scientific way.

When running experiments to test hypotheses in syntax (within the framework of generative grammar), native speakers' judgments of acceptability more often than not provide an important key to uncovering the nature of I-language. This is precisely because there is little hope of knowing the precise system of human language merely by looking at good or grammatical sentences that are available around us. Unacceptable or ungrammatical sentences crucial for confirming the adequacy of a hypothesis are generally not produced at all in ordinary speech, except perhaps by mistake. Thus, even if we check thousands and thousands of sentences in newspapers, there will be no guarantee that we can find the one single crucial example needed to verify the proposed hypothesis. For this reason, we often ask native speakers for judgments on carefully constructed (and sometimes ungrammatical) sentences that enable us to check the validity of our hypothesis and see whether the predictions are borne out on the basis of these sentences.

For Further Research

(A) The concepts of I-language and E-language are first discussed in Chomsky (1986). There are a number of research questions that need to be addressed in the investigation of the knowledge of language. Chomsky lists the following research questions for linguistic investigations.

(i)   a. What constitutes knowledge of language?
        b. How is such knowledge of language acquired?
        c. How is knowledge of language put to use?

The discussion of the first question figures prominently in current research on syntax in generative grammar.

(B-1) Japanese school children learn the columns of the multiplication table up to 9×9 by memorizing fixed expressions (called "kuku" (九九)). Some of the fixed expressions are given in (ii).

(ii)   ni-nin-ga si;   ni-san-ga roku;   ni-si-ga   hati;   ni-go zyuu;   ni-roku
        2×2-NOM 4   2×3-NOM 6   2×4-NOM 8   2×5 10   2×6
        zyuuni....
        12
        '2 times 2 is 4; 2 times 3 is 6; 2 times 4 is 8; 2 times 5 is 10; 2 times 6 is
        12...'

In (ii), multiplication operations (with multiplicands and multipliers) are expressed as arguments, and their products are given as (nominal) predicates. Some arguments are marked with nominative case, but others are not. On the basis of (ii), formulate as many hypotheses as possible that can account for the case-marking pattern of the examples at hand. Extend your observations, and check which hypothesis best describes the full set of *kuku* data. (Exactly how other columns in the multiplication table are expressed can easily be checked by searching for the *kuku* table over the Internet.)

(B-2) We can easily find linguistic expressions around us whose syntactic behavior looks rule-governed. Choose some set of such expressions and formulate more than one hypothesis to account for the regularity governing them. Then, evaluate the hypotheses and determine which one is most plausible by checking them against some further data available around you.

CHAPTER 2

Rationalism versus Empiricism [A]

2.1 Some Mysteries Escaping Our Attention

When we look around, we easily recognize the fact that our communities are flooded with linguistic signs. Linguistic expressions produced by human language are found so commonly that we are often not conscious of their existence. We usually take it for granted that language can produce an unlimited number of linguistic messages, but how can this be possible? This ability is not immediately obvious, and a little reflection shows that this is one mysterious aspect of human language. In this chapter, let us consider some mysteries surrounding language that often go unnoticed.

To begin, recall that only humans have the ability to acquire a language: every human acquires at least one language as his/her native tongue, but no other animals are capable of acquiring a language (see Chapter 1). It is important to keep in mind here that some social animals (chimpanzees as well as many species of birds) use "calls" to communicate with each other. But the repertoire of their calls is severely limited, and only a small, fixed set of calls are used in their communication. Moreover, such social animals cannot create new signs to communicate in new circumstances. Human language crucially differs in this respect since we can create messages to convey whatever message we may have. This is due to the fact that human language is a rule system that can produce (new) complex signs by combining discrete signs.

Now, the question that arises is: Why is it that humans are distinguished from other animals in their possession of language? An answer to this question in generative grammar is that humans, but not other animals, are endowed with a **Faculty of Language**—a mental organ that enables us to acquire a langauge, developed perhaps by chance in the process of our evolution. Thanks to the Faculty of Language, any human child can acquire his/her language through a short period of exposure to it. Since other animals do not have this ability, they cannot acquire the kind of language that humans use. This amounts to saying that language is specific to humans, i.e. language is an endowment unique to human beings. The hypothesis that humans are born with an innate knowledge of the grammar of language is often referred to as the **innateness hypothesis.**

There is a group of scientists who are suspicious of the idea that only humans are endowed with the ability to acquire language. Some of these scientists have attempted to disprove this idea by conducting experiments with chimpanzees to see whether they can learn and speak a (human) language. In spite of the attempts by the scientists skeptical about the innateness hypothesis, none of the experiments on chimpanzees so far have been reported to be successful; they have not provided any meaningful results or conclusive evidence showing that chimpanzees can acquire a language in just the same way as humans. In the absence of definite evidence showing that other animals can acquire a language, at least at present, there is no reason to abandon the initial hypothesis that only human beings can acquire a language (although, in the future, we might find evidence showing that the contrary is true).

Chimpanzees are not radically different from humans physically; they have hands, legs, eyes, ears, etc., just like humans. Chimpanzees can manipulate tools and instruments, and we are sometimes surprised to see behaviors on their part demonstrating their intelligence. In point of fact, they appear to be much smarter in some respects than human infants who have just begun to speak a language. It was recently reported that the genetic difference between humans and chimpanzees is as little as 1.23 %, i.e. we share almost 99 % of our genes with chimpanzees. Interestingly, this ratio is smaller than the genetic difference between zebras and horses, which is only 1.5 %. Physically, the only prominent visible difference between the two kinds of animal is that while zebras have stripes on their body, horses do not. Given these facts, it is quite natural to wonder how this small genetic difference leads to a big gap in the ability to acquire a language, an ability that distinguishes humans from chimpanzees (as well as other animals).

Of course, the innateness hypothesis is not the only possible view of **language acquisition.** It could also be hypothesized that human children come into possession of language solely by way of learning. In point of fact, the idea that language is a kind of acquired habit that must be learned by studying or through experiences is also found in the literature. This idea is based on the premise that our brain starts out, as it were, as a "blank slate," on which nothing is written. This view is referred to as **empiricism,** which essentially says that a language can only be learned through experiences. Standing in contrast is the view called **rationalism,** which says that language is built upon reason, and therefore innate, i.e. language is one of the abilities with which only humans, but not other animals, are endowed. Generative grammar adopts the second view. There are a number of *a priori* reasons for favoring the second view over the first.

2.2 The Secret Revealed

Since every human can acquire a language, it is fair to say, as postulated by the innateness hypothesis, that we are endowed with an innate (or genetic) mechanism that allows us to acquire a language. The idea lying behind this innateness hypothesis becomes clearer if we consider how children develop their language abilities. Needless to say, babies cannot speak a language when they are born. (Incidentally, you might have encountered an anecdote of a noble man who began to speak the instant he was born, but this cannot be true if he was a human.) Typologically, a broad range of variation is observed among languages (consider the grammatical differences between English and Japanese). Interestingly, despite the fact that the world's languages appear to be so diverse and differ widely in their complexities, the process as well as the speed of language acquisition by children is surprisingly uniform across languages.

Children start making cooing and babbling sounds three or four months after birth. It is around 12 months of age that children begin to produce intelligible words. At this stage, children's verbal expressions are limited to one-word utterances, although a certain degree of minor individual variation might be observed. (Often, their utterances still include babbling, so we need to be attentive to understand what they say.) This period of child language development is called the **one-word stage**. Since sentences are not constructed at the one-word stage, we cannot really tell whether the children at this stage possess what can be regarded as grammar (for obvious reasons). About six months later (approximately in the period of 18 to 24 months after birth), they reach the stage where they can produce what can be regarded as sentences (or quasi-sentences) by combining words. Children at this stage can generally combine no more than two words to produce a sentence, and thus this period of child language is referred to as the **two-word stage**. (1) provides a sample of utterances elicited from a child acquiring Japanese at the two-word stage, more precisely, at the age of 18 months.

(1)   a. Aaka   buubuu!   b. Moo   tyoo.
          red   car   still   more
          '(A) red car!'   '(Give me) some more.'
      c. Buubuu   kita.   d. Aikuen   kuu.
          car   came   nursery go
          '(A) car came.'   '(I will) go to the nursery.'
      e. Otete   pai.
          hand   full
          '(My) hands (are) full.'

After the two-word stage, children begin to display their rich grammatical knowledge of their mother tongue. Children who have passed 30 months after birth are able to produce fairly complex utterances with inflections (and agreements). (2) is a sample of utterances uttered by the same child that produced the utterances in (1).

(2) a. Otoosan   pekepon   ar-u.
        father   cross.out   be-PRS
        'Father is no good.'

     b. Okaasan-ga   moo-tyotto   nenne   si-toku   yuu-te-hat-ta.
        mother-NOM   a.little-more sleep   do-put   say-GER-HON-PST
        'Mother said that (she would) have a sleep a little more.'

     c. FATHER: Kore-wa   toosuto.
                        this-TOP   toast
                        'This is toast.'

        CHILD: Kore-wa   syokupan   to   iu   mono   ya.
                        this-TOP   white.bread   that   say   thing   PRT
                        'This is what is called 'white bread'.'

There are qualitative differences between the utterances in (1) and those in (2). Just one year after the child produced the utterances in (1), she articulated the utterances in (2), which were formed by combining multiple words. The utterances given in (2) are by far more complex than those in (1). Note that when the child produced the utterances in (2), she was still in the process of acquiring Japanese (the Kansai dialect of Japanese) as her native tongue, and the grammar was not yet perfect; she was capable of using a Kansai dialect honorific form, as in (2b), but the way she used it is somehow a bit strange.

A number of interesting facts are observed in language acquisition. Young children everywhere acquire languages at almost the same pace even though they may be exposed to languages that appear to differ in complexity. The children will eventually come to know every detail of the grammar of the language they are acquiring. The result of language acquisition is always perfect even without explicit instruction by parents or people around them. Children can create and use various kinds of constructions even though they are not aware of the precise grammatical rules for constructing them. This stands in stark contrast with processes that require learning. For instance, children would never know the four arithmetic operations of addition, subtraction, multiplication, and division unless they are explicitly taught. The learning process is not always perfect: some children are likely to be poor in performing certain arithmetic calculations even if they know how to calculate.

Also notable is the fact that there is a **critical period** for language acquisition, just like our bodily organs, such as eyes and ears. Generally speaking, our bodily organs can fully develop their functions if they receive appropriate stimulus in a critical period. Our eyes begin to work after they are exposed to light, which serves as the stimulus. If, for any reason, children are not exposed to light during the critical period, it would be extremely difficult, or even impossible, for them to have proper eyesight. To a large extent, this holds true of language acquisition; children are not able to fully develop their first language after they have passed their "critical period." If children fail to receive the stimulus in a timely manner, they face extreme difficulty in acquiring a language, if, in fact, it is not totally impossible. The existence of a critical period for language acquisition can be inferred from a report on Genie, a girl who was not able to fully develop her first language due to the deprivation of the stimulus at the critical period resulting from social isolation and abuse (as well as cases of "feral" children like Victor of Aveyron).

Even by observing children around us, we can find evidence suggesting that language acquisition does not depend on learning. In the first place, adults do not necessarily speak to children in an optimal way for the purpose of language acquisition. Adults often speak to children using simplified expressions that differ from adult speech, i.e. their utterances (directed toward children) are often imperfect or are not formed properly from the viewpoint of adult grammar. Furthermore, their linguistic expressions are likely to contain errors, improper omissions, fragments, slips of the tongue, and the like. Secondly, if children learn their language by hearing imperfect or incorrect sentences, there would be very little hope of their attaining perfection, as repeated exposure to incorrect sentences would put them in danger of learning the grammar incorrectly—but this simply does not happen. Somehow, they eventually come to possess the grammar of the language perfectly, without regard to the quality of the adult speech that serves as stimulus for their language acquisition. Young children can have knowledge of language even without instruction (by parents and other people) and there is little individual variation in the speed of developing the grammar of their first languages. This suggests that children are equipped with a Faculty of Language innately as a mental/biological mechanism.

Under the empiricism view, language is a product of learning, which amounts to saying that the input (i.e. the stimulus) is straightforwardly reflected in the children's knowledge of grammar, as depicted in (3).

(3)   stimulus   →   language

Obviously, the facts of children acquiring their first languages cannot be accounted for if, as the empiricists claim, knowledge of the grammar of a language is obtained solely by learning. On the other hand, the rationalist view, held in generative grammar, maintains that we humans innately possess a Faculty of Language, i.e. we are endowed with the knowledge of language hereditarily.

(4)   stimulus   →   Faculty of Language (FL)   →   language

Under the rationalism view, the stimulus to which children are exposed serves as a trigger to activate the Faculty of Language, by way of which children construct the grammar of the language spoken around them. The children do not come into possession of knowledge of language simply by the process of learning; rather it is innately given, and this knowledge of grammar, referred to as **Universal Grammar (UG)**, is installed in our brain as an initial state. UG eventually evolves into individual languages like English and Japanese, with exposure to different types of stimulus (i.e. various sorts of linguistic expressions produced in the community where the children acquiring their language are raised).

Furthermore, there is evidence that children construct the grammar of their language without memorizing the adults' utterances. For example, observe that the utterance in (5), which was produced by a child at two years and a half of age, is not well-formed from the viewpoint of adult grammar of Japanese.

(5)   Okaasan   kore   oi-te   ppanasi.
      mother   this   put-GER   let
      'Mother keeps leaving this.'

At this stage, the child, who was in the process of acquiring Japanese, appeared to know how the verb *oku* inflects when combined with the gerundive *-te*, but did not have the knowledge that a *-te* gerundive verb cannot be combined with *ppanasi* to produce a compound verb, as shown by the fact that *oi-te ppanasi* in (5) was uttered instead of the well-formed *oki-ppanasi* [put-let]. It is difficult to imagine that the child heard this type of ungrammatical sentence before. Rather, it is more likely that the utterance was produced by the grammatical rules that the child constructed in the course of language acquisition, which are not yet correct or complete from a viewpoint of adult grammar.

Apparently, children acquiring a language produce utterances following grammatical rules that differ from adult grammar. Parents rarely tell their children whether their utterances are grammatical or not (from the viewpoint of adult grammar). Interestingly, children do not listen to the parents even if they are told that their utterances are not grammatical. Nevertheless, the production of ungrammatical sentences does not last long, and, despite the fact that they initially make grammatical errors in producing sentences, children acquire the (correct) grammar of adult language perfectly in a relatively short period of time. For example, young children acquiring Japanese often make a persistent and incorrect choice between the inanimate verb *aru* and animate verb *iru*, producing utterances like *Wanwan aru*. [doggie be.INANIMATE] 'There is a dog.' instead of *Wanwan iru*. [doggie be.ANIMATE]) even if they are told that this use of *aru* is not grammatical. Nevertheless, this kind of grammatically incorrect utterance disappears completely in due course. This provides another piece of evidence suggesting the adequacy of the hypothesis in generative grammar that the grammatical knowledge of language originates from the Faculty of Language, the biologically given mental organ, and that children do not come into possession of their first languages solely through learning or experiences, although input is required to allow them to tailor their grammar to that of the language they are acquiring.

Adult speech serving as input to the children's language acquisition is known to be notoriously incomplete or imperfect. Children are capable of acquiring the highly complex rule system of their language perfectly even though they may not necessarily receive stimuli in an optimal way. The impoverished nature of the input available for language acquisition poses a problem referred to as **the poverty of stimulus**. The question of how we know so much about the grammar of language with so little and imperfect experience is known as **Plato's problem**, named after the Greek philosopher Plato. (Plato's *Meno* includes a Socratic dialogue with one of Meno's slaves, which provides an argument for the human's inborn knowledge.) Under the rational view, language acquisition is guided by the Faculty of Language—a cognitive ability rooted in biology.

For Further Research

(A) One of the major research questions in generative grammar is how we are able to acquire a language. Children acquiring a language construct their grammar, which may differ significantly from adult grammar, in the course of language development. Data from children in the process of acquiring a language often offer evidence allowing us to verify some linguistic hypotheses, which cannot be found if we look at only adult language. Some anecdotes on children acquiring English are discussed in Pinker (1994). There are several open databases available for use in child language acquisition studies, one of which is CHILDES (Child Language Data Exchange System). This database can be found on the TalkBank project website by Carnegie Mellon University.

(B-1) The example in (i) is an utterance produced by a child of two and a half years old and is deviant from the perspective of adult grammar.

(i) Simare-nai.   Okaasan,   simat-te.
     close-NEG   mother   close-GER
     'Close not. Mom, close!'

By the two underlined words in (i), the child intended to mean 'close (tr.)', but the verb forms are not correct. What kind grammar is the child likely to have as her grammar at this stage? What would be the grammatical rule that gives rise to the utterance in (i)?

(B-2) The utterance given in (ii), which was elicited from a child acquiring Japanese, is not grammatical by the adult grammar of Japanese.

(ii) Siroi   kami-ni   siroi   mazikku-sika   kakeru   n   da   yo.
      white   paper-on white   marker.pen-only   write.can   PRT   COP   PRT
      '(I) can write only with the white pen on the white paper.'

In this particular case, the use of *sika* is deviant. What kind of grammatical rule did the child have at the time when it was uttered? How does this child's grammar differ from the adult grammar of Japanese?

CHAPTER 3

Universal Grammar [A]

3.1 Language as a Creative System

We are capable of generating and understanding an unlimited number of novel sentences, all created by following the algorithms (or rules) specified by the grammar of the language we know (even if we are not aware of their existence). We constantly encounter new situations not merely on some special occasions but also in our daily life. Nevertheless, we have no difficulty in coping with them because language allows us to express and understand new, novel thoughts and respond verbally to new situations. The kind of linguistic creativity in linguistic production and comprehension that makes it possible for us to deal with new experiences is often mentioned as the creative aspect of language use. This flexibility could not be attained if we simply replicated sentences stored in our memory.

Language has a grammatical system in which sentences are constructed in accordance with specified grammatical rules. This can easily be seen by the fact that we can create infinitely long sentences, as exemplified in (1).

(1) a. Mari-ga   ki-ta.
         Mari-NOM   come-PST
         'Mari came.'
     b. [Mari-ga   ki-ta   to]   Ken-ga   it-ta.
         Mari-NOM   come-PST   that   Ken-NOM   say-PST
         'Ken said that Mari came.'
     c. [[Mari-ga   ki-ta   to]   Ken-ga   it-ta   to]
         Mari-NOM   come-PST   that   Ken-NOM   say-PST   that
         Eri-ga   omot-ta.
         Eri-NOM   think-PST
         'Eri thought that Ken said that Mari came.'

d. [[[Mari-ga   ki-ta   to]   Ken-ga   it-ta   to]
    Mari-NOM   come-PST   that Ken-NOM say-PST   that
    Eri-ga   omot-ta   to]   Masao-ga   kangae-ta.
    Eri-NOM   think-PST   that   Masao-NOM   consider-PST
    'Masao considered that Eri thought that Ken said that Mari came.'

(1a) is a sentence that stands on its own. This sentence can be placed inside another sentence, as in (1b), i.e. it can be used as an embedded clause if the quote marker *to* 'that' is added to it. Since the embedding rule may apply iteratively (by **recursion**), we can create (1c) from (1b), and (1d) from (1c), and so on. In theory, if the application of this rule continued ad infinitum, infinitely long sentences would be derived. This proves that sentences are not simply memorized but are constructed according to the grammatical rules of the language. If language is a rule system, it makes sense that we can easily understand a very long sentence that we have never heard or encountered before (although there may be physical limitations such as memory or attention span that restrict our actual processing).

As discussed previously, there is good reason to believe that only human beings are endowed with the ability to acquire language. Since other animals cannot acquire a language, at least in the same way that humans can, we can think of the Faculty of Language as an inborn language program encoded in our brain, and this program is the device that children use for their language acquisition. The grammar of language before developing into individual languages (like Japanese and English) is called **Universal Grammar (UG)**. This is, as it were, the initial state of language. One of the important goals of research in generative grammar is discovering what UG is like. This is not a simple enterprise because of the complex nature of language, but a hypothesis has been proposed, formulated on the basis of indirect evidence.

To be a little more specific, language, which is a highly complex system, has the important property that children can acquire it without explicit instruction. Furthermore, the process and speed of acquisition do not vary across languages. On the other hand, it is also true that the grammars of individual languages differ quite widely, and that individual languages often look totally different (such as Japanese, English, Swahili, etc.). These facts suggest that languages, which are derived from UG, appear to be furnished with the two conflicting properties of **uniformity** and **variation**. To account for this paradoxical aspect of language, it is hypothesized that knowledge of language (UG), an innate biological program, has a predetermined core, so that all natural languages have essentially the same system, but there is also a part of grammar that needs to be fixed or modified by the stimulus or input received.

If the fundamental part of the grammar of human language does not vary across languages, UG must be constant, in large part, but there must be a variable part that allows us to produce a wide range of language variations. The constant part is called **principles** and the variable part **parameters**. Thus, UG can be thought of as consisting of these two components, as in (2).

(2)   UG = Principles + Parameters

Principles, the core part of UG, cannot be altered, presumably because they are pre-determined (genetically). During the process of language acquisition, parameters are set based on the input to which children acquiring a language are exposed, i.e. the language spoken around them. If parameter setting is done by a simple procedure, like flipping up or down a light switch, we can provide a natural account for the fact that children can acquire their languages without difficulty in a short period of time, as well as the fact that the acquisition process is uniform across languages.

Children starting the process of language acquisition will observe the individual language people around them speak. This linguistic experience serves as the stimulus to Faculty of Language (FL), which constitutes UG, and, as a consequence, FL produces the grammar of the individual language as its output, as (3) illustrates.

(3)   stimulus   →   FL (UG)   →   individual language

Language acquisition requires exposure to the stimulus (input) due to the presence of parameters that need to be fixed. The language that children acquire changes depending on their linguistic environment (like the body color of chameleons). On the other hand, since the large part of UG, i.e. principles, is constant and does not vary across languages, children can come to know the grammar in a very short period of time.

Note that observable linguistic phenomena are the products of the grammar of an individual language developed out of UG. What we hear or speak is produced by the rules of the individual language, but strictly speaking, the grammar of an individual language is not UG by itself. Given that we only have access to the products of individual languages, our quest of UG is essentially an attempt to uncover the initial state of the program (UG) built into the human brain, by observing the external linguistic phenomena which are closely related, but not identical, to the products of the internalized grammar of individual languages, which comes from UG. Since we cannot directly view the biologically given program of UG, it is easy to imagine how difficult it is to achieve the ultimate goal of the research program.

UG is the initial state of the rule system of language converting our thoughts into their representations. Modified through the process of parameter setting, UG becomes the grammar of a particular language that can be used for producing sentences. It is hypothesized in generative grammar that sentences are produced by **computation**. We can think of computation here as a discrete system that can be defined in terms of logical formulae, which means that sentences are built by applying certain logical algorithms to words. In general, human cognitive capacities are considered to constitute analogue systems, where there are no clear-cut boundaries. For instance, human visual fields do not necessarily have clear-cut boundaries and the visual acuity of recognizing shape and motion gradually declines as it goes toward the periphery. This holds true also of human auditory perception. Sounds are not discrete but range gradually in volume from minute to loud, and our auditory perception does not have a clear-cut dividing point between "loudness" and "non-loudness". Notably, it is claimed in generative grammar that the grammar of language, unlike other human cognitive abilities, constitutes a discrete system (like the natural numbers: 0, 1, 2 ...). In other words, even though UG is considered to represent one type of human cognitive capacity, it is distinguished from other cognitive capacities. This view leads to the idea of the autonomy of natural language, called the **autonomy thesis**.

Alternatively, one might think of language as a product arising from an interaction of human cognitive capacities. Under this perspective, language is regarded as an analogue system that is not different in type from other cognitive abilities, such as visual and auditory perception. This is the perspective taken by cognitive linguistics, which has enjoyed popularity in recent years. At first sight, it looks as if generative grammar places too much emphasis on the autonomy of language, but so far, no evidence has been found that counterexemplifies this hypothesis. As a matter of fact, the autonomy thesis is one (concrete) hypothesis posited for the purpose of conducting research on the nature of human language. Until much more is known about the nature of human language, it will not be possible to provide a definitive answer to the question of whether or not the autonomy thesis is adequate. Given this state of affairs, we will maintain the autonomy thesis as a working hypothesis.

3.2 Parameters

If the premise that the grammatical system of human language, i.e. UG, is comprised of principles and parameters is accepted, the next task is to determine what properties principles and parameters possess. The invariant part of UG is the main topic of the later chapters, so let us here restrict our attention to the variable part of UG, i.e. parameters, which children set with exposure to stimuli when acquiring a language. Needless to say, from the present perspective, many syntactic variations among languages are accounted for by the parametric differences.

For the purpose of identifying some parameters available in UG, it is instructive to make a comparison between Japanese and English, which possess quite different structural properties in a number of respects. First of all, Japanese and English differ in their basic word order. To make this point, let us consider (4).

(4)   a. Mary (S)   ate (V)   cookies (O)
       b. Mari-ga (S)   kukkii-o (O)   tabe-ta (V)
          Mari-NOM   cookie-ACC   eat-PST
          'Mari ate cookies.'

The Japanese sentence in (4b) is syntactically equivalent to the English sentence in (4a). Both are transitive sentences, comprised of the subject (S), the object (O), and the verb (V). In both English and Japanese, the subject (S) comes first. The object (O) and the verb (V), however, are ordered differently in the two languages. In English, the verb (V) precedes the object (O), but in Japanese, the verb (V) follows the object (O). The facts suggest that the arrangement of subject, object, and verb to build a transitive sentence is subject to parametric variation.

In English, the basic word order is Subject (S) – Verb (V) – Object (O), and thus English is referred to as an **SVO language**. On the other hand, Japanese is an **SOV language** because the language has the basic word order of Subject (S) – Object (O) – Verb (V). Importantly, the word order difference between Japanese and English comes from the way in which the most important element (the verb) is ordered relative to a less important one (the object). In fact, languages in the world can be divided into two types, depending on how the head (the verb) is ordered relative to a dependent element (the object). From this point of view, Japanese is classified as a **head-final language** and English, a **head-initial language**. The parameter at issue here is known as the **head parameter**, and a language has the option of choosing either head-initial or head-final as its parameter value.

Another parametric difference between Japanese and English is found in how *wh*-questions are formed. English has a grammatical rule placing a *wh*-phrase at the beginning of a clause, but Japanese lacks this fronting rule, so that a *wh*-phrase can appear in a middle of the clause.

(5)   a. *What* did Mary eat?

     b. Mari-ga   *nani-o*   tabe-ta   no?
       Mari-NOM   what-ACC   eat-PST   Q
       'What did Mari eat?'

Natural languages can be divided into two types according to whether they have a grammatical rule moving a *wh*-phrase to the front of the clause. This parameter, which has to do with the applicability of *wh*-movement, is referred to as the **wh-parameter**. On this parameter, English is identified as a *wh*-movement language, but Japanese is classified as a non-*wh*-movement language.

Furthermore, languages can be partitioned into two classes depending on whether a subject needs to be overtly realized or not. In English, finite clauses need to have an overtly realized subject, but Japanese does not have such a requirement. Accordingly, we observe the contrast given in (6).

(6)   a. *(Mary) ate cookies.

     b. (Mari-ga)   kukkii-o   tabe-ta.
       Mari-NOM   cookie-ACC   eat-PST
       '(Mari) ate cookies.'

In English, the subject must be realized, as shown in (6a). (The sign *( ), i.e. the starred parentheses, means that the sentence is not acceptable if the element enclosed in the parentheses is not overtly realized.) In Japanese, by contrast, it is possible to elide the subject, as shown in (6b); subjects can remain unpronounced as long as their referents are recoverable from context, which is signified by the parentheses ( ). Thus, Japanese is often referred to as a **pro-drop language** (pro-drop = "pronoun-dropping"). Since the variation emerges depending on whether or not a null subject is allowed, the relevant parameter is called the **null-subject parameter**. The examples in (6) illustrate that there is parametric variation between English and Japanese with regard to the null-subject parameter.

Note here that English is a language where subjects need to be overtly realized in finite clauses even when they are not required semantically. The meteorological sentence in (7) illustrates this point.

(7)   *(It) rained.

The English word *rain* in (7) expresses the meaning of 'rain falls', so that the sentence is semantically complete even without a subject. Nevertheless, since English requires the presence of a subject in a finite clause, the pronoun *it*, which does not have a substantive meaning, appears as a subject in (7). No such requirement is imposed on Japanese.

(8)   a. Ame-ga   hut-ta.
             rain-NOM   fall-PST
             'It rained.'
    b. Sigure-ta.
        drizzle-PST
        'It drizzled.'

(8a) is a case where the verb *huru* 'fall' selects an argument denoting 'rain' as its subject.(Note that *huru* can also take subjects referring to other entities that fall from the sky (e.g. *yuki* 'snow', *kazanbai* 'volcanic ash')). On the other hand, the subjectless sentence in (8b) is acceptable since a meteorological verb like *sigureru* 'drizzle' expresses a complete meaning (without a subject). The entity referred to as 'drizzling' is included as part of the meaning of the verb, so it is not possible to have a subject denoting such an entity. Accordingly, it does not make sense to construct a *wh*-question like (9), which asks for what kind of entity "drizzles".

(9)   *Nani-ga   sigure-ta   no?
        what-NOM   drizzle-PST   Q
        'What drizzled?'

Since what is "drizzling" is referred to as part of the verb meaning, but not as a subject, a *wh*-question like (9) cannot be constructed. The distinct behavior observed between English and Japanese with regard to meteorological verbs comes from a difference in parameter setting on null subjects.

For Further Research

(A) Natural languages can be classified by a number of different criteria. One well-known classification based on morphological properties is given in (i).

(i)   a. Isolating language: All words are invariable, i.e. there is no morphological variations in words.
       b. Agglutinative language: A word may consist of more than one morpheme with a clear morpheme boundary.
       c. Fusional language: A word may contain more than one morpheme, but there are no clear-cut boundaries between morphemes in a word.
       d. Polysynthetic language: A large number of morphemes can be combined into a word, and a complex word can often correspond to a sentence.

This is a typological classification of languages in the world discussed by Comrie (1989). Japanese is of the agglutinative type, where the components of predicates are visible, but form "tight" units morphologically (but not necessarily syntactically).

(B-1) There are many linguistic phenomena that come from parametric differences between Japanese and English other than the ones discussed in this chapter. In (ii), for instance, the main verb *hasiru* 'run' is combined with the causative suffix *(s)ase* to form a morphologically complex predicate, where *(s)ase* is agglutinated to the main verb.

(ii)   Ken-ga   kodomo-o   hasir-ase-ta.
       Ken-NOM   child-ACC   run-CAUS-PST
       'Ken made the child run.'

The type of causative formation that yields a morphologically tight unit by combining a main verb with a causative verb is not available in English. English causative constructions have an analytic form, as indicated by the translation. What causes this difference in causative formation between Japanese and English? What kind of parameter can we posit?

(B-2) Japanese has a time-denoting verb *tatu* 'pass, elapse'. This verb can take a subject like *zikan* 'time', as in (iiia), or the subject may be left unrealized, as in (iiib).

(iii)   a. Zikan-ga   iti-zikan   tat-tara,   watasi-wa   kaer-u.
            time-NOM   one-hour   pass-if   I-TOP   return-PRS
            'If one hour passes, I will go home.'
        b. Iti-zikan   tat-tara,   watasi-wa   kaer-u.
            one-hour   pass-if   I-TOP   return-PRS
            'If one hour passes, I will go home.'

Japanese has another time-denoting verb *suru* 'pass, elapse', which cannot take
a subject, as shown in (iv).

(iv)   a. *Zikan-ga   iti-zikan   si-tara,   watasi-wa   kaer-u.
            time-NOM   one-hour   pass-if   I-TOP   return-PRS
            'If one hour passes, I will go home.
        b. Iti-zikan   si-tara,   watasi-wa   kaer-u.
            one-hour   pass-if   I-TOP   return-PRS
            'If one hour passes, I will go home.'

The verb *suru* 'pass, elapse' does not allow the nominative-marked argument
zikan 'time' to appear as its subject, which the verb *tatu* 'pass, elapse' can take.
Why is it that the time-denoting verb *suru*, as opposed to *tatu*, cannot take a
subject?

CHAPTER 4
Lexical and Functional Categories [B]

4.1 Two Kinds of Words

A sentence is usually constructed by combining a number of different words. (Single word sentences are possible but are not frequently found.) The term **syntax** refers to the way in which **words** (or **lexical items**) are put together to form sentences, which are used to package various thoughts; needless to say, syntax constitutes the core unit of the grammar of human language. A sentence may be likened to a house in that both consist of various kinds of parts; a house has walls, doors, and windows that have distinct functions; there are also nails, hinges, or glues that are used to put them together. If they are positioned in the right places, the house will function properly. (A house without a door would be totally dysfunctional; it is very easy to imagine how uncomfortable and inconvenient it would be for us to live in such a queer house!) The same is true of sentences—the main target of our investigation. Even a simple sentence like (1) is composed of a variety of elements serving different functions, just like walls, doors, and nails in houses.

(1) Ken-wa   asu   hoteru-ni   tomar-u.
     Ken-TOP   tomorrow   hotel-at   stay-PRS
     'Ken will stay at a hotel tomorrow.'

When words are arranged properly according to the grammar of Japanese, the sentence functions appropriately. A sentence like (1) is **well-formed**, for it is constructed properly in accordance with Japanese grammar. The sentence can therefore be understood by any Japanese speaker. On the other hand, an unintelligible word salad is produced if the same set of words is assembled randomly, as in (2).

30

(2) *Hoteru   asu-(r)u   Ken   tomar-wa-ni.
     hotel   tomorrow-PRS   Ken   stay-TOP-at

It is clear from (2) that a sentence, just like a house, does not function properly unless its parts are placed properly.

Various parts of speech are necessary for constructing sentences. Parts of speech are largely divided into two classes. One class includes words that carry substantive meanings, such as *Ken*, *asu* 'tomorrow', *hoteru* 'hotel' and *tomar(u)* 'stay'. These lexical items, which are comparable in their functions to the walls and windows used in a house, belong to the class referred to as **lexical categories**. Words like *wa*, *ni*, and *(r)u* are dependent elements morphologically, and have functions comparable to glue, nails, and hinges that prevent house walls and windows from falling apart. These lexical items fall into **functional categories** and play an important role in signaling the grammatical relations of the elements with which they are associated, although they do not carry substantive meanings by themselves.

4.2 Lexical Categories

As noted above, words (lexical items) are categorized into either lexical or functional categories. In this section, we will consider the nature of lexical categories (open word classes). There are several kinds of words that fall into lexical categories. From a typological perspective, many languages have nouns, verbs, and adjectives; nevertheless, it is also true that some languages do not have all of these categories, while other languages have more categories than those mentioned here. In Japanese, at least three major lexical categories can be identified, as in (3).

(3)   a. **Nouns** (*meishi*):   *hon* 'book', *heiwa* 'peace', *zitensya* 'bicycle', *mizu* 'water', etc.
      b. **Verbs** (*dōshi*):   *hataraku* 'work', *taberu* 'eat', *tatu* 'stand', *hanasu* 'speak', etc.
      c. **Adjectives** (*keiyōshi*):   *utukusii* 'beautiful', *sizuka-da* 'quiet', *yoi* 'good', etc.

The classification given in (3) is not the same as the classification found in traditional grammar (or school grammar) because **adjectives** (*keiyōshi*) ending in *-i* and **nominal adjectives** (*keiyōdōshi*) ending in *-da* are combined into the class of adjectives. The main reason for this coalescence is that these two types of expressions behave in the same way in syntactic terms, although they show distinct inflections. It is also possible to classify words in other ways, and/or to present finer-grained (or coarser-grained) classifications. For instance, some researchers set up an independent category of **verbal nouns** (**VNs**). Verbal nouns (e.g. *ryokoo* 'travel') behave both as verbs (*ryokoo-suru* [travel-do]) and as nouns (*ryokoo-o suru* [travel-ACC do]), and their categorization has sometimes been a controversial issue in Japanese syntax.

Verbs and adjectives are inflecting words and consist of (non-inflecting) stems and inflectional elements. In Japanese generative grammar, it is a common practice to separate inflectional elements from verbs and adjectives and put them into the class of functional categories. Strictly speaking, then, the dictionary forms of verbs and adjectives each consist of the two items of stem and inflectional ending, although they are often regarded as forming single words. In Japanese, verbs are divided into two major types according to the morphological status of their stems, i.e. consonant-stem and vowel-stem verbs. The verb *ageru* 'give' has the inflectional pattern: *age-ru* [give-PRS. PLAIN], *age-masu* [give-PRS. POLITE], *age-reba* [give-PROVISIONAL], *age-yoo* [give-HORTATIVE], etc. This inflectional pattern suggests that the stem of *ageru* is *age-*, which ends in a vowel, and hence, this class of verbs is called vowel-stem verbs. On the other hand, the inflection of the verb *kaku* 'write' is: *kak-u* [write-PRS. PLAIN], *kak-imasu* [write-PRS. POLITE], *kak-eba* [write-PROVISIONAL], *kak-oo* [write-HORTATIVE], etc., which indicates that the verb stem of *kaku* is *kak-*, ending in a consonant, so it is identified as a consonant-stem verb. (Incidentally, consonant-stem verbs cannot be segmented into their stems and inflections by appeal to their representation in the moraic *kana* orthography (*hiragana* 平仮名 or *katakana* 片仮名) —writing systems whose basic unit is the cluster 'consonant-vowel (CV)'.

There are important features that are shared by lexical categories. One notable property is that their meanings can be understood even when they stand alone. Since lexical words carry substantive meanings, it is easy to see what meanings words like *hon* 'book', *hasiru* 'run', and *kawaii* 'pretty' carry, independently of the grammatical contexts in which they appear. The next, and perhaps the most prominent property associated with lexical categories is that the inventory of words belonging to lexical categories (i.e. words categorized as content words) is virtually unlimited: Hundreds of thousands of Japanese words are listed in a voluminous dictionary like *Nihon Kokugo Daijiten* [The Grand Dictionary of Japanese], but this cannot be the whole list of Japanese lexical words. New lexical words are constantly being coined for the purpose of expressing new ideas and concepts or merely for novelty (**neologisms**), and words that fall out of use are often rendered "obsolete". Owing to these characteristic properties, it is not possible to make a comprehensive list of lexical words.

There are a number of ways of determining the categories (parts of speech) of lexical words. One way of doing this is to classify them on the basis of their meanings (**semantic criterion**). While this is a commonly used method for categorization, it turns out that this does not necessarily provide a useful way of evaluating the category of lexical words. For instance, verbs are often said to describe an act, an event, or a state. If this is taken to be the criterion for the categorical identification of a given word, the word *hasiru* 'run', which denotes the act of running, can be classified as a verb. However, *hasiri* 'running' appearing in (4) would be erroneously categorized as a verb under the same criterion.

(4) Eri-no   hasiri-wa   subarasikat-ta.
    Eri-GEN   running-TOP   wonderful-PST
    'Eri's running was wonderful.'

Needless to say, the word *hasiri* 'running' falls into the noun, not the verb, class although it refers to an event of running semantically. Similarly, adjectives are often said to describe a state or a quality (e.g. *utukusii* 'beautiful', *kurai* 'dark'). This description does not suffice to identify the class member of adjectives, however, for there are verbs that describe a state (e.g. *aru/iru* 'be', *dekiru* 'can do'). This shows that semantic criteria are not so useful for the purpose of identifying the category of lexical words, because, in many, if not all, cases, they do not demarcate categories in a reliable manner.

In generative grammar, therefore, semantic criteria are not used for classifying lexical categories (word classes, parts of speech), but they are determined on the basis of their shared morphological and syntactic properties.

(5)
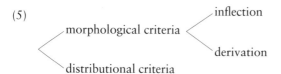

The criteria used for identifying word classes come in several types. Specifically, words can be distinguished on the basis of their morphological properties, and the **morphological criteria** can be derivational or inflectional. Inflecting words display unique inflection patterns depending on their class. Thus, lexical words, if they inflect, can be classified by looking at the inflectional forms. Obviously, verbs do inflect differently from adjectives in Japanese, as seen in *hasir-eba* [run-PROVISIONAL], *hasit-ta* [run-PST], *hasir-oo* [run-HORTATIVE] (for *hasiru* 'run') versus *utukusi-kereba* [beautiful-PROVISIONAL], *utukusi-kat-ta* [beautiful-PST] (for *utukusii* 'beautiful'). Another method of identifying word classes is to consider derivation—the morphological process whereby one word is formed from another by attaching an affix. For instance, in Japanese, the suffixes *-sa* and *-mi* are used to derive a noun from an adjective, as in *utukusii* 'beautiful' + *-sa* → *utukusi-sa* 'beauty'. Notably, these suffixes can be attached to only adjectives (as well as nominal adjectives, which we take to fall into the class of adjectives). Accordingly, we can easily determine that the bases (e.g. *utukusii*) to which they can attach are adjectives, while their outputs (e.g. *utukusi-sa*) are nouns.

When using the derivational criteria, a caution needs to be exercised, however, because some affixes can be associated with more than one category. For instance, the prefix *hu-* 'non-' can attach to Sino-Japanese words (e.g. *hu-kakuzitu* 'uncertain') as well as native Japanese words (e.g. *hu-tasika* 'uncertain'), and both original base words and the derived words can be either nouns or nominal adjectives. In the case of the complex word *hu-benkyoo* 'idle', the derived form could be either a noun or a nominal adjective, as the two forms *hu-benkyoo-no* [NEG-study-GEN] and *hu-benkyoo-na* [NEG-studious-ATTRIBUTIVE] are possible; on the other hand, the base *benkyoo* 'study' must be a noun, as seen by the contrast in acceptability: *benkyoo-no* [study-GEN] versus **benkyoo-na* [studious-ATTRIBUTIVE].

Distributional/syntactic criteria can also be utilized for deciding on the categories of words. In the distributional/syntactic criteria, the category of words is determined according to where they appear syntactically. For example, expressions that can be inserted into the underlined position in (6) are nouns because only nouns can appear in that position.

(6) Watasi-wa   ____-ga   hosi-i.
     I-TOP   -NOM   want-PRS
     'I want ____.'

A given word is categorized as a noun if it can appear in the underlined position in (6), but this does not mean that all nouns can appear in that position, since nouns are often susceptible to additional conditions that further restrict their distribution.

In linguistics, it is fairly standard to apply morphological and distributional (or syntactic) criteria to words to identify their classes. This means that the organization of lexical categories is defined in terms of their morphological and distributional patterns. As far as their classifications are concerned, however, there are no absolute criteria that enable us to classify all words into their categories. Owing to the absence of a single diagnostic that can be used at any time for distinguishing one class of words from another, it is often necessary to apply a number of criteria to lexical words so as to assess their categorical status.

4.3 Functional Categories

Let us next consider the characteristic properties of functional categories. In general, function words (belonging to the functional categories) are conceived of as possessing the following general properties: A) they signal the grammatical relations of elements that they are associated with, and it does not make much sense to use them independently of grammatical contexts, B) they are limited in number, and they are rarely introduced into the inventory of words as new items. Broadly speaking, functional categories constitute a closed class, and the properties of functional words noted above are orthogonal to the properties of lexical words. At first sight, it might look as if functional words are trivial, because they are often appended to lexical words as dependent elements morphologically. On the contrary, they play a vital role in defining the grammatical relations of their associated expressions, and they are in fact the key elements that guarantee the expressiveness of language; if no functional categories existed in language, the range of ideas we could express would be severely limited.

There is no general consensus among scholars about the inventory of functional categories, but at least the categories listed in (7) are generally considered to fall into the functional class.

(7)   a.   **Postpositions:** *kara* 'from', *de* 'with', *made* 'until', etc.
       b.   **Determiners:** *kono* 'this', *ano* 'that', *arayuru* 'every', etc.
       c.   **Pronouns:** *kare* 'he', *watasi* 'I', *anata* 'you', *nani* 'what', etc.
       d.   **Complementizers:** *to* 'that', *yooni* 'that', *no* [NOMLZ], *ka* [Q], etc.
       e.   **Auxiliaries:** *daroo* 'will', *soo-da* 'I hear', *kamosirenai* 'might', etc.
       f.   **Tense:** *-ru* [PRS], *-ta* [PST]

To illustrate the terms briefly, **postpositions** are functional words that attach to noun phrases, as *de* 'in' in *niwa-de* 'in the garden'. They are called "postpositions" because they occur after nouns (*post-* means 'after'). If they occurred before nouns, they would be called "prepositions" (*pre-* means 'before') (e.g. English *on* is a preposition because it occurs on the left side of a noun, as in *on the wall*). Postpositions and prepositions differ in their surface order relative to their hosts, but their grammatical functions are the same. In Japanese, particles (e.g. *kara* 'from', *de* 'in') serve as postpositions. Note that there are also other types of particles, which include syntactic case markers (e.g. *ga* [NOM], *o* [ACC]), adverbial particles (e.g. *dake* 'only', *sae* 'even'), which serve to add additional meanings (like adverbs), and discourse particles (e.g. *wa, yo, ne*), which express the speaker's attitude toward the propositions expressed by the sentences. **Determiners** include a range of article-like elements, such as demonstratives (e.g. *sono* 'its') and quantifiers (e.g. *arayuru* 'every', *subete-no* 'all'). **Pronouns** are further classified into personal pronouns (e.g. *watasi* 'I', *anata* 'you') and indeterminate pronouns (e.g. *dare* 'who', *nani* 'what'). **Complementizers** introduce subordinate clauses. **Auxiliaries** add a variety of subsidiary (or secondary) meanings to predicates. In Japanese, auxiliaries are dependent elements that do not stand on their own morphologically but are generally considered to be separate from predicates syntactically. Finally, **tense** includes elements like *-ru* [PRS] and *-ta* [PST], which encode temporal information. The tense forms an integral part of predicates in morphological terms but are considered to occupy a syntactic position distinct from that filled by the predicate (in Japanese generative grammar).

Some lexical words may be turned into functional words via a grammatical process referred to as **grammaticalization**. In Japanese, complex postpositions like *nitotte* 'for' and *nituite* 'about' originated from complex 'postposition + verb' forms (e.g. *ni* 'in' + *toru* 'take', *ni* 'in' + *tuku* 'attach'), but they now serve as single-word function words.

(8)   Sore-wa   kare-nitotte   yokat-ta.
      that-TOP   he-for   good-PST
      'That was good for him.'

The complex postposition *nitotte* includes the verb *toru* 'take', which takes an o-marked complement when used in isolation. Nevertheless, morphologically speaking, *totte* takes a *ni*-complement, as shown in (8). This is one indication that the *totte* 'take' of *ni-totte* 'for' no longer serves as a verb. There are also postpositions like *nikansite* 'concerning' that retain part of their original inflection as verbs, as in (9).

(9)   gengo-nikansuru   mondai
      language-concerning   problem
      'the problems concerning language'

The postposition *nikansuru* originated from the complex from *ni* 'in' + *kansuru* 'concern'. What is notable here is that when followed by a nominal element, the complex postpositon *nikansite* takes the noun-modifying form *nikansuru*.

For Further Research

(A) Studies of grammatical and lexical categories in Japanese have a long tradition, and a number of different classifications on parts of speech have been proposed. All of the four great traditional Japanese grammarians, Yoshio Yamada, Daizaburō Matsushita, Shinkichi Hashimoto, and Motoki Tokieda, proposed their own classifications. Different categorizations have been proposed in recent linguistic research based on generative grammar and cognitive linguistics as well (see Kishimoto and Uehara (2016) for an overview of various analyses on parts of speech).

(B) In traditional Japanese grammar, *tai* 'want', which expresses a desiderative meaning, is classified as an auxiliary. It inflects like an adjective but differs from full-fledged adjectives in that it is a morphologically dependent element. In this connection, observe that *tai* (combined with a verb) qualifies as an embedded predicate without a complementizer (embedded to *omou* 'think'), but another auxiliary *nai* 'not', which also inflects like an adjective, does not.

(i)   a. Watasi-wa   [kono   biiru-o   nomi-taku]   omo-u.
             I-TOP   this   beer-ACC   drink-want   think-PRS
             'I want to drink this beer.'
    b. *Watasi-wa   [kono   biiru-o   noma-naku]   omo-u.
             I-TOP   this   beer-ACC   drink-NEG   think-PRS
             'I think I will not drink this beer.'

Note that a full-blown adjective like *oisii* 'tasty' is allowed to appear as such an embedded predicate.

(ii)   Watasi-wa   [kono   biiru-o   oisiku]   omo-u.
       I-TOP   this   beer-ACC   tasty   think-PRS
       'I think this beer tasty.'

Is it possible to classify the desiderative *tai* as an adjective in light of the distribution above? If not, what category can be assigned to *tai*? How about *nai*, which shows the same inflectional pattern as *tai*? Do *tai* and *nai* fall into the same class or belong to distinct classes? Discuss the advantages and disadvantages of an analysis taking *tai* and *nai* to belong to the same category versus an analysis taking them to be classified into two distinct categories drawing on morphological and syntactic/distributional criteria.

PART II

Ingredients of
Clauses

CHAPTER 5

Syntax: The Core of Grammar [B]

5.1 What Is a Constituent?

Having discussed what elements are necessary to build up sentences, we are now in a position to talk about the syntactic structures of Japanese. Sentences are the constructs derived by combining words in accordance with the rules of a language. Before discussing the syntactic forms or expressions that can be derived by the grammar, it is important to understand a very basic syntactic concept—the notion of **constituent**. A constituent can be defined as "a group of words that works as a syntactic unit". In many cases, we can identify constituents by looking at whether syntactic operations, such as **replacement** or **movement**, can be applied to a given string of words.

To be concrete, let us consider the dialogue in (1) and examine what constituents comprise the underlined part of the sentence in (1a).

(1) a. A: Mari-wa   <u>totemo   kookana   yubiwa-o</u>   kat-ta.
         Mari-TOP   very   expensive   ring-ACC   buy-PST
         'Mari bought a very expensive ring.'
     b. B: Naze   <u>sonna   yubiwa-o</u>   kat-ta   no?
         why   such   ring-ACC   buy-PST   Q
         'Why did she buy such a ring?'
     c. A: Mari-wa   <u>sore-o</u> totemo ki-ni-it-ta kara   da
         Mari-TOP   it-ACC very   like-PST because   COP
         sooda.
         I.hear
         'I heard that this was because Mari liked it very much.'

The underlined part in (1a) is a **noun phrase**, which consists of three words (or lexical items) *totemo* 'very', *kookana* 'expensive', and *yubiwa-o* 'ring'. (Informally, a noun phrase can be defined as a constituent comprising more

than one word and having the same syntactic function as a noun.) Note that
sonna yubiwa-o, uttered by B in (1b), and *sore-o*, uttered by A in (1c), both refer
to *totemo kookana yubiwa-o* in (1a). This means that the pronominal *sonna*
(1b) substitutes for the two-word sequence *totemo kookana*, and *sore-o* in (1c),
the entire phrase *totemo kookana yubiwa-o*. (2) illustrates how pronominal
replacement has applied to the underlined string of words in (1a).

(2) a. totemo kookana (yubiwa-o)   b.   totemo kookana yubiwa-o
                ↓   ↓
            sonna   sore-o

Since replacement is a syntactic operation that applies to a string of words
forming a unit, we can state that *totemo kookana* 'very expensive' and *totemo
kookana yubiwa-o* 'very expensive ring' are constituents (i.e. syntactic units).

For the purpose of representing constituents in syntactic terms, **tree diagrams**
(or simply **trees**) are often used. Tree diagrams are handy tools that allow us to
understand the way in which words are combined structurally. A constituent is
indicated by two lines connected to a single point, as illustrated in (3).

(3)

In the first place, *totemo* and *kookana* form a constituent (because the two
words can be replaced with *sonna*). This grouping of words is reasonable
because what *totemo* modifies or describes is *kookana*, but not *yubiwa-o* (and
thus *totemo kookana* is well-formed with a legitimate interpretation 'very
expensive', but **totemo yubiwa-o* 'very ring' is not; the latter expression is as
semantically deviant as its English equivalent **very ring*). This structural relation is represented in the tree diagram on the left, where both words are connected into a single **node**—the point where the two lines (**branches**) are united.
The three words *totemo*, *kookana*, and *yubiwa-o* form a constituent because
the string of these words can be replaced by *sore-o*. This syntactic unit can be
formed by adding *yubiwa-o* to the constituent *totemo kookana*, as shown in the
tree diagram on the right in (3). In the expanded tree diagram, the three words
totemo, *kookana*, and *yubiwa-o* are connected to the top node, and thus, they
are identified as a constituent.

Looking at the tree diagrams in (3) alone, we cannot tell what parts of speech
are used in constructing the noun phrase structure. To solve this problem,

various labels are added above the words and the nodes (as conventions); *totemo* 'very' is an adverb and is assigned the category label Adv (=Adverb). *Kookana* 'expensive' is an adjective (or to be more precise, a nominal adjective), and the label A (=Adjective) is allocated to it. *Yubiwa* 'ring' is a noun, and thus is assigned the lablel N (=Noun). The syntactic unit which includes *totemo* and *kookana*, but not *yubiwa-o*, functions as an adjective phrase, so it bears the label AP (=Adjective Phrase). The sequence of *totemo kookana yubiwa-o* functions as a noun phrase in its entirety and is assigned the label NP (=Noun Phrase). If all the words and the nodes in the tree diagram are labeled, the noun phrase comes to have the representation in (4a).

(4)   a.

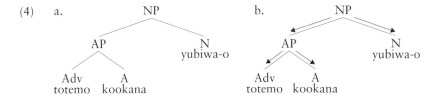

The diagram in (4a) is a complete noun phrase structure. In (4a), *totemo*, *kookana*, and *yubiwa-o* are all connected to the uppermost node, which has the label NP. The top node **dominates** all these three words (meaning that they can be reached by going down the lines from the top node, as shown in (4b)). We also say that in (4a), *totemo*, *kookana*, and *yubiwa-o* are "constituents" of the NP. (Note that the term "constituent" expressed in the form "constituent of" here is used in another closely related sense, meaning 'the members (of the NP)'.) *Sore*-replacement as seen in (1c) is a syntactic operation that applies to the NP. In addition, in (4a), *totemo* and *kookana* are constituents of the AP because these words can be reached by going down the lines from the AP node. (Note that *yubiwa-o* is located outside the AP and is not dominated by the AP node.) *Sonna*-replacement in (1b), which has produced the sequence *sonna yubiwa-o*, is a syntactic operation that applies to this AP.

In the noun phrase structure in (4a), there is no node that includes *kookana* and *yubiwa-o*, but excludes *totemo*. In other words, there is no single node such that we can reach *kookana* and *yubiwa-o*, but not *totemo*, by going down the branches. When a node includes *yubiwa-o*, it must also include *totemo* and *kookana*. This means that *kookana* and *yubiwa-o* cannot form a constituent, excluding *totemo*. This leads us to the prediction that no syntactic operation will apply to the sequence of *kookana yubiwa-o* in (1a). Indeed, there is no such syntactic operation. If pronominal replacement is forced on the non-constituent sequence *kookana yubiwa-o*, ungrammatical phrases are derived, as shown by the ungrammaticality of **totemo sore-o* and **totemo sonna*.

5.2 Sentence Structures

Let us now turn to the discussion of how sentences are constructed. In general, subjects are said to have a special status from other arguments. It is often assumed that the verb and its object form a VP constituent, while the subject is placed outside. In Japanese, it is possible to test for sentence structures by appeal to a syntactic operation often referred to as **pseudo-clefting**, which separates focus from presupposition. While maintaining the assumption that a syntactic operation may apply to a constituent, let us next consider the examples in (5b-c), which are derived from the simple sentence in (5a) via pseudo-clefting.

(5) a. Ken-ga   kodomo-o   home-ta.
         Ken-NOM child-ACC   praise-PST
         'Ken praised the child.'

     b. [Ken-ga si-ta]   no   wa   [kodomo-o   homeru]   koto   da.
         Ken-NOM do-PST that TOP   child-ACC   praise   that   COP
         'What Ken did was praise the child.'

     c. *[Kodomo-o si-ta]   no   wa   [Ken-ga   homeru] koto   da.
         child-ACC   do-PST that TOP   Ken-NOM   praise   that   COP
         'What did the child was Ken praise.'

Pseudo-clefting is an operation that places some constituent in its focus position. In (5b-c), the verb *homeru* 'praise' appears before copula *da*. The examples show that the subject *Ken-ga* and the object *kodomo-o* do not have equal syntactic status. In (5b), what appears in focus position is a combination of the verb and its object, showing that these two words form a constituent, i.e. VP. On the other hand, the subject and the verb cannot be placed in focus position together, as in (5c), which indicates that they do not form a constituent. Furthermore, in (5b), only the verb in the bare from (i.e. the dictionary form), but not one in the past form, can appear in focus position, and thus, *homeru* 'praise' cannot be replaced by *home-ta* 'praised'. Note that the tense is realized on the verb *suru* in the pseudo-clefted version, as seen in (5b) and (5c). This fact suggests that the tense element appears outside the verb phrase syntactically, although it attaches to the verb morphologically in (5a).

The data in (5) illustrate that the object and the verb form a constituent, but that the subject and the verb do not form a constituent excluding the object. This means that the object and the verb are first combined to form a syntactic unit, as represented by the left-hand tree diagram in (6).

(6) a.   b.

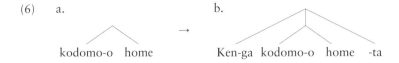

Then, the subject and the tense are added to the combined structure of the object and the verb. The resultant structure, represented in the tree diagram on the right, is a sentence structure that can be assigned to (5a).

Category labels can be assigned as follows. First, the top node is labeled S (=Sentence). The tensed element -*ta* has the category label Aux (=Auxiliary) (since it is a tense auxiliary). If the verb is labeled V (=Verb), the syntactic unit into which the verb and the object are combined is labeled as VP (=Verb Phrase). The subject *Ken-ga* and the object *kodomo-o* are noun phrases (which are accompanied by their case marking), so they have the label NP (=Noun Phrase). The proper noun *Ken-ga* stands alone in (5a), but strictly speaking, it can be identified as a phrase. This can be seen by the fact that pronouns can substitute for it, as in *Ken-ga* [Ken-NOM] → *kare-ga* [he-NOM], *dare-ga* [who-NOM], in much the same way as it can substitute for a more complex noun phrase, as in *sono hito-ga* [that man-NOM] → *kare-ga* [he-NOM], *dare-ga* [who-NOM]. Note that *sono hito-ga* 'that man' forms an NP by virtue of combining *hito-ga* with the determiner *sono*, as in (7a), where *sono* appears in D (=Determiner).

(7) a.   NP   b.   NP   c.   NP   d.   NP

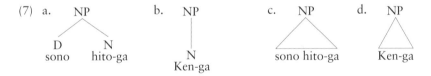

The facts of pronominalization applying to *sono hito* illustrates that the pronouns *kare* and *dare* replace the NP, but not N. Since *Ken* can be replaced with the same pronouns, the proper noun *Ken* can be assumed to have the NP structure represented in (7b). The abbreviation symbol △ in (7c-d) is sometimes used to indicate that the internal structure is being left unanalyzed. This simplifying symbol makes it possible to avoid presenting irrelevant details and allows us to pay attention to what we really need to look at when analyzing syntax. If all labels are assigned to the relevant nodes, the tree diagram for (5a) is complete. Since we are concerned with the sentence structure, but not noun phrase structures here, the abbreviated notation is used for NPs (with accompanying case markers) in (8).

44

(8)

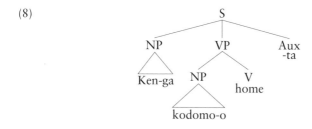

Given the structure in (8), we can account for the contrast in acceptability between (5b) and (5c) as follows. In (5b), the VP constituent, consisting of the verb and the object, is placed in focus position. Hence, (5b) is acceptable. On the other hand, it is not possible to place the subject and the verb in focus position omitting the object, since the subject and the verb do not form a constituent excluding the object, i.e. there is no node that includes the subject and the verb but excludes the object. Thus, (5c) is not well-formed.

English differs from Japanese in the order of the verb and object, as well as the position of the Aux. Nevertheless, English, too, has a syntactic structure where the verb forms a constituent with an object while its subject occurs outside. In English, the structure is easy to confirm, because the sequence of an object plus the verb behaves as a unit that may undergo **VP-preposing**, as in (9b).

(9)   a. John will kick the ball.
       b. John intends to kick the ball, and [kick the ball] he will _____.

Since syntactic operations apply to a group of words forming a constituent, the fact of VP-preposing in (9b) illustrates that the object and the verb form a constituent that does not incorporate the subject or the auxiliary *will*. The English sentence in (9a), thus, has the sentence structure represented in the tree diagram (10).

(10)

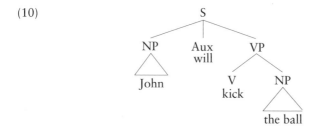

English has essentially the same hierarchical structure as Japanese, but Aux and the verb appear in different linear word order. This word order difference comes from a word order parameter, which is set when children acquire Japanese or English.

It is worth noting that the information represented in the tree diagram in (8) can also be represented by a **labeled bracketing representation** like that in (11).

(11)   [$_S$ [$_{NP}$ Ken-ga] [$_{VP}$ [$_{NP}$ kodomo-o] [$_V$ home]] [$_{AUX}$ -ta]]

In (11), constituents are indicated by [ ], which encloses a word or a set of words, and the labels are appended to the left brackets to signify their categories. The procedure to construct the bracketing representation in (11) is essentially the same as that by which a tree diagram is constructed. The representation in (11) can be constructed by putting words together to form constituents one by one, as in (12).

(12)   a. [$_{NP}$ kodomo-o] + [$_V$ home]
           → [$_{VP}$ [$_{NP}$ kodomo-o] [$_V$ home]]
       b. [$_{NP}$ Ken-ga] + [$_{VP}$ [$_{NP}$ kodomo-o] [$_V$ home]] + [$_{AUX}$ -ta]
           → [$_S$ [$_{NP}$ Ken-ga] [$_{VP}$ [$_{NP}$ kodomo-o] [$_V$ home]] [$_{AUX}$ -ta]]

First, in (12a), the labeled bracket containing the verb, i.e. [$_V$ home] is combined with [$_{NP}$ kodomo-o] to give a verb phrase, which is labeled [$_{VP}$]. After the VP is constructed, the labeled brackets containing the subject and the tense, i.e. [$_{NP}$ Ken-ga] and [$_{AUX}$ -ta], are added to the VP [$_{VP}$ [$_{NP}$ kodomo-o] [$_V$ home]]. Once the subject, AUX, and VP are enclosed in [$_S$], as in (12b), the bracketing representation in (11) for (5a) is derived. In the bracketing representation, multiple brackets indicate that constituents are nested and the need to count and match up opening and closing brackets can make it harder to process the hierarchical structure. This bracketing method of representing structures is useful, however, especially when there is not enough space to place a big tree diagram.

For Further Research

(A) Derivations of syntactic structures are often specified by rewriting rules, called **phrase structure rules**. For instance, the syntactic structure of a transitive sentence (like *Ken-ga kodomo-o home-ta* 'Ken praised the child') can be derived by the phrase structure rules in (i).

(i)   a.   S   →   NP   VP   Aux
       b.   VP   →   NP   V
       c.   NP   →   N

The rule in (ia) states that S expands to NP, VP, and Aux. The rule (ib) states that VP expands to NP and V, and the rule (ic) states that one realization of an NP is simply a noun (N). The first rule gives rise to the phrase structure in (iia). The second rule creates the internal structure of VP, and the phrase structure in (iib) is constructed by adding the VP-internal structure to (iia). Finally, the rule expanding an NP as N applies to yield (iic).

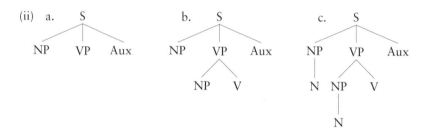

Once individual lexical items (i.e. words) are placed at the bottom of the category labels in (iic), a complete tree representation is derived, as in (iii).

(iii)

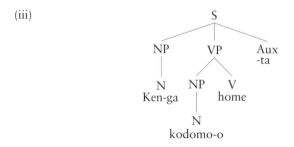

(B) In coordination, categories of the same syntactic status are connected and set side by side with a coordinator. Coordination is possible at many different levels of phrase structure. In Japanese, the coordinate particles *tari...tari...* can be attached to verbs, as in (iv).

(iv)   Eri-ga   kabe-o   tatai-tari   ket-tari   si-ta.
        Eri-NOM   wall-ACC   hit-CONJ   kick-CONJ   do-PST
        'Eri hit and kicked the wall.'

In the coordinate structure in (iv), where two verbs are coordinated, constituents (including the verbs) can be reordered by scrambling. The examples in (v) show that the object and the verb can be scrambled together across the subject, but that the subject and the verb cannot be placed before the object by scrambling.

(v)   a. Kabe-o   ket-tari   tatai-tari,   Eri-ga   si-ta.
          wall-ACC   kick-CONJ   hit-CONJ   Eri-NOM do-PST
          'Both kicked and hit the wall, Eri did.'
      b. *Eri-ga   ket-tari   tatai-tari,   kabe-o   si-ta.
          Eri-NOM   kick-CONJ   hit-CONJ   wall-ACC do-PST
          'Eri both kicked and hit the wall did.'

Do the examples in (v) constitute evidence that the verb and its object form a constituent, to the exclusion of the subject (i.e. VP)?

CHAPTER 6

Generalizing Phrase Structures: X′-Theory [B], [E]

6.1 Word Order

Japanese and English differ in their basic word order. Japanese is an SOV language in which the verb follows the object, whereas English is an SVO language in which the verb precedes the object. Interestingly, the same kind of word order difference is found in many other places, as exemplified in (1).

(1) Japanese   English
   a. [hon-o]   kau   ←→ buy [books]   (VP)
      book-ACC   buy
   b. [gengogaku-nituite-no] hon ←→ books [on linguistics] (NP)
      linguisitics-on-GEN   book
   c. [hoteru]   kara   ←→ from [the hotel]   (PP)
      hotel   from
   d. [watasi-ga hon-o   kau] nara ←→ if [I buy books] (Adverbial Clause)
      I-NOM   book-ACC buy if

The Japanese and English examples have equivalent meanings, and their structures are also comparable. Nevertheless, the underlined expressions and the expressions enclosed in the square brackets have the opposite order between Japanese and English. The underlined and the enclosed constituents on the two sides in (1a-d) are arranged as if reflected in a mirror (e.g. "NP-V" versus "V-NP"), and thus the expressions constitute **mirror image** pairs.

The "mirror image" arrangement of constituents in (1) reflects a parametric difference between the two languages. It is important to see that in all the examples in (1), the underlined part has semantically missing information, while the part enclosed by the square brackets serves to fill the gap. For instance, the transitive verb *kau* 'buy' in (1a) cannot stand alone and needs to be accompanied by an object like *hon-o* 'books', which counts as a complement, in order to express a complete meaning as VP. The same holds true of the other cases in (1). In all the cases, the underlined expressions are identified as **heads**, which are indispensable elements for constructing their phrases, while the expressions enclosed in square brackets serve as **complements**, which provide required supplementary information for their heads. Japanese has the "complement-head" order, but English has the reverse "head-complement" order. One interesting fact is that the ordering of constituents within a language is fairly constant across categories, including noun phrases, postpositional/prepositional phrases, and verb phrases. This suggests that the order of the constituents is produced via the same grammatical rule regardless of the category, i.e. a given language has a single word-ordering rule (generating the same linear order of heads and complements in most, if not all, categories).

6.2 Semantic Functions in Phrase Structure

Heads and complements are not the only elements that can be included in phrases; other kinds of elements are also allowed to occur, as shown in (2).

(2) Ken-no   aka-byoosi-no   ryoori-no   hon
     Ken-GEN   red-front.cover-GEN   cooking-GEN   book
     'Ken's book on cooking with a red front cover'

In (2), the noun *hon* 'book' functions as the head of the entire phrase, and thus the phrase is identified as a noun phrase. Since the noun phrase shares the same categorical information with the noun head, we say that the noun phrase is a **projection** of the noun head, or that the noun (head) projects to the noun phrase. The noun head transmits its categorical information to higher syntactic units formed by combining with other elements, and the largest unit is identified as a noun phrase. The top node that does not project any further is a **maximal projection**.

In the noun phrase in (2), three genitive-marked phrases, which function as modifiers to the noun, are included. One may think of the noun phrase as having a "flat" structure in (3), where all the genitive phrases are directly dominated by the topmost NP.

(3)

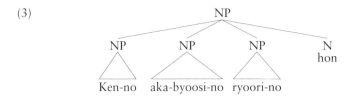

Nevertheless, there are good reasons to believe that the flat structure in (3) is not the correct one. We can confirm this by considering how so-called **no replacement** applies to the noun phrase in (2).

(4)   a. [Ken-no   [aka-byoosi-no   ryoori-no   hon]]-wa
            Ken-GEN   red-front.cover-GEN   cooking-GEN   book-TOP
            kari-ta-ga,   Mari-**no**-wa   kari-nakat-ta.
            borrow-PST-CONJ   Mari-one-TOP   borrow-NEG-PST
            'I borrowed Ken's book on cooking with a red front cover, but not Mari's.'

       b. [Ken-no   aka-byoosi-no   [ryoori-no   hon]]-wa
            Ken-GEN   red-front.cover-GEN   cooking-GEN   book-TOP
            kari-ta-ga,   [Mari-no   ao-byoosi-**no**]-wa
            borrow-PST-CONJ   Mari-GEN   blue-front.cover-one-TOP
            kari-nakat-ta.
            borrow-NEG-PST
            'I borrowed Ken's book on cooking with a red front cover, but not Mari's with a blue front cover.'

In (4), the *no* in bold type is a pronoun replacing a string of words. In (4a), *no* substitutes for the two genitive phrases plus the noun, i.e. [*aka-byoosi-no ryoori-no hon*], showing that they form constituents. In (4b), *no* substitutes for one genitive modifier plus the noun, i.e. [*ryoori-no hon*]. (Note that if the pronoun *no* follows the genitive *no*, the sequence of *-no no* is obtained, but in actuality this duplicated form is reduced to a single *no* by a phonological process called "haplology".) Since *no* replacement applies to a constituent, the data in (4) show that the noun phrase has three different levels of constituents, possessing the layered structure given in (5).

52

(5)

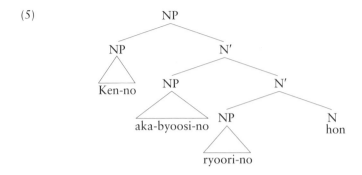

In (5), the N head projects to NP, but there are two other nodes intervening between them. The two nodes cannot be N (indicating the head) nor can they be NP (indicating the maximal projection), and thus they are called **intermediate projections**, which are labeled as N′ (pronounced 'N-bar'). In (5), the lower N′ node includes the genitive phrase *ryoori-no* and the noun *hon*, and thus *no* can substitute for the set of the two words *ryoori-no hon*, as in (4b). The higher N′ node includes the two genitive phrases *aka-byoosi-no* and *ryoori-no* plus the noun head *hon*, but *Ken-no* is not included. Accordingly, *no* can replace the three-word sequence of *aka-byoosi-no ryoori-no hon*, as in (4a).

The three genitive phrases in (5) have different semantic functions. The noun structure conveys the meaning of 'Ken has the book whose front cover is red, which is about cooking'. The topmost genitive phrase *Ken-no*, which specifies the individual who possesses the book, is called a **specifier**. The lowest genitive phrase *ryoori-no*, which provides supplementary (and necessary) information concerning the book, is a **complement** to *hon*. The middle genitive phrase *aka-byoosi-no*, which provides additional information describing the color of the front cover, is an **adjunct**. The important fact is that the distinct hierarchical positions that the three genitive phrases occupy in the noun phrase structure reflect their semantic relations relative to the noun head.

The noun phrase in (2) has a structure where the three genitive phrases are placed in distinct syntactic positions. This fact can further be confirmed by looking at the facts of **coordination**. A coordinate construction is formed when two or more phrases with the same status are poisitoned side by side, making use of a connective like *to* 'and', as in (6).

(6)   a. [[Ken-to   Mari]-no aka-byoosi-no   ryoori-no]   hon
            Ken-and Mari-GEN red-front.cover-GEN cooking-GEN book
            'Ken and Mari's books on cooking with a red front cover'

b. [Ken-no   [aka-byoosi-to   ao-byoosi]-no   ryoori-no]
   Ken-GEN   red-front.cover-and blue-front.cover-GEN cooking-GEN
   hon
   book
   'Ken's books on cooking with a red front cover and a blue front
   cover'

c. [Ken-no   aka-byoosi-no   [ryoori-to   geemu]-no] hon
   Ken-GEN   red-front.cover-GEN   cooking-and game-GEN   book
   'Ken's books on cooking and games with a red front cover'

The examples in (6) are all fine because genitive phrases of the same status are coordinated. (6a), (6b), and (6c) can be interpreted as meaning 'Ken's book and Mari's book', 'a book with a red front cover and a book with a blue front cover', and 'a book on cooking and a book on games', respectively. By contrast, if genitive phrases with different functions are coordinated, unacceptability results.

(7)   a. *[Ken-to   aka-byoosi]-no   hon
       Ken-and   red-front.cover-GEN   book
       'books of Ken's and with red front cover'

   b. *[aka-byoosi-to   ryoori]-no   hon
       red-front.cover-and   cooking-GEN   book
       'books on cooking and with a red front cover'

   c. *[ryoori-to   Ken]-no   hon
       cooking-and   Ken-GEN   book
       'books on cooking and of Ken's'

The examples in (7) are not acceptable since the coordinated phrases do not have the same syntactic status. Since only phrases of the same syntactic status can be coordinated with *to* 'and', the contrasts in acceptability between the sentences in (6) and those in (7) show that the three genitive phrases in (2) appear in distinct syntactic positions. (Note that some examples could be acceptable if the coordinated genitive phrases are interpreted as belonging to the same type; for instance, (7c) would be acceptable if it means 'a book on cooking, as well as a book on Ken'.)

6.3 X'-Theory

As noted above, if the basic phrase structures are the same across categories, it is possible to think about a general format (the **X'-schema**) used for constructing all types of phrasal expressions. This general format is given in (8a).

(8) a.

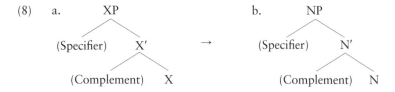

In the general format (8a), X, X′, and XP represent **variables** where X can be filled by any category label. If (8a) is a noun phrase (NP), the label N can be used in the position of X, and thus, we can have the NP-structure which has labels N, N′, and NP, as represented in (8b). If (8a) is an adjective phrase (AP), the label A appears in place of X, thus, having A, A′, and AP. In a postpositional phrase (PP), P appears in place of X. If V is used in place of X, the resulting structure represents VP. These phrase structures are shown in (9).

(9) a.

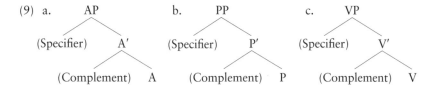

The theory of generalized phrase structure outlined here is called **X′-theory** (Note that when X′-theory was introduced, X̄ was used to represent an intermediate projection, but later, X̄ was changed to X′ for type-setting reasons (i.e. the bar is moved to the side and changed to a prime sign). But since the over-bar terminology was retained, X′ is still conventionally pronounced 'X-bar'.)

In X′-theory, specifiers and complements may or may not appear, and the optionality of these elements is indicated by the parentheses ( ). In general, if no coordination is involved, only one complement is permitted within a phrase. In point of fact, a noun phrase does not allow more than one complement, as illustrated in (10).

(10) *bunpoo-no   gengogaku-no   hon
       grammar-GEN   linguistics-GEN   book
       'a book on linguistics, on grammar'

A similar restriction is imposed on specifiers as well, such that a noun phrase does not easily allow multiple occurrences of specifiers of the same type.

(11) a. *aru   sono   hon
         some   that   book
         'some that book'
      b. *Ken-no   Mari-no   hon
         Ken-GEN   Mari-GEN   book
         'Ken's, Mari's book'
      c. sono   Ken-no   hon
         that   Ken-GEN   book
         'that book of Ken's'

(11a) shows that the determiners *aru* and *sono* cannot co-exist in an NP, and
(11b) shows that two possessor arguments are not allowed in an NP. On the
other hand, a determiner like *sono* can occur with a possessive NP, as shown in
(11c), perhaps because they assume different functions.

   By contrast, adjuncts can readily be iterated (even without coordination). For
instance, a single noun can be modified by more than one adjective.

(12)   kirei-na,   ookii,   siroi   hon
       pretty   big   white   book
       'a pretty, big, white book'

Both determiners and adjectival modifiers (appearing in the noun-modifying
form) modify nouns in a broad sense. Strictly speaking, they assume different
semantic functions; accordingly, they occupy different syntactic positions in
phrase structure. The behavioral differences observed between determiners and
adjectives come from a difference in their syntactic status.

   Parametric variations of word order can be characterized in X'-theoretical
terms. Japanese differs from English in the position of a complement relative to
the head in a phrase structure. Japanese has complement-head order, while
English has head-complement order. Thus, English has the X'-format in (13),
where the order of a head and a complement is reversed.

(13)

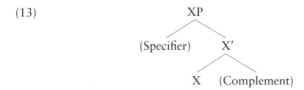

The difference in the position of the complement relative to the head in the
X'-schema in (8a) and (13) mirrors the fact that while Japanese is an SOV language where O precedes V, English is an SVO language where O follows V. In

both Japanese and English, specifiers appear to the left of the head. This can be taken as reflecting the fact that in both languages, S precedes V.

The fact that the same X'-format applies to many kinds of phrases within a language (e.g. NP, VP, PP) brings out an interesting consequence for the theory of language acquisition. Recall that children can acquire their native languages in a short period of time. In the Principles and Parameters theory, language acquisition can be accomplished to a large extent simply by setting parametric values (plus or minus). Once children set the head parameter in their language, i.e. the order of complement and head, they know instantly how complements and heads are ordered in all types of phrases because the head-complement order is constant across categories, as dictated by X'-theory. This suggests that once parameters are set in one place, the same parameters apply in other places. If the same grammatical rules apply across many categories, we can solve one paradox pertinent to language acquisition, which is the fact that children come to know every detail of the grammar of their language even with the very limited amount of stimulus available for them.

For Further Research

(A) In X'-theory, phrase structures are specified in a category-neutral manner, and this allows us to capture cross-categorical generalizations on phrase structure. It is possible to formulate the X'-format in terms of rewriting rules, as in (i).

(i) a. XP → (Spec) X'
     b. X' → X (Comp)

Since the ordering of complement (Comp) and X is subject to parametric variation, as seen by their ordering difference between Japanese and English, we can postulate that their orders are irrelevant for the purpose of the X'-format. XP can generally have one specifier and one complement. If more than one specifier or complement can be included in a structure, it can be hypothesized that the structure consists of two or more phrasal projections. In Japanese, noun phrases can have two specifiers if they belong to distinct types, i.e. if they are heads of distinct projections, which suggests that an NP contains more than one phrasal projection (see Chapter 12).

(B) The mirror image pairs of expressions in Japanese and English discussed in this chapter are determined by the head parameter. Japanese has the complement-head order, and English has the head-complement order. (The position of specifiers does not differ between English and Japanese.) There are other expressions that reflect a difference in the head parameter between the two languages, as in (ii).

(ii) a. Ken did <u>not</u> come.
      b. Ken-wa   <u>ko-nakat</u>-ta.
          Ken-TOP   come-NEG-PST
          'Ken did not come.'

As shown in (ii), the sequence of "negation + verb" is ordered differently in English and Japanese. In English, the negator occurs before the verb, but in Japanese, the order is reversed, showing that they have a mirror image relation. Discuss how these orders are determined. Also, find other mirror image pairs of expressions in English and Japanese, and discuss what structural relations they may have.

CHAPTER 7

Reformulating Clause Structures [B]

7.1 X'-Schema for Clause Structures

X'-theory dictates that the linear order of specifier, head, and complement is constant across categories within a given language. This ordering is determined according to the head parameter, which can be easily set by looking at basic transitive clauses (with either SOV or SVO order). X'-theory brings us a number of desirable consequences. In particular, this theory can provide a principled account for the fact that children can easily acquire a language without looking at every detail of its grammar (or its grammatical phenomena).

The X'-format specified by X'-theory applies to many different types of phrases. Nevertheless, we can find one important exception where X'-format fails to apply. To be concrete, consider the tree diagram in (1b) constructed for the transitive sentence in (1a).

(1)   a. Sensei-ga   Mari-o   home-ta.
          teacher-NOM   Mari-ACC   praise-PST
          'The teacher praised Mari.'
       b.

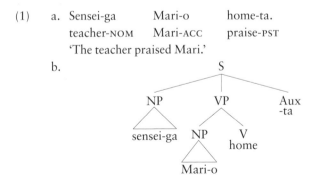

The clause structure in (1b) does not follow the X'-schema. If phrase structures are constant across categories, the clause structure (starting with S) would be expected to be in keeping with the X'-schema, just like other phrases. Nevertheless, the clause structure has a form that does not conform to the

X'-format applying to various types of phrases.

Moreover, the clause structure in (1b) does not comply with two important general principles that are considered to apply universally. One principle is called the **Headedness Principle**, which states that a phrase is formed by way of projection from its head. According to the Headedness Principle, a verb can never form a postpositional phrase. Thus, (2a), where V projects to VP, is a possible structure, but (2b), where V projects to PP, is not.

(2)   a.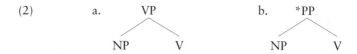

Another principle relevant for the present discussion is the **Binarity Principle**, which states that the branching from a node is always binary. Given this Principle, the binary branching VP structure in (3a) is well-formed, but the ternary branching structure in (3b) is not.

(3)   a.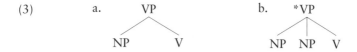

The Binarity Principle implies that when there are two or more phrases inside a phrase, they are always combined in such a way that binary branching is created; if the sequence of NP + NP + V has the structure in (4a), it obeys the Binarity Principle, as there is no ternary branching.

(4)   a.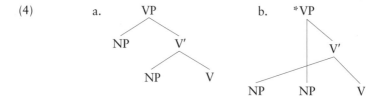

The well-formed VP in (4a) has a structure where binary branching is iterated, i.e. VP branches down into V' and NP, and V' branches down into V and NP. (There is also a general constraint prohibiting branches from crossing that is observed in (4a) but is violated in (4b).)

The two basic principles (the Headedness Principle and the Binarity Principle) are not observed in (1b). For one thing, the sentence structure in (1b) has ternary branching. For another, the sentence is not a projection of any head, i.e. "S" is simply an abbreviated label for "sentence". It would be tempting to say that the clause is a level of representation different from the phrase level representations (VP, NP, etc.), so that its representation does not have to follow the X′-schema. But this is hardly explanatory, and it would be nice if the clause structure could be made to conform to the two general principles. As a matter of fact, this is possible: In (1b), there are three constituents that appear just below S. One is Aux, which is filled by a tense element. Note, however, that Aux is a kind of head, but does not project to a phrase, which violates the Headedness Principle. On the other hand, if Aux is taken to project to a phrase, i.e. S, the structure can be made consistent with the Headedness Principle. Suppose here that S is the maximal projection of tense (T), occupied by tense -*ta*. If so, S can now be relabeled as TP (=Tense Phrase). Furthermore, if the subject NP is a specifier to TP, and VP is a complement, the structure in (5) can be constructed.

(5)

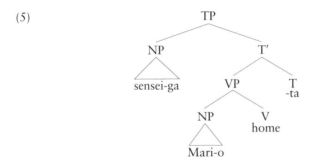

In the clause structure in (5), there is no phrasal projection that violates the two principles noted above. In this structure, the subject, which refers to the person or the thing being mentioned by the statement, is identified as the specifier of TP. On the other hand, VP, which describes an event, functions as a complement to TP, while serving to add semantic content to the tense, so to speak.

Needless to say, the clause structure is identical between Japanese and English with the exception of the complement-head order; i.e. English differs minimally from Japanese in that an object appears to the right of the verb. To be concrete, let us consider the clause structure of the English sentence in (6).

(6)   John praised Mary.

In English, a simple tense element ([PRS] or [PST]) forms part of the verb, but when the clause is negated by *not*, it appears independently of the verb, as in *John did not praise Mary*. Thus, we can postulate that in (6), the fused verb form *praised* is derived by applying a morphological rule to the two elements: [PST]+*praise* → *praised*. This being the case, the structure in (7) can be posited for the sentence in (6).

(7)

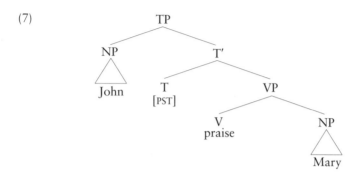

The TP projections in (5) for Japanese and in (7) for English not only conform to the two principles (the Headedness Principle and the Binarity Principle) but also reflect the parametric difference in the order of complement and head between the two languages, in that TP has a complement-head order in Japanese, and a head-complement order in English. Furthermore, in the new, revised clause structure, TP constitutes the maximal projection of a tense (T), which is in full conformity with the X′-schema. This indicates that X′-theory applies to the sentence-level projection, as well as other phrasal projections.

The present analysis can also provide a theoretical account for a phenomenon that looks at first sight mysterious. This has to do with the fact that tense marking is obligatory on predicates (in English and Japanese), even though there are sentences that do not have to specify a temporal relation semantically. For instance, a sentence stating a universal truth like (8) is valid at any time, place, and circumstance, but somehow the sentence must include tense marking that specifies a temporal relation, as seen by the present tense marking on the predicate.

(8) Tikyuu-wa   maru-i.
     earth-TOP   round-PRS
     'The earth is round.'

Why is it the case that tense must be indicated on the predicate in order to construct a full-fledged sentence? The answer to this question is that a sentence must have a tense (T) head because TP, which is an indispensable projection to construct a sentence, needs to be projected from a T head.

7.2 The Hidden Upper Structure

If a sentence has a TP projection projected from a T head above the VP, then the clause structure observes the X'-schema even at the sentence level. The question arises, then, whether the TP projection provides a complete representation of sentence structure. The examples in (9) show that there must be an additional projection above TP.

(9) a. Watasi-wa [Ken-ga   Mari-o   home-ta   to]   omo-u.
         I-TOP   Ken-NOM   Mari-ACC   praise-PST   that   think-PRS
         'I think that Ken praised Mari.'
     b. Ano hito-wa   [Ken-ga   Mari-o   home-ta   ka]
         that man-TOP   Ken-NOM   Mari-ACC   praise-PST   Q
         tazune-ta.
         ask-PST
         'That man asked if Ken praised Mari.'

In the embedded clauses in (9), additional elements such as *to* 'that' and *ka* 'whether' appear to the right of the tense. Since these elements (typically) occur in complement clauses, they are called **complementizers**.

   If a full sentence is complete with TP, with no other phrases projected above it, the fact that complementizers appear in the embedded clauses remains a mystery. This puzzle is solved if a clause completes with a phrasal projection that accommodates a complementizer like *to* or *ka*, i.e. the head of C (=Complementizer), which includes a complementizer, projects to CP (=Complementizer Phrase). Under this analysis, the structure in (10) can be posited for the complement clauses in (9).

(10)

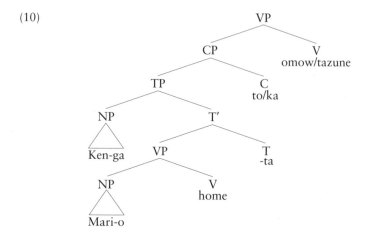

(The slash notation (/), as seen in '*omow/tazune*' in the tree, indicates alternative choices of words.) In (9a), the complementizer *to* 'that', which occupies the C-head position, signals that the embedded clause is declarative. In (9b), the complementizer *ka*, which is the Japanese counterpart of *whether* or *if*, signals that the matrix verb selects an interrogative clause as its complement. When a C head, which contains a complementizer, is combined with TP, it projects to CP. Note that Japanese is a head-final SOV language, and given that in Japanese a higher head appears to the right of a lower head (in linear order), it is naturally expected that complementizers are always ordered to the right of the tense. (Needless to say, CP is placed above TP in English as well. However, English is an SVO language, so a complementizer appears to the left of the subject.)

Embedded clauses have CP projections, as evidenced by the fact that they occur with complementizers. What about matrix clauses (or main clauses)? Since there is no *a priori* reason to think that matrix clauses differ from embedded clauses in structural terms, it can be hypothesized that they also have a projection above TP. In point of fact, in Japanese, complementizer-like elements occur to the right of tense even in matrix clauses, as exemplified in (11).

(11) Sensei-ga   Mari-o   home-ta   no?
      teacher-NOM   Mari-ACC   praise-PST   Q
      'Did the teacher praise Mari?'

In Japanese, a particle used to form an interrogative clause may be placed to the right of the tense in both matrix and embedded clauses. If a question particle appears in the C-head position, CP must be projected in matrix clauses, just as it is in embedded clauses.

(12)

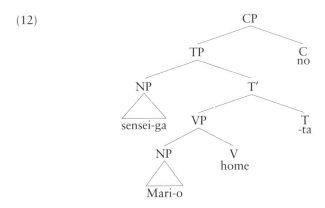

Given the phrase structure in (12), it may seem inappropriate to give the rele-vant projection the name CP (=Complementizer Phrase), for it does not neces-sarily indicate the presence of a complement clause in the strict sense of a clause serving as the complement to some head. Nevertheless, we follow the conven-tion of using this term even for the projection positioned above TP in matrix clauses. In declarative matrix clauses, complementizers do not occur on the sur-face, but we can assume that they have CP projections whose head is left unfilled (or filled by a phonologically null element).

In Japanese, questions are formed by putting a question particle in the C-head position. In English, a complementizer (*if* or *whether*) is inserted into C when forming an embedded yes-no question.

(13) a. I wonder if Mary will come.
      b. I wonder [$_{CP}$ if [$_{TP}$ Mary will come]]

On the other hand, a direct yes-no question implements so-called **subject-auxil-iary inversion**, as seen in (14).

(14) a. Mary will come.
      b. Will Mary come?

An auxiliary verb like *will* appears in different positions depending on whether a matrix clause is a question or not. In (14b), the auxiliary *will* appears to the left of the subject *Mary*, which follows if it undergoes a syntactic operation moving it from the T-head position to the C-head position, as illustrated in (15).

(15)

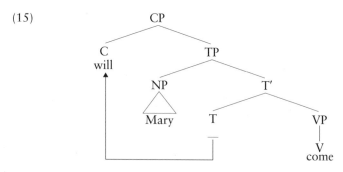

The facts concerning complementizers and subject-auxiliary inversion point to the conclusion that in English, just as in Japanese, both matrix and embedded clauses have CP projections which can host complementizers.

For Further Research

(A) There are constraints imposed on phrase structure other than the Binarity Principle and the Headedness Principle. One such constraint is that a node can branch off downward, but not upward.

(i)

The structure in (i) is not well-formed, because a single head is not allowed to project two distinct maximal projections.

(B-1) In Japanese, a noun complement clause can be introduced by the complementizer *toiu* 'that'. It has the morphological form of *to* + *iu* [that + say], but this sequence cannot be divided by movement, as shown in (iib).

(ii) a. Ken-wa   [sensoo-ga   oki-ru   toiu]   uwasa-o
         Ken-TOP   war-NOM   break.out-PRS   that   rumor-ACC
         kii-ta.
         hear-PST
         'Ken heard the rumor that a war will break out.'
      b. *[Sensoo-ga   oki-ru   to]   Ken-wa   iu   uwasa-o
          war-NOM   break.out-PRS   that   Ken-TOP   say   rumor-ACC
          kii-ta.
          hear-PST
          'That a war will break out, Ken heard the rumor.'

On the other hand, *soo* replacement can apply to the sequence of the noun complement plus *to*, a part of *toiu*, while leaving *iu* intact, as in (iii).

(iii) a. Soo-iu   uwasa-mo   ar-u.   b. Doo-iu   uwasa?
          so-say   rumor-also   be-PRS   how-say   rumor
          'There is also such a rumor.'   'What rumor?'

Discuss whether it is appropriate to treat *toiu* as a single complementizer. How can the facts mentioned in (ii) and (iii) be accounted for?

(B-2) The discussion on the discourse particles *to*, *no* and *ka* appearing at the end of a clause suggests that clause structure has a hidden CP structure projected over the TP structure. Can there be only one projection that projects above TP? Or is there more than one projection above TP? A close look at the distribution of discourse particles provides us with a clue to understanding this issue.

CHAPTER 8

Thematic Roles [B]

8.1 How Are Logical Meanings Determined in Syntax?

If we only look at possible syntactic structures of a language, we cannot provide an accurate description of the grammar. The reason is that not all syntactically possible structures are well-formed. Japanese has intransitive sentences
with the sequence "subject + verb" and also transitive sentences with the
sequence "subject + object + verb". These structures are allowed by the syntactic rules, but in actuality, they can be either well-formed or ill-formed, as illustrated in (1).

(1)   a. Mari-ga   nai-ta.
           Mari-NOM   cry-PST
           'Mari cried.'
      b. *Mari-ga   Ken-o   nai-ta.
           Mari-NOM   Ken-ACC   cry-PST
           'Mari cried Ken.'

The two sentences in (1) have structures that conform to the syntactic rules of
Japanese. Nevertheless, (1a) is a good sentence and (1b) is not. The difference
comes from the fact that the verb *naku* 'cry' does not take an object. This verb
can occur in an intransitive clause but not in a transitive clause. Thus, only (1a)
is a grammatical sentence. A similar contrast is observed between (2a) and (2b).

(2)   a. Ken-ga   Mari-o   home-ta.
           Ken-NOM   Mari-ACC   praise-PST
           'Ken praised Mari.'
      b. (*)Ken-ga   home-ta.
            Ken-NOM   praise-PST
           'Ken praised.'

70

(2a) is a well-formed sentence. But (2b) is ill-formed, or at best, it is considered to be incomplete. This is because the verb *homeru* 'praise' is a transitive verb, which requires an object in addition to its subject. Since *homeru* is a transitive verb, (2b) is ungrammatical if it is taken to be an intransitive clause. Note that in Japanese, arguments are often omitted if their reference can be recovered from the context, so (2b) could be used as an elliptical transitive clause. Thus, (2b) is not felt to be totally ungrammatical, unlike (1b), which includes an object argument that cannot possibly occur in an intransitive clause. (The symbol (*) in (2b) indicates that the sentence can be acceptable under some conditions.)

It is important to see here that the verb determines the number of arguments that can appear in a clause, and hence the sentence pattern. This can be confirmed by looking at how the frames in (3) can be interpreted.

(3) a. *[X]-ga   [Y]-o   nak-u.
           -NOM   -ACC   cry-PRS
          '[X] cries [Y].'
     b. [X]-ga   nak-u.
           -NOM   cry-PRS
          '[X] cries.'

Since the verb *naku* 'cry' cannot appear in a transitive clause with a subject and an object, we can immediately see that (3a) is not a well-formed sentence frame, even if we do not know what expression fills in [X] and [Y]. In the same vein, we know, at the very least, that (3b) is a (potentially) well-formed sentence frame independent of what fills [X] since the verb *naku* is intransitive. In contradistinction, in (4), the variable Z appears in a position that is filled by a verb.

(4) Sensei-ga   [Z]-ta.
     teacher-NOM   -PST
     'The teacher [Z]-ed.'

In (4), we cannot tell whether or not this is a well-formed sentence frame, due to a lack of the information needed to determine the sentence pattern. This illustrates that the number of arguments appearing in a sentence varies according to the properties of the verb, which means that it is the verb that carries the semantic information that determines the overall pattern of the sentence.

To determine whether a given sentence is well-formed or not, it is not sufficient to check only the number of arguments that the verb allows. It is also necessary to determine what kind of argument is allowed in the sentence.

(5)   [X]-ga   [Y]-o   home-ta.
                -NOM   -ACC   praise-PST
       '[X] praised [Y].'

In the transitive frame in (5) with the verb *homeru* 'praise', X must be filled by an argument referring to an individual capable of performing the act of praising, and Y, by an argument referring to an individual or entity counting as the target of the act. These restrictions on argument selection (called **selectional restrictions**) must be satisfied to derive a legitimate sentence. Thus, (6) is not acceptable.

(6)   *Yakan-ga   Mari-o   home-ta.
       kettle-NOM   Mari-ACC   praise-PST
       'The kettle praised Mari.'

The sentence in (6) is odd on the normal interpretation. If *tyabin* 'kettle' is replaced by a human noun like *Ken*, the sentence is fine. The oddity of the sentence in (6) is semantic in nature, i.e. it is a matter of semantic interpretation. The sentence could be uttered felicitously in a "fairy tale" context where the kettle behaves like a human, in which case the argument *tyabin* satisfies the selectional restriction imposed on the subject.

   The data illustrate that in order to derive a legitimate sentence, it is necessary for the verb to specify not only a proper sentence pattern (e.g. whether it takes an object or not) but also the semantic types of the arguments it selects. In generative grammar, these two sorts of information are encoded in *θ*-roles (or **thematic/semantic roles**), and the kinds of *θ*-roles are specified in the verb's **argument structure** (or *θ*-grid): for instance, the verbs *homeru* 'praise' and *naku* 'cry' have the argument structures in (7).

(7)   a.   homeru: <Agent, Theme>
       b.   naku: <Experiencer>

(7a) indicates that the verb *homeru* bears the *θ*-role of "agent", which specifies an individual who performs the act of praising, and the *θ*-role of "theme", which specifies the target to which the praising act is directed. (7b) indicates that the verb *naku* has the *θ*-role of "experiencer", referring to an individual experiencing the feeling of sadness.

   How can the verbs specify the nature of arguments in terms of *θ*-roles? This is accomplished by *θ*-role **assignment**—the grammatical process of the verb assigning *θ*-roles to its arguments, as represented in (8).

72

(8)　　[Ken-ga　　[Mari-o　　home_{<Agent, Theme>}] -ta]

In (8), as indicated by the dotted arrows, the verb *homeru* assigns an agent role
to its subject, and a theme role to its object. Accordingly, the subject is interpreted as an agent, and the object, as a theme. Once the θ-roles are assigned
correctly, the sentence is properly interpreted.

It is worth noting that θ-roles do not provide precise descriptions of the arguments (i.e. the exact characterizations of the participants of a particular event
described by the verb), but rather, their role labels provide some general descriptions in a rather coarse-grained manner. For instance, the subjects of the verbs
hasiru 'run' and *hataraku* 'work' refer to individuals taking some kind of intentional action, so the θ-roles they receive are both called "agent". θ-roles do not
have specific labels which vary from verb to verb (e.g. "kicker" and "kickee" for
the verb *keru* 'kick', and "praiser" and "praisee" for the verb *homeru* 'praise'),
but carry general labels, such as "agent" and "theme". If θ-roles are characterized in this manner, we can easily capture semantic generalizations covering the
same types of arguments.

A number of restrictions are imposed on the way in which the verb assigns
θ-roles, which are necessary for sentences to have a proper semantic interpretation. One such restriction is that the two θ-roles of the verb *homeru*—agent and
theme—are never assigned to the arguments in the way illustrated in (9).

(9)　　*[Ken-ga　　[Mari-o　　home_{<Agent, Theme>}] -ta]

In (9), the agent role is assigned to the object and the theme role is assigned to
the subject. With this θ-role assignment, the sentence in (2a) would carry the
meaning of 'Mari praised Ken', but this interpretation is not permitted for this
sentence. The unavailability of the intended interpretation in (9), where the
subject is interpreted as theme, and the object as agent, naturally falls out if
θ-roles are assigned in accordance with **the thematic hierarchy**: Agent > Theme.
This hierarchy indicates that the higher agent role is assigned to the higher
argument, and the lower theme role, the lower argument. In point of fact, (2a) is
interpreted properly only if the agent role is assigned to the subject, which is
higher than the object structurally, and the theme is assigned to the lower
object. The priority of agent over theme in θ-role assignment to the subject
position is sometimes indicated by an underline, as in <Agent, Theme>.

θ-role assignment is subject to other restrictions. For instance, there is a
restriction such that one θ-role can never be assigned to more than one argument. If the agent role were assigned to both subject and object, the sentence in

(2a) would be interpreted as 'Ken and Mari praised.'

(10)   *[Ken-ga   [Mari-o   home_{\<Agent, Theme\>}] -ta]

The impossibility of assigning this interpretation to the sentence in (2a) shows that there is a ban on assigning one and the same θ-role to two or more arguments. (Note also that the theme role remains unassigned in (10), which is also considered to be illegitimate). (11) illustrates another kind of constraint on θ-role assignment.

(11)   *[[Ken-ga   home_{\<Agent, Theme\>}] -ta]

In (11), a single argument receives two distinct θ-roles from the verb. If this type of θ-role assignment is possible, the sentence in (12) would be acceptable with the interpretation that Ken praised Ken (himself).

(12)   *Ken-ga   home-ta.
        Ken-NOM   praise-PST
        (lit.) 'Ken praised.'

(In (12), 'lit.' signifies that the translation is literal, i.e. a word-to-word translation into English.) The intended interpretation is not available for the sentence in (12). In order to express this meaning, the sentence needs to have the form in (13) instead, which has a reflexive pronoun *zibun* 'self' in object position to receive the theme role.

(13)   Ken-ga   zibun-o   home-ta.
        Ken-NOM   self-ACC   praise-PST
        'Ken praised himself.'

In (13), the reflexive pronoun *zibun* needs to be coreferential with the subject *Ken*, i.e. *zibun* refers to the same individual that *Ken* does. The reason why the verb *homeru* must have a transitive sentence comprised of two arguments is that the verb has two θ-roles to assign and one argument cannot receive more than one θ-role.

In short, θ-role assignment is constrained in such a way that the thematic relations of arguments are uniquely determined, and there is a one-to-one correspondence between θ-roles and arguments (alongside the thematic hierarchy constraint). This one-to-one relationship is regulated by the way in which

θ-roles are assigned to arguments, and this condition is called the **θ-criterion**. The θ-criterion is a mechanism that enables us to understand the meaning of sentences, because it imposes a grammatical condition that guarantees that all and only the arguments required by the verb are properly realized in the sentence (by way of θ-role assignment).

8.2 Kinds of Thematic Roles

It is a commonly held assumption that natural language makes available a restricted list of θ-roles. Although there is no general consensus about the θ-roles that can be used for a syntactic analysis, the following list represents some of the common labels allocated to θ-roles, although it is by no means exhaustive. (The underlined arguments in the (a-g) examples bear the named θ-roles).

(14) a. **Agent:** Ken-ga   hasit-ta.
                   Ken-NOM   run-PST
                   'Ken ran.'

    b. **Experiencer:** Mari-ni   Ken-ga   mie-ta.
                   Mari-DAT   Ken-NOM   see-PST
                   'Mari saw Ken.'

    c. **Theme:** Kodomo-ga   osara-o   wat-ta.
                   child-NOM   dish-ACC   break-PST
                   'The child broke the dish.'

    d. **Location:** Kodomo-wa   beddo-de   ne-ta.
                   child-TOP   bed-on   sleep-PST
                   'The child slept on the bed.'

    e. **Source:** Watasi-wa   kinoo   Tookyoo-o   de-ta.
                 I-TOP   yesterday   Tokyo-ACC   leave-PST
                   'I left Tokyo yesterday.'

    f. **Goal:** Kanozyo-wa   eki-ni   tui-ta.
                 she-TOP   station-at   arrive-PST
                   'She arrived at the station.'

    g. **Instrument:** Ano hito-wa   ohasi-de   udon-o   tabe-ta.
                   that man-TOP chopstick-INS   noodle-ACC eat-PST
                   'That man ate noodles with chopsticks.'

The θ-roles are characterized as follows. **Agent** represents an individual instigating some intentional action. **Experiencer** is an individual experiencing some psychological state. An experiencer does not have to perform an agentive action, while an agent does. **Theme** is a target to which an action is directed or an entity undergoing a change. Theme is sometimes divided into two subcategories, one is **theme** (in a narrow sense), which undergoes movement, and the other is **patient**, which undergoes a change of state. **Location** refers to a place where an action or an event takes place. **Source** represents a starting point of movement, and **goal**, a place in which movement ends (i.e. a destination). **Instrument** specifies a tool or a device used to make an agentive (or a causative) event happen.

Finally, subjects and objects are most typically realized as NPs syntactically, bearing nominative case *ga* and accusative case *o*. These case markers specify the grammatical relations of expressions to which they attach. There are also postpositions like *de* 'with (or in)', *kara* 'from', *made* 'to', and the like, which assign fixed semantic meanings to the arguments that accompany them. Arguments with such postpositions do not undergo syntactic operations like passivization, so they are considered to be realized as PPs, just like English PPs.

For Further Research

(A) The θ-criterion has been proposed by Chomsky (1981) as a constraint falling under θ-theory. Chomsky (1981: 35) defines it as:

(i) θ-criterion: Each argument bears one and only one θ-role, and each
       θ-role is assigned to one and only one argument.

This criterion is closely related to the Projection Principle, the condition which requires that selectional information on lexical items be represented at every syntactic level (Chomsky (1986: 86)). These principles cannot account for the fact that agent has priority over other roles in θ-role assignment to subject position. Instead, this fact is accounted for by positing a thematic hierarchy. Various versions of thematic hierarchies have been proposed in the literature (e.g. Fillmore (1968), Jackendoff (1972), Van Valin and LaPolla (1997), Baker (1988, 1997); see Levin and Rappaport Hovav (2005) for an overview).

(B) Japanese has verbs of asking such as *tazuneru* 'ask' and *situmon-suru* 'question'. These verbs select for interrogative clauses but show a difference as to whether or not they can take a noun phrase as their complement. The verb *tazuneru* can take both types of complements.

(ii)   a. Ken-wa   [Mari-ga   doko-ni   ik-u   ka]   tazune-ta.
          Ken-TOP   Mari-NOM   where-to   go-PRS   Q   ask-PST
          'Ken asked where Mari would go.'
       b. Ken-wa   [Mari-no   ik-u]   basyo-o   tazune-ta.
          Ken-TOP   Mari-GEN   go-PRS   place-ACC   ask-PST
          'Ken asked the place where Mari would go.'

The predicate *situmon-suru* 'question' cannot take a noun phrase as its complement, while it can take a clausal complement.

(iii) a. Ken-wa   [Mari-ga   doko-ni   ik-u   ka]   situmon-si-ta.
          Ken-TOP   Mari-NOM   where-to   go-PRS   Q   question-do-PST
          'Ken questioned where Mari would go.'
       b. *Ken-wa [Mari-no   ik-u]   basyo-o   situmon-si-ta.
          Ken-TOP   Mari-GEN   go-PRS   place-ACC   question-do-PST
          'Ken questioned the place where Mari would go.'

What makes the two verbs behave differently? Note that (iib) takes a noun phrase syntactically, but it is understood as a kind of question asking for the identity of the place where Mari would go (i.e. as a "concealed question").

CHAPTER 9

Passivization: Case and NP-movement [B]

9.1 Active-Passive Pairs and Their Derivations

Cross-linguistically, including Japanese and English, it is true that many active sentences have passive counterparts. If we follow the common practice of assuming a derivational relationship between the two, we can take a passive clause to be derived from its active counterpart in many cases, at least. The pair of active and passive sentences in (1) describes the same event from a different perspective.

(1)   a. Sensei-ga   Ken-o   sikat-ta.
             teacher-NOM   Ken-ACC   scold-PST
             'The teacher scolded Ken.'
      b. Ken-ga   sensei-ni   sikar-are-ta.
             Ken-NOM   teacher-by   scold-PASS-PST
             'Ken was scolded by the teacher.'

The active sentence in (1a) describes an event viewed from the teacher's side (i.e. as the teacher's event), but the passive sentence in (1b) describes the same event from Ken's side. Despite this difference, the two sentences have the same logical meaning because they both describe a scolding action in which *sensei* 'the teacher' is an agent and Ken, a theme.

Normally, the same logical meaning will no longer be expressed if arguments are simply exchanged. In (2), *Ken* appears in initial position marked with nominative case, and *sensei* is marked with accusative case.

(2)   Ken-ga   sensei-o   sikat-ta.
        Ken-NOM   teacher-ACC   scold-PST
        'Ken scolded the teacher.'

Unlike (1b), (2) does not have the same logical meaning as (1a). This raises the question of why (1a) and (1b) carry the same logical meaning despite the fact that the arguments are aligned differently.

To understand how the passive and active sentences are linked to the same logical meaning, let us consider the structural properties of a passive clause. (The discussion here is confined to cases involving so-called **direct passivization**, although Japanese has another type of passivization referred to as indirect passivization: see Chapter 18). Direct passivization effects a number of notable structural changes, as can be confirmed by the pair of active and passive sentences in (3).

(3) a. Kodomo-ga   omotya-o   tukut-ta.
        child-NOM   toy-ACC   make-PST
        'The child made a toy.'   (Active)
     b. Omotya-ga   kodomo-niyotte   tukur-are-ta.
        toy-NOM   child-by   make-PASS-PST
        'A toy was made by the child.'   (Passive)

In the first place, passivization induces a change in verb form; a passive verb carries the passive morpheme *(r)are*, but an active verb does not. Secondly, the subject of an active transitive sentence loses its status by passivization and is marked with a postposition *ni*, *niyotte* or *kara* in its passive counterpart (the actual choice of postposition may vary depending on the type of passivized verb). This postpositional phrase, which is derived by passivization, can often be dropped, i.e. its presence is optional, just like adjuncts, so the subject argument is regarded as having been **demoted** to the status of an adjunct via passivization. Finally, the original object of the active sentence appears as the subject of the passive clause, marked with nominative *ga*. Here, the object is **promoted** to subject under passivization.

In generative grammar, the fact that active and passive sentences express the same logical meaning is accounted for by assuming that both share essentially the same **underlying structures**, where the thematic relations of arguments are determined. Let us discuss how a passive clause is formed syntactically under this perspective.

In the derivation of a passive clause from an active one, an erstwhile object is promoted to become a subject. This structural change is effected by **NP-movement**, which moves an argument (i.e. NP) from its original object position to the subject position, as in (4).

(4) [TP omotya-ga [VP ……. ~~omotya-ga~~ tukur-are]-ta]

The strikethrough in (4) indicates the position from which the passive subject is originated, and the arrow indicates the path of movement. It is reasonable to posit the derivation in (4), where the passive subject appears in subject position as a result of movement, given the fact that no argument can be realized in object position in the passive clause. (Although we cannot literally see anything that actually moves, we can infer that movement is involved in the derivation, and it is a common practice to say that movement takes place (metaphorically) when some element appears in a position distinct from its original position, as seen in passive clauses.)

In Japanese, case marking is required on NPs when they occur in a sentence (although it is sometimes omitted in colloquial speech). Subjects bear nominative *ga*, and objects, accusative *o*. Arguments appear with case marking in passive clauses as well, but, as can be seen from the pair of sentences in (3), a change of case marking occurs. While *omotya* 'toy' in the active clause in (3a) is marked with accusative case, the same argument in the passive clause in (3b) is marked with nominative case; the change here is from accusative *o* to nominative *ga*: *omotya-o* → *omotya-ga*. On the other hand, the transitive verb *tukuru* 'make' has the argument structure <Agent, Theme>, and the subject is identified as bearing the agent role, and the object, the theme role in (3a). In the passive clause in (3b), the subject bears a theme role.

As noted above, the promotion of an object to a passive subject is invoked by virtue of passive NP-movement. To illustrate how a passive clause is derived via NP-movement, let us first consider an active clause like (3a). In (3a), the verb *tukuru* 'make' assigns an agent role to a subject and a theme role to an object, as illustrated in (5).

(5)   [$_{TP}$ kodomo [$_{VP}$ omotya tukut$_{<Agent, Theme>}$] -ta]

In (5), the arguments receive their θ-roles in a proper way, so the sentence can be assigned an appropriate semantic interpretation. Nevertheless, (5) is not well-formed yet, because, as it stands, the arguments have not been assigned case marking.

θ-roles are necessary for the semantic interpretation of arguments. But why is it that case marking is needed for arguments? The answer is that unless an NP is assigned Case, it is not allowed to occupy a position in the clause even if it has a θ-role. This Case constraint imposed on arguments is called the **Case filter**, which is often considered to follow from the condition that arguments cannot be interpreted unless they are assigned Case (called the **visibility condition**). This state of affairs may be likened to a case of theater performance: Even if an actor has been given the script of a play, the actor is not allowed to perform his role on the stage unless he is officially licensed to take the designated position by some authorized person (like a director). The theoretical construct to license the occurrence of NPs in a clause is called **structural Case** (with the upper-case "Case"), whereas its actual morphological realization is called **morphological case** (with the lower-case "case"). The important point is that an argument must be assigned Case in order for the θ-role it bears to be recognized (or visible).

Arguments are Case-licensed if they receive structural Case; the generally accepted assumption on Case-assgignment is that a finite T assigns nominative Case to the subject position, and that a transitive V assigns accusative Case to the object position. In (3a), if the arguments get structural Case from the verb and the tense, as in (6), they are structurally licensed to occur in the sentence.

(6)   [$_{TP}$ kodomo [$_{VP}$ omotya   tukut$_{[ACC]}$] -ta$_{[NOM]}$]

In the active clause in (3a), the subject and object each receive both Case and θ-role in their original positions, as seen in (5) and (6). In this case, no NP-movement is invoked in the derivation.

The assumption on Case-assigning heads, i.e. finite T and transitive V assign nominative and accusative Case, respectively, can be empirically justified. To begin with, observe that an accusative argument cannot appear if the verb is intransitive, as in (7).

(7)   Mari-ga   (*Ken-o)   taore-ta.
        Mari-NOM   Ken-ACC   fall.down-PST
        'Mari fell down (Ken).'

This suggests that a transitive verb is the assigner of accusative Case. For nominative Case, finite T is the Case assigner because the nominative *ga* is assigned to subjects appearing in finite clauses. In a non-finite embedded clause like (8), the logical subject cannot be marked with nominative *ga*, but must be marked with accusative *o*.

(8)   Ken-wa   [Mari-o/*-ga   kawaiku]   omot-ta.
        Ken-TOP   Mari-ACC/-NOM   cute   think-PST
        'Ken thought Mari cute.'

(The notation -*o*/*-*ga* in (8) indicates that the accusative marking is acceptable, while the nominative marking (with the asterisk) is not.) The embedded predicate is not finite, since it does not carry a tense marker like -*ru*/-*ta* (and an embedded clause with no tense marker is often called a **small clause**). Given that a finite tense is needed for an NP to be marked with nominative case, we can state that finite tense (T) is an assigner of nominative Case.

In the passive clause in (3b), the passivized verb behaves like a kind of intransitive verb, because the original subject is demoted to an adjunct. In (3b), the transitive *tukuru* 'make' bears the passive morpheme *(r)are*, which changes its argument structure as follows: *tukuru*:<Agent, Theme> → *tukur-are-ru*:<Theme>. Passivization makes an agent role unavailable in the verb's argument structure. It is often stated that the absence of the agent role is due to the passive morpheme's absorbing the agent role from the argument structure. Nevertheless, the agent can appear in the clause if marked with *niyotte* 'by', which suggests that the postposition *niyotte* assigns an agent role to the demoted subject. In the passive clause in (3b), the θ-roles are assigned, as in (9).

(9)   [$_{TP}$ [$_{VP}$ (kodomo niyotte$_{<Agent>}$) omotya   tukur-are$_{<Theme>}$] -ta]

If the derivation stopped here, the theme argument would appear in object position in the passive sentence. But this argument is moved to the subject position for Case reasons. The transitive verb *tukuru* loses its ability to assign accusative Case when passivization applies. Accordingly, the argument in the object position needs to move into the subject position to receive nominative Case, as depicted in (10a) and (10b).

(10)   a. [$_{TP}$ [$_{VP}$(kodomo niyotte$_{[OBL]}$) omotya tukur-are]-ta$_{[NOM]}$]

        b. [$_{TP}$ omotya [$_{VP}$(kodomo niyotte$_{[OBL]}$) ~~omotya~~ tukur-are]-ta$_{[NOM]}$]

The demoted subject occurs with *niyotte*. The postposition *niyotte* is a Case assigner and a θ-role assigner at the same time, so the demoted NP is allowed to occur in the sentence (optionally). (It is assumed here that P assigns oblique Case to its complement.) NP-movement is triggered in a passive clause because the passive subject, which first appears in object position to receive a θ-role, needs to have Case in order to serve as an argument in the passive sentence. (The argument in its original position before movement is indicated by a strikethrough in (10b).)

84

9.2 Evidence for NP-movement

The foregoing discussion on the derivation of passive clauses presupposes that the theme role is uniformly assigned to an object position in both active and passive sentences. This presumption is based on a hypothesis referred to as the **Uniformity of Theta Assignment Hypothesis (UTAH)**. This hypothesis requires that the same θ-roles are assigned to the same structural positions. Under this perspective, a passive subject generated in object position first receives a theme θ-role and then is moved to the subject position to receive nominative Case. (On the other hand, if a theme θ-role were assigned to the subject position in a passive clause, the passive subject would receive both the theme θ-role and nominative Case in subject position and thus no NP-movement would be induced for a passive clause.)

There is empirical evidence in support of the analysis taking the passive subject to originate from an object position. To make this point, let us consider the sentence in (11), which contains the secondary **resultative predicate** *konagona-ni* 'into pieces'.

(11) Robotto-ga   kabe-o   konagona-ni   kowasi-ta.
      robot-NOM   wall-ACC   pieces-to   break-PST
      'The robot broke the wall into pieces.'

The sentence in (11) describes the event of the robot's breaking the wall, and *konagona-ni* specifies the resultant state of the wall. The sentence cannot mean that the robot was broken into pieces by hitting an especially sturdy wall, although it is not difficult to imagine such a situation. The resultative predication has a constraint such that its target is limited to direct objects (i.e. **the direct object constraint**). This predicative relation is indicated by the double-headed arrow in (12).

(12) [$_{TP}$ robotto   [$_{VP}$ kabe   konagona-ni   kowasi] -ta]

The passive sentence in (13) appears not to conform to the generalization, as the resultative predicate *konagona-ni* describes the resultant state of the subject.

(13) Kabe-ga   konagona-ni   kowas-are-ta.
      wall-NOM   pieces-to   destroy-PASS-PST
      'The wall was broken into pieces.'

The acceptability of (13) follows, however, if the passive subject starts out as an object, as in (14).

(14) [$_{TP}$ kabe   [$_{VP}$ ~~kabe~~   konagona-ni   kowas-are] -ta]

In the passive sentence, the resultative predication appears to target the passive subject on the surface, but if the passive subject originates as an object, it turns out that this predication observes the direct object constraint at the underlying level, where NP-movement has not yet been instantiated.

A similar pattern is found in modification by the quantity adverb *takusan* 'a lot'. First, (15a) can mean that the child made a lot of toys but lacks the interpretation that a lot of children made toys. In (15b), *takusan* cannot specify the number of children (although it can specify the amount of running, in which case it serves as a verbal modifier).

(15) a. Kodomo-ga   omotya-o   tebayaku   takusan   tukut-ta.
          child-NOM   toy-ACC   quickly   a.lot   make-PST
          'The child made a lot of toys quickly.'
      b. #Kodomo-ga   kinoo   takusan   hasit-ta.
          child-NOM   yesterday   a.lot   run-PST
          'The child ran a lot yesterday.'

The examples in (15) show that *takusan* can modify an object, and not the subject, and that its modification is constrained by the direct object constraint. (The sign # in (15b) indicates that the interpretation in which it modifies the subject is absent). In spite of this generalization, the subject can be targeted by *takusan* in a passive sentence like (16).

(16) Omotya-ga   kono   kodomo-niyotte   takusan   tukur-are-ta.
      toy-NOM   this   child-by   a.lot   make-PASS-PST
      'A lot of toys were made by that child.'

The fact that *takusan* can modify the passive subject falls out if it appears in the subject position as a consequence of undergoing NP-movement from an object position, which takes place by the requirement that an argument needs to have Case. The facts concerning resultative predicates and quantifiers like *takusan* lend empirical support for the analysis taking a passive subject to originate from the object position.

For Further Research

(A-1) The Uniformity of Theta Assignment Hypothesis (UTAH), which regulates syntactic structures at the underlying level before NP-movement takes place (called "D-structure"), was proposed by Baker (1988: 46):

(i)   The Uniformity of Theta Assignment Hypothesis: Identical thematic relationships between items are represented by identical relationships between those items at the level of D-structure.

This hypothesis provides a rationale for the view that a passive subject, which assumes a theme role, originates from an object position, since it is the object position that is assigned the theme role by the verb.

(A-2) The Case filter is a condition that requires an overtly realized NP to be Case-marked, which is specified as :*NP if NP has phonetic content and has no Case (Chomsky (1981: 49)). This requirement may be captured by the visibility condition, which states that an element is visible for θ-marking only when it is assigned Case (Chomsky (1986: 94)). Needless to say, if an NP does not satisfy the visibility condition, it receives no interpretation, which leads to ungrammaticality. In passive clauses, the transitive verb is deprived of the ability to assign accusative Case by the addition of a passive affix. This process is called "Case absorption" because the passive affix is taken to absorb the Case from the verb (see Baker, Johnson, and Roberts (1989)).

(B) Ditransitive verbs taking two objects display divergent behavior in regard to passivization. Firstly, *ataeru* 'give' allows both accusative and dative objects to be promoted to a passive subject by passivization.

(ii)   a. Ken-ga   Mari-ni   hon-o   atae-ta.
          Ken-NOM   Mari-DAT   book-ACC   give-PST
          'Ken gave Mari a book.'
       b. Mari-ga   Ken-ni   hon-o   atae-rare-ta.
          Mari-NOM   Ken-by   book-ACC   give-PASS-PST
          'Mari was given a book by Ken.'
       c. Hon-ga   Ken-niyotte   Mari-ni   atae-rare-ta.
          book-NOM   Ken-by   Mari-DAT   give-PASS-PST
          'A book was given to Mari by Ken.'

Secondly, *semaru* 'urge' allows a dative object, but not an accusative object, to be promoted to a passive subject.

(iii) a. Ken-ga   Mari-ni   kekkon-o   semat-ta.

            Ken-NOM   Mari-DAT   marriage-ACC   urge-PST

            'Ken urged marriage (to him) on Mari.'

      b. Mari-ga   Ken-ni   kekkon-o   semar-are-ta.

            Mari-NOM   Ken-by   marriage-ACC   urge-PASS-PST

            'Mari was uged marriage (to him) by Ken.'

      c. *Kekkon-ga   Ken-niyotte   Mari-ni   semar-are-ta.

            marriage-NOM   Ken-by   Mari-DAT   urge-PASS-PST

            'Marriage (to him) was urged Mari by Ken.'

Thirdly, the reverse pattern of passivization is found with *nagasu* 'pass on, leak'.

(iv) a. Ken-ga   Mari-ni   zyoohoo-o   nagasi-ta.

            Ken-NOM   Mari-DAT   information-ACC   pass.on-PST

            'Ken passed on the information to Mari.'

      b. *Mari-ga   Ken-ni   zyoohoo-o   nagas-are-ta.

            Mari-NOM   Ken-by   information-ACC   pass.on-PASS-PST

            'Mari was passed on information by Ken.'

      c. Zyoohoo-ga   Ken-niyotte   Mari-ni   nagas-are-ta.

            information-NOM Ken-by   Mari-DAT   pass.on-PASS-PST

            'Information was passed on to Mary by Ken.'

Why do the ditransitive verbs in (ii)-(iv) show a difference with regard to the promotion of the two objects by passivization?

PART III

Nominal Structures

CHAPTER 10

Anaphors, Pronominals, and R-Expressions [B]

10.1 Pronouns

Nouns are most typically used for naming people, places, things, or ideas. This class of expressions includes common nouns (e.g. *tatemono* 'building') and proper nouns (e.g. *Ken, Tokyo*). Pronouns (e.g. *sore* 'it', *kare* 'he') pattern with nouns in terms of their syntactic distribution, since they occur in exactly the same positions that nouns (or noun phrases) do. In Japanese, just as ordinary nouns do not inflect, so pronouns also do not inflect. Nevertheless, pronouns differ from nouns in not having their own denotations and hence not directly referring to entities in the outside world. To be concrete, consider the sentence in (1).

(1)   Sore-wa   omosiro-i.
           it-TOP   interesting-PRS
           'It is interesting.'

The pronoun *sore* 'it' in (1) could mean anything (e.g. *eiga* 'movie', *benkyoo* 'study', *hanasi* 'talk') insofar as it refers to an inanimate entity, and we cannot understand its precise meaning if we do not know what *sore* refers back to. Pronouns have the property that their exact meanings can be retrieved only when the references of their antecedents are known because they do not have references of their own.

     In school grammar, pronouns are treated as constituting a uniform class with no further classifications, but if their syntactic behaviors are taken into consideration, we need to divide them into the two subclasses of **pronominals** and **anaphors**. *Sore* 'it', *sorera* 'they', *kare* 'he', *kanozyo* 'she', and the like belong to the pronominal class. On the other hand, **reflexive** *zibun-zisin* 'self' and **reciprocal** *otagai* 'each other' are included in the anaphor class. Pronominals and anaphors share the property that their referents need to be fixed by reference to their antecedents, but they display distinct syntactic behaviors. The most prominent difference between the two is that anaphors like *zibun* 'self' are not legitimate unless their antecedents are found in the sentences in which they occur, but no such requirements are imposed on pronominals like *kare* 'he', as illustrated in (2).

(2)   a. Kare-ga   hasit-ta.
           he-NOM   run-PST
           'He ran.'
      b. *Zibun-ga   hasit-ta.
           self-NOM   run-PST
           'Oneself ran.'

Since pronouns, unlike anaphors, do not have to find their antecedents in the sentences in which they occur, they are often not treated in the realm of syntax. But it must be stressed that pronouns are subject to some syntactic constraints, as we will discuss below. (Note also that *zibun* has another "non-reflexive" use, where it refers to a first or second person. When *zibun* serves as a personal pronoun rather than a reflexive, it typically refers to an individual identifiable in context, i.e. its referent typically does not appear as an argument in the clause.)

10.2 Structural Relations

As remarked above, anaphors (such as reflexive *zibun* 'self' and reciprocal *otagai* 'each other') are subject to grammatical constraints restricting their syntactic behavior. Let us illustrate this point by making use of the reflexive *zibun*.

(3)   a. Ken$_i$-ga   **zibun**$_i$-o   home-ta.
           Ken-NOM   self-ACC   praise-PST
           'Ken praised himself.'
      b. Ken$_i$-wa   [**zibun**$_i$-ga hasit-ta   to]   it-ta.
           Ken-TOP   self-NOM   run-PST   that   say-PST
           (lit.) 'Ken said that self ran.'
      c. ***Zibun**$_i$-ga [Ken$_i$-ga   hasit-ta   to]   it-ta.
           self-NOM   Ken-NOM   run-PST   that   say-PST
           (lit.) 'Self said that Ken ran.'

In (3a), the reflexive *zibun* 'self' must refer to the same individual as the subject *Ken*, which appears in the same clause. (The two arguments share the same index, shown with the subscript *i*, indicating that they refer to the same individual or entity.) If we look at slightly more complex cases, it becomes clear that the antecedent does not have to be located in the same clause in which *zibun* resides. For example, in (3b), the antecedent of *zibun* is *Ken* in the matrix clause, but in (3c), *zibun* cannot take the embedded subject *Ken* as its antecedent. Informally, we can state, on the basis of these examples, that the anaphor *zibun* needs to take its reference from a subject located in a structurally higher position.

The structural condition restricting the distribution of *zibun* can be captured more accurately by the very important structural notion of **c-command**. C-command is the most important and basic structural relation countenanced in generative grammar, and can be defined as follows: α c-commands β if α is in a higher position than β or in an equal position to β and α does not dominate β. Let us first illustrate how this works, using the abstract tree representations in (4).

(4)   a.

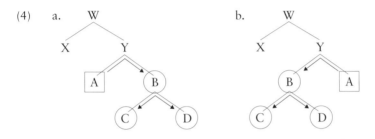

b.

What node does the boxed A c-command in (4a)? To find out, we first need to spot the point where we can evaluate the height of nodes relative to A, and this is the first branching point (or node) above A (i.e. the node Y in (4a)). This node can be reached by going up the branch on A. Then, we go down the other branch from Y, and reach some other nodes. This is the set of nodes that A c-commands. This downward movement can be repeated as many times as we wish. Specifically, if we go down from Y, we first reach B, and if we go down further, then we reach C or D depending on which branch we follow. The nodes that can be reached by following the arrows, i.e. the circled B, C, and D, are the nodes that A c-commands, and the other nodes are not c-commanded by A. In other words, A c-commands B, C, and D, but not the nodes W, X, or Y.

In (4b), the linear positions of A and B are switched, so A is preceded by B. In accordance with this change, the linear order of C and D to A is also switched in such a way that both C and D precede A. Despite these changes in linear order, the boxed A in (4b) c-commands exactly the same nodes as (4a), i.e. the circled B, C, and D. These c-command relations can easily be confirmed by following the arrows depicted in (4b). This shows that c-command is a hierarchical relation, and that precedence is not relevant, i.e. the c-command relation does not

94

depend on whether A precedes or follows B, C, and D.

In regard to the question of how reflexive *zibun* finds its antecedent, we can state that *zibun* takes its reference from an antecedent that c-commands it. To lend concreteness, let us consider how the contrast in acceptability between (3b) and (3c) can be characterized by the notion of c-command. The tree diagrams (5a) and (5b) represent the relevant part of the sentence structures for (3b) and (3c), respectively.

(5) a.   b.

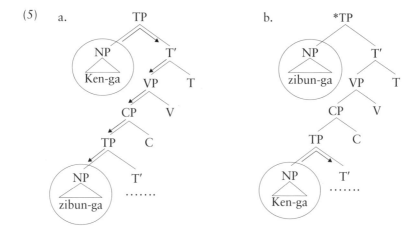

In (5a), the antecedent *Ken* can find the anaphor *zibun* in a lower structural position by following the "c-command" arrows. This shows that the NP *Ken* c-commands *zibun*, so that *Ken* can serve as the antecedent of *zibun*. By contrast, in (5b), the NP *Ken* cannot reach the anaphor by following the arrow, which means that the NP *Ken* does not c-command *zibun*, and hence cannot be the antecedent of *zibun*. (Similarly, in (3a), the NP *Ken* c-commands *zibun*, so that the intended interpretation is available, which may be easily confirmed by drawing a tree diagram for (3a).)

A case like (6), where the reflexive *zibun* is embedded inside an NP in subject position, can be handled in the same way.

(6)   *Ken$_i$-no   imooto-ga   **zibun**$_i$-o   home-ta.
       Ken-GEN   sister-NOM   self-ACC   praise-PST
       'Ken's sister praised herself/*himself.'

In (6), the NP *Ken* cannot be the antecedent of *zibun*, although Ken is, in a sense, located in a syntactic position higher than the anaphor *zibun*. As shown in the English gloss, *zibun* can only refer to the whole (c-commanding) NP *Ken-no imooto*. The impossibility of *Ken* serving as the antecedent of *zibun* in

(6) comes from the failure of *Ken* to c-command *zibun*.

(7)

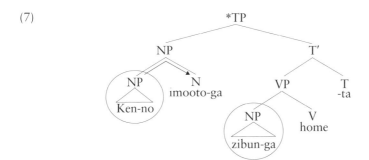

In (7), *the NP Ken* cannot reach *zibun* by following the arrow, which means that *Ken* does not c-command *zibun*. Thus, *Ken* cannot be the antecedent of *zibun* in (6). On the other hand, the entire NP *Ken-no imooto* c-commands *zibun* and can therefore be the antecedent of *zibun*.

Note also that a genitive phrase embedded in NP can be a potential target for reflexivization, as shown in (8).

(8)   Ken$_i$-no   **zibun**$_i$-e-no   taido
      Ken-GEN   self-to-GEN   attitude
      'Ken's attitude toward himself'

In (8), the intended anaphoric relation can be established because the NP *Ken* c-commands the reflexive *zibun*, as (9) illustrates.

(9)

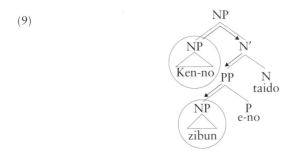

In (9), the genitive NP *Ken-no* c-commands the anaphor *zibun*, as indicated by the arrows, and thus a legitimate antecedent-anaphor relation can be established between the two.

In short, the possible anaphoric relation of the reflexive *zibun* can be defined in terms of the structural notion of c-command. Generally, the reflexive *zibun* has subject orientation, meaning that it takes its reference from a subject. Nevertheless, this does not suffice to characterize its syntactic behavior because the *zibun* must be c-commanded by its antecedent to establish an anaphoric relation between them.

10.3 Binding Theory

Let us now turn to the question of how pronominals behave in the sentences in which they occur. The following examples illustrate that there is a syntactic constraint applying to pronominals constraining the determination of their references.

(10) a. *Ken_i-wa $kare_i$-o home-ta.
        Ken-TOP he-ACC praise-PST
        'Ken praised him.'

     b. Ken_i-wa [Mari-ga $kare_i$-o home-ta to] it-ta.
        Ken-TOP Mari-NOM he-ACC praise-PST that say-PST
        'Ken said that Mari praised him.'

     c. $Kare_i$-no tomodati-ga Ken_i-o home-ta.
        he-GEN friend-NOM Ken-ACC praise-PST
        'His friend praised Ken.'

In (10b), *kare* 'he' in object position can refer to the same person as the subject *Ken* in the matrix clause (i.e. *kare* can take its reference from *Ken*), so that the two expressions may be coreferential. But the same pronominal *kare* cannot be coreferential with *Ken* in (10a), even though it is easy to imagine a situation where Ken praised himself. This fact suggests that a pronominal is subject to a grammatical constraint preventing it from taking its reference from an NP in a higher position in the same clause. Note further that *kare* in (10c) can be coreferential with *Ken*, even though the pronoun precedes the proper noun. ((10c) is a bit harder to process, but the coreferential relation can be easily identified if it constitutes an answer to the question *Dare-no tomodati-ga Ken-o home-ta no?* [who-GEN friend-NOM Ken-ACC praise-PST Q] 'Whose friend praised Ken?'.) Since *kare* is embedded in the subject NP in (10c), the fact shows that the relevant constraint restricting the possible antecedent of the pronoun is a "c-command" rather than a "precedence" relation: the pronoun cannot take its reference from the noun that c-commands it in the same clause.

Anaphors such as *kare-zisin* 'himself' as well have a grammatical constraint restricting their syntactic behavior which differs from the constraint conditioning the syntactic distribution of pronominals.

(11) a. Ken$_i$-ga   **kare-zisin$_i$**-o   home-ta.
          Ken-NOM   him-self-ACC   praise-PST
          'Ken praised himself.'

     b. *Ken$_i$-wa   [Mari-ga   **kare-zisin$_i$**-o   home-ta   to]   it-ta.
          Ken-TOP   Mari-NOM   him-self-ACC   praise-PST   that   say-PST
          'Ken said that Mari praised himself.'

In (11a), the anaphor *kare-zisin* 'himself' refers to the same individual as the subject *Ken*. In (11b), *kare-zisin* cannot take its reference from the subject *Ken* located outside the embedded clause. (Since *kare* is a masculine pronoun, *Mari* cannot be a possible antecedent in (11b).) This fact shows that the anaphor *kare-zisin* needs to take its reference from an NP located in the same clause. Note that this behavior of *kare-zisin* differs from what we observed for *zibun* in our earlier discussion.

Finally, a proper noun like *Ken* is called a **referring expression** (or **R-expression**), and the examples in (12) show how an R-expression behaves in a sentence.

(12) a. *Kare$_i$-ga   **Ken$_i$**-o   home-ta.
          he-NOM   Ken-ACC   praise-PST
          'He praised Ken.'

     b. *Kare$_i$-wa   [Mari-ga   **Ken$_i$**-o   home-ta   to]   it-ta.
          he-TOP   Mari-NOM   Ken-ACC   praise-PST   that   say-PST
          'He said that Mari praised Ken.'

In (12a), *Ken* cannot be coreferential with the subject *kare* 'he' appearing in the same clause. In (12b), *Ken* in the embedded clause cannot be coreferential with the matrix subject *kare*. The data illustrate that an R-expression like *Ken* cannot be coreferential with a pronoun that c-commands it.

What we have seen above is that pronouns do not refer to entities by themselves but take their reference from their antecedents. Pronouns are divided into two classes. Anaphors (e.g. *zibun* 'self', *otagai* 'each other') must find their antecedent in the sentential domain. Pronominals (e.g. *kare* 'he') may have their antecedent in the sentential domain, but are prohibited from finding the antecedents in the same clause. R-expressions (e.g. *Ken*) are capable of referring to entities without taking their reference from other arguments. If a pronoun takes its reference from an antecedent that c-commands it, the antecedent is said to **bind** the pronoun. The theory that treats the syntactic constraints on anaphors, pronominals, and R-expressions in the sentential domain is called **binding theory**.

For Further Research

(A-1) The term "c-command" is an abbreviation of "constituent command". The notion of c-command is formally defined as follows.

(i) α c-commands β iff (=if and only if) every γ that dominates α also dominates β, and neither α nor β dominates the other.

In (i), γ is taken to be a branching node when it defines "c-command". If γ is taken to be a maximal projection, it will define "m-command", i.e. a structural relation based on maximal projections.

(A-2) Binding theory identifies the possible syntactic relationships between pronouns (anaphors and pronominals) and their antecedents in a sentential domain. Chomsky (1986: 166) defines the three binding conditions in (ii).

(ii)   a. <u>Condition A</u>: An anaphor must be bound in a local domain.
        b. <u>Condition B</u>: A pronominal must be free in a local domain.
        c. <u>Condition C</u>: An R-expression must be free.

There are several versions for the definition of "a local domain", but it roughly corresponds to a clause or an NP containing the anaphor or the pronominal. Note that if X shares the same index with the antecedent Y that c-commands it (i.e. X takes its reference from a c-commanding Y), we say that X is **bound** by Y, and that if X is not bound, then X is **free**.

(B-1) In Japanese, when R-expressions (or proper nouns) are repeated in a clause, they can refer to the same individual, as in (iii).

(iii)   Ken$_i$-ga   Ken$_i$-o   home-ta.
        Ken-NOM   Ken-ACC   praise-PST
        'Ken praised Ken (=Ken praised himself).'

This fact seems to suggest that the R-expression *Ken* in object position can take its reference from the R-expression *Ken* in subject position which c-commands it. This happens only when the same noun is repeated, as shown by the fact that (iv) is not acceptable if *Ken* is taken to be coreferential with the subject.

(iv)   a. *Ano   hito$_i$-ga   Ken$_i$-o   home-ta.
           that   man-NOM   Ken-ACC   praise-PST
           'That man praised Ken.'

b. *Kare_i-ga   Ken_i-o   home-ta.
 he-NOM   Ken-ACC   praise-PST
 'He praised Ken.'

One puzzling fact is that the intended interpretation is available only if the same NP appears in subject and object position. What constraint can be set up to account for the facts on this type of coreference?

(B-2) Japanese has two kinds of reciprocal constructions, one with reciprocal pronouns and one with reciprocal verbs, as in (v).

(v) a. [Ken-to Mari]-ga **otagai**-o   home-ta.
    Ken-and Mari-NOM each.other-ACC praise-PST
   'Ken and Mari praised each other.'
  b. [Ken-to Mari]-ga home-**at**-ta.
    Ken-and Mari-NOM praise-RECP-PST
   'Ken and Mari praised each other.'

Does the reciprocal pronoun in (va) show syntactic behaviors that are expected from binding theory? In (vb), a reciprocal relation is indicated by the verb. How can the reciprocal relation be characterized syntactically?

CHAPTER 11

Quantifier Scope [B], [C]

11.1 Quantifiers

Pronominal expressions such as *someone/everyone* (English) and *dareka* 'some-one'/*daremo* 'everyone' (Japanese) constitute a special kind of pronominal expression known as **quantifiers** (or **quantified expressions**). Quantifiers fall into the class of functional categories, like other pronouns (such as pronominals and anaphors) but possess distinct syntactic functions. Quantifiers specify quantities rather than referring to specific individuals. Quantifiers generate **scope**, and the English sentence in (1) has **scope ambiguity**, in the sense that two distinct scope interpretations are obtained, distinguished according to how the two quantifiers are interpreted.

(1)   Someone admires everyone.

One interpretation available for (1) is that there is one person who admires everyone. Another interpretation is that for each person, there is a person whom he admires. These interpretations are represented in (2).

(2)   a. 'admirer'   'admiree'   b. 'admirer'   'admiree'
                          X   A ——————— X
              A <   Y   B ——————— Y
                          Z   C ——————— Z

(2a) represents the first interpretation in which there is one person who admires all the people. This interpretation is derived by first fixing A as the individual that the subject *someone* refers to, and then deciding on the individuals *every-one* refers to (X, Y, and Z). (2b) represents the interpretation in which there is more than one pair of admirers and admirees. The second interpretation is derived by first determining the individual *everyone* refers to (A, B and C), and then fixing the individual loved by each of them (X, Y, and Z). Accordingly, while there is one person A who loves X, Y, and Z on the first interpretation, there are three persons A, B, and C, who love X, Y, and Z, respectively, on the second interpretation.

The ambiguity of the sentence in (1) is generally observed for scope-bearing expressions, i.e. quantifiers. How the quantifiers are interpreted is captured by the notion of (**relative**) **scope**. Specifically, in the interpretation in (2a), the admiree *everyone* (the object) is interpreted relative to the admirer *someone* (the subject) because there is one specific individual who admires all. (2a) is obtained when the **existential quantifier** *someone* takes wider scope than the **universal quantifier** *everyone*, and this scope relation is represented as "some > every" (using the greater-than sign ">"). By contrast, in (2b), the admirer *someone* (the subject) is interpreted relative to the admiree *everyone* (the object), since (2b) means that for every admiree, there is at least one admirer. The scope relation is reversed here. The interpretation in (2b) is obtained when the admiree *everyone* takes scope over the admirer *someone* (i.e. "every> some").

How about Japanese? Of course, Japanese, too, has quantified expressions, but their scope behavior seems to differ from what is observed in English quantifiers. To understand this point, consider how the sentences in (3) can be interpreted.

(3)　a.　Dareka-ga　　　daremo-o　　　sonkei-si-te　　i-ru.
　　　　　someone-NOM　everyone-ACC　admire-do-GER　be-PRS
　　　　　'Someone admires everyone.'
　　　b.　Daremo-o　　　dareka-ga　　　sonkei-si-te　　i-ru.
　　　　　everyone-ACC　someone-NOM　admire-do-GER　be-PRS
　　　　　'Everyone, someone admires.'

The sentence in (3a) has the basic SOV order, and (3b) is derived from (3a) by moving the object to the front of the sentence via scrambling. Although there might be individual speaker variation, many speakers of Japanese find (3a) unambiguous and (3b) ambiguous with regard to the relative scope of the two quantifiers. (It might take a little time to understand what scope interpretation is available for the sentences in (3).) The only scope interpretation available for (3a) is the one on which *dareka* takes scope over *daremo* ("some > every"), represented in (2a), but the scrambled sentence in (3b) has the scope interpretation on which *daremo* takes scope over *dareka*, represented in (2b) ("every > some"), as well as the one on which *dareka* takes scope over *daremo*, represented in (2a) ("some > every").

(3a) and (3b) differ in the surface order of the two quantifiers, and it is generally considered that the difference in scope interpretation is a consequence of a difference in their syntactic structures; that is, one quantifier takes scope over another if the former is located in a higher position than the latter. In (3a), the subject *dareka* is expected to take scope over the object *daremo*, given the constituent structure in (4), which can be assigned to (3a).

(4)

In (4), the subject c-commands the object, which means that the existential quantifier *dareka* 'someone' is located in a position higher than the universal quantifier *daremo* 'everyone', so that the scope interpretation "some > every" is available. By contrast, if the object is moved across the subject by scrambling, as in (3b), the syntactic structure in (5) is derived.

(5)

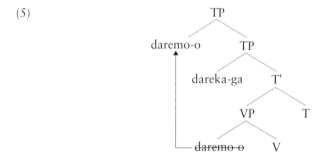

In (5), the object quantifier is scrambled to a position higher than the subject. When the object is added to TP by scrambling, as in (5), the maximal projection TP is split into two segments, i.e. another projection label TP is created. This syntactic operation is called **adjunction**; in (5), *daremo-o* is moved by scrambling, and adjoined to TP. (On the other hand, NP-movement of an argument from an object position to an unfilled (or empty) subject position, as found in passive clauses, is called **substitution**.)

Suppose that the scrambled quantifier *daremo* can be interpreted in either the original or the moved position for the purpose of the scope interpretation. If the option of interpreting it in the original position is chosen, *dareka* c-commands *daremo*; hence the scope interpretation "some > every" is obtained.

(6)

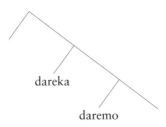

On the other hand, if the quantifier *daremo* is interpreted in the moved position, it c-commands the subject *dareka*, and thus, the reverse scope interpretation "every > some" is obtained.

(7)

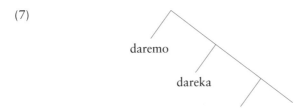

If the scrambled quantifier can be interpreted in two distinct syntactic positions (i.e. in either the original or the moved position), the availability of the two interpretations ("some > every", "every > some") is naturally expected. In effect, the Japanese facts suggest that the relative scope relations of quantifiers are determined according to where they are located in syntactic structures.

Recall at this moment that an English sentence like (1) is ambiguous, allowing either the subject or the object to take wide scope over the other. Example (1) does not involve visible movement of the object over the subject, but still the sentence is ambiguous. How can the sentence be ambiguous then? If, as noted above, the relative scope of the two quantifiers *someone* and *everyone* is determined on the basis of their syntactic positions, it must be the case that a structure generating the scope ambiguity is available. In point of fact, abstracting away from (many) details that do not concern us here, we can account for the fact that the sentence in (1) has scope ambiguity if the structure in (8) is created via invisible movement.

(8)

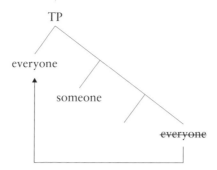

The relative scope of quantified expressions is defined in terms of c-command. If *everyone* is interpreted in its original position, *someone* c-commands *everyone*, and thus, the interpretation "some > every" is derived. On the other hand, if *everyone* is interpreted in the moved position, *everyone* c-commands *someone*. Then, the interpretation "every > some" is obtained. (The invisible movement indicated by the arrow in (8) is often called **Quantifier Raising (QR)**, since it raises quantifiers to higher structural positions than those in which they actually occur on the surface.)

Although the hypothesized movement of *everyone* to a higher position in (8) is never audible, it is generally assumed in generative grammar that invisible movement can be utilized to generate scope for quantifiers. Since QR is inaudible, its effect can be detected only through scope interpretations in English. In Japanese, by contrast, scope interpretations may change depending on how arguments are ordered, i.e. scrambling changes the hierarchical structure of arguments, and at the same time, it changes the possibility of scope interpretations. In this respect, scrambling bears some resemblance to QR. Such being the case, Japanese provides an interesting argument for the hypothesis that quantifier scope is determined on the basis of syntax.

11.3 The T-Model of Grammar

Syntactic operations change or transform syntactic structures. When movement takes place in the derivation, we have derived structures different from their base structures. In the Principles and Parameters approach, the system of grammar includes distinct levels of syntactic representation, called **D-structure, S-structure, Logical Form (LF)**, and **Phonetic Form (PF)**, as shown in (9).

(9)   Lexicon ┈┈┈➤ D-Structure (=Deep Structure)

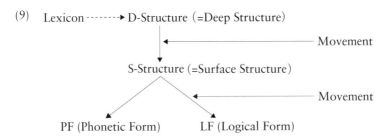

The model in (9) illustrates how the syntactic derivations proceed. First, D-structure representations, where the thematic relations of arguments are determined, are constructed by combining lexical items chosen from the Lexicon. Then, S-structure representations are derived, which are closer to the forms that we actually hear since they directly feed into Phonetic Form (PF). LF representations represent the structural aspects of semantic interpretations (e.g. scope relations of quantifiers) and are derived from the S-structure representations.

As we saw above, changes in syntactic structures could be either overt (audible)(e.g. scrambling in Japanese) or covert (inaudible)(e.g. QR in English). How can we capture this fact under this model? In (3b), where an object is scrambled over the subject, we can posit the derivation in (10).

(10)   a.   [$_{TP}$ NP [NP V]]   (D-structure)

        b. [$_{TP}$ NP [$_{TP}$ NP [___ V]]   (S-structure)

Since the object is overtly fronted to the left of the subject in (10) by scrambling, this movement must take place in the derivation from D-structure to S-structure. Note that when no movement (e.g. scrambling) is induced in the syntactic derivation from D-structure to S-structure, these two representations are (virtually) identical.

In passive clauses, the subject originates in object position but is moved into the subject position by NP-movement. Thus, passive sentences provide another case where movement takes place in the derivation from D-structure to S-structure.

(11)   a. [$_{TP}$ [$_{VP}$ NP V]]   (D-structure)

        b. [$_{TP}$ NP [$_{VP}$ ___ V]]   (S-structure)

The difference between passivization and scrambling lies in the fact that the passive movement involves substitution, moving the (original) object NP into an unfilled subject position, whereas the object scrambling involves adjunction to TP.

Because LF movement takes place after S-structure is input to PF, it does not change the way in which sentences are pronounced. QR in English is an operation that takes place in the derivation from S-structure to LF.

(12)   a.   [$_{TP}$ someone [V   everyone]]   (S-structure)

   b.   [$_{TP}$ everyone [$_{TP}$ someone [V _____]]   (LF)

S-structure and LF representations would be identical if no movement takes place in the derivation from S-structure to LF.

The figure in (9) represents a model of syntax in the Principles and Parameters framework. Since part of the figure illustrating the derivations from D-structure to LF and PF through S-structure has a Y or T shape (if we look at it upside down), this model of syntax is called the **Y-model** or the **T-model**. Models of syntactic analysis have been modified in accordance with developments within the theory. Even the most recent model of syntax is likely to be further modified or changed when new insights into syntax are brought to light. Importantly, however, the idea that movement, which is used to characterize linguistic **displacement** phenomena (e.g. passivization, scrambling), is a general or universal rule of natural language remains constant and unchanged throughout the history of generative grammar.

108

For Further Research

(A) Quantifier Raising (QR) creates an operator-variable structure by virtue of moving quantifiers at LF. If QR applies to (ia), the LF structure in (ib) is derived, where *someone* is moved and adjoined to TP leaving a copy in its original position, which is indicated by the strikethrough "~~someone~~".

(i)   a.   Someone walks.

      b.   [$_{TP}$ someone [$_{TP}$ ~~someone~~ walks]]

With a view to deriving a logical representation, the copy is converted into a variable to be linked to the moved *someone*, which serves as an operator. Then, (ib) is interpreted as having an operator-variable structure akin to the logical formula: $\exists x$: person [x walks] (= 'there is some person who walks'), and thus (ia) has the interpretation 'there is someone such that he walks'.

(B-1) There are cases where pronouns are interpreted as variables which co-vary with the variable created by QR, as exemplified in (ii).

(ii)   Daremo$_i$-ga   zibun$_i$-no   koto-o   hanasi-ta.
        everyone-NOM   self-GEN   fact-ACC   talk-PST
        'Everyone$_i$ talked about himself$_i$.'

Where there are three individuals A, B, and C, (ii) means that A talked about A, B talked about B, and C talked about C. What structure can be assigned to (ii) as an LF representation?

(B-2) The particle *sika* generates the meaning of 'only' when combined with a sentential negator. The presence of a sentential negator is required for *sika* to appear in the clause, and thus (iiib) is not acceptable.

(iii)   a.   Ken-sika   hasira-nakat-ta.
          Ken-only   run-NEG-PST
          'Only Ken ran.'
      b.   *Ken-sika   hasit-ta.
          Ken-only   run-PST
          'Only Ken ran.'

What LF structure can be assigned to (iiia)? Why is it necessary for *sika* to be combined with a negator?

On the other hand, the possibility of licensing *sika* differs between (iva) and (ivb) despite the fact that a negative marker is present in the two examples.

(iv)   a.   Ken-sika   kodomo-o   kamawa-na-i.
             Ken-only   child-ACC   care-NEG-PRS
             'Only Ken cares about the children.'

       b. *Watasi-wa   sore-de-sika   kamawa-na-i.
             I-TOP   that-with-only   care-NEG-PRS
             'I am all right only with that.'

(iva) shows that the negator *nai* licenses the occurrence of *sika*, but in (ivb), the same *nai* does not license *sika*. What causes the difference in acceptability between the two sentences?

CHAPTER 12

NP/DP and PP [D]

12.1 Case Particles

There are a number of important differences in the organization of clauses between Japanese and English, many of which may be subsumed under the rubric of parametric variations, but some variations receive independent accounts. One such notable difference between the two languages has to do with the surface morphological fact that in Japanese, but not in English, arguments (as well as adjuncts) almost always occur with particles indicating **grammatical relations.**

(1) a. Eri-ga   heya-de   gurasu-o   otosi-ta.
             Eri-NOM   room-in   glass-ACC   drop-PST
             'Eri dropped the glass in the room.'
    b. Gurasu-ga   otos-are-ta.
             glass-NOM   drop-PASS-PST
             'The glass was dropped.'

The particles that appear on the subject *Eri* and the object *gurasu* 'glass' in (1a) are **structural case markers.** *Ga* and *o* represent **nominative case** and **accusative case**, respectively. The distribution of structural case markers is determined by the syntactic context in which they appear, and no one-to-one correspondence can be posited between the semantic relation of arguments and their case markers. For instance, the nominative arguments *Eri* in (1a) and *gurasu* in (1b) both function as subjects, but their semantic relations differ. *Eri* in (1a) is an agent, and *gurasu* in (1b) is a theme. The subject *gurasu* in (1b) has the same theme role as the object *gurasu* in (1a) (because *gurasu* in (1b) is promoted from the object to become the passive subject via passivization). Despite the fact that they bear the same θ-role, their case marking differs. These facts illustrate that it is not possible to pinpoint the exact semantic roles of arguments by looking at the structural case marking that they are associated with.

In (1a), another type of particle, i.e. *de* 'in', occurs with the location *heya* 'room'. Unlike nominative and accusative case markers, the particle *de* specifies the fixed semantic relation of location. This type of expression does not undergo syntactic operations that affect its grammatical relation (such as passivization).

(2) *Heya-ga   gurasu-o   otos-are-ta.
      room-NOM   glass-ACC   dropped-PASS-PST
      'The room was dropped the glass (in).'

The locative expression *heya-de* 'in the room' stands in contrast with the accusative argument *gurasu* in (1b) in not undergoing passivization. Particles (such as *de* 'in', *made* 'till', *kara* 'from', and *to* 'with') that specify fixed semantic relations are **postpositions**. The PPs (=Postpositional Phrases) projected from the postpositions are most typically construed as adjuncts, just like English PPs.

In English, no overt case marking appears on nouns, but morphological case marking is manifested in the inflectional forms of pronouns, as in *She scolded him*, where *she* is a nominative form and *him* is an accusative form. Syntactically, arguments serving as subjects and objects form NPs (=Noun Phrases), but arguments with prepositions constitute PPs (=Prepositional Phrases). Thus, the structures of the NP *this daughter* and the PP *in the room* differ, as illustrated in (3).

(3)   a.

In (3a), the NP *this daughter* is formed by combining the noun N *daughter* with the determiner D *this*. In (3b), the PP *in the room* is derived by combining the P *in* with the NP consisting of the N *room* plus the D *the*.

In Japanese, on the other hand, both arguments and adjuncts accompany particles in the same way, at least on the surface, as in *Eri-ga* and *heya-de* in (1a). Given the morphological fact of particles marking both arguments and adjuncts, it is tempting to say that Japanese does not distinguish between NPs (for arguments) and PPs (for adjuncts) in syntactic terms. On the contrary, there is good reason to assume that arguments appear as NPs while adjuncts (such as locatives) constitute PPs: e.g. an accusative nominal like *sono tomodati-o* 'that friend' forms an NP as a whole, and the nominal *sono tomodati-kara* 'from that friend' counts as a PP, which includes an NP in it (i.e. *kara* is a postposition that projects to PP), as represented in (4).

(4) a.

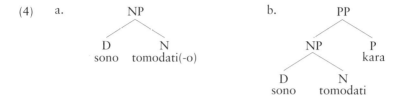

In Japanese, numeral quantifiers (NQs), such as *huta-ri* 'two-persons' and *mit-tu* 'three-things', have the structural property that they can be floated off from certain kinds of host nominals, but not others. It is often claimed that **numeral quantifier floating** (NQ floating) serves to distinguish between NPs and PPs. To illustrate this point, consider (5).

(5) a. [_{NP} Huta-ri-no   kodomo-ga]   hasit-ta.
            two-CL-GEN   child-NOM   run-PST
         'Two children ran.'
     b. [_{NP} Kodomo-ga]   (kinoo)   huta-ri   hasit-ta.
            child-NOM   yesterday   two-CL   run-PST
         'Two children ran (yesterday).'

In (5), the elements in the square brackets are constituents of the nominative argument. In (5a), the numeral quantifier *huta-ri* 'two-persons', which is marked with genitive *no*, is included in the NP. By contrast, in (5b), the numeral quantifier *huta-ri* is launched off the NP as a floated quantifier, so that it does not constitute part of the NP constituent. Accordingly, it is possible for an adverb like *kinoo* 'yesterday' to occur to the left of *huta-ri*—that is, between the quantifier and the nominal element it quantifies.

Similarly, it is possible to float a numeral quantifier from arguments carrying accusative *o*, as in (6).

(6) a. Ken-ga   [_{NP} huta-ri-no   kodomo-o]   home-ta.
         Ken-NOM   two-CL-GEN   child-ACC   praise-PST
         'Ken praised two children.'

b. Ken-ga   [_NP kodomo-o]   (minna-no   mae-de)
   Ken-NOM   child-ACC   everyone-GEN   front-LOC
   huta-ri   home-ta.
   two-CL   praise-PST
   'Ken praised two children (in front of everyone).'

In (6a), the numeral quantifier *huta-ri* is marked with genitive case and serves as a prenominal modifier to the NP. But as shown in (6b), it can also occur outside the host by virtue of NQ floating. By contrast, particles (like *kara* 'from', *de* 'in', *made* 'until', etc.) are postpositions, and numeral quantifiers are not allowed to float off from arguments that occur with them, as illustrated in (7).

(7)   a. Ken-ga   [_PP huta-ri-no   tomodati-kara] hon-o   kari-ta.
         Ken-NOM   two-CL-GEN   friend-ABL   book-ACC borrow-PST
         'Ken borrowed the books from two friends.'
      b. Ken-ga   [_PP tomodati   huta-ri-kara]   hon-o   kari-ta.
         Ken-NOM   friend   two-CL-ABL   book-ACC borrow-PST
         'Ken borrowed the books from two friends.'
      c. *Ken-ga   [_PP tomodati-kara]   (kinoo)   huta-ri hon-o
         Ken-NOM   friend-ABL   yesterday two-CL book-ACC
         kari-ta.
         borrow-PST
         'Ken borrowed the books from two friends (yesterday).'

The numeral quantifier marked with genitive case in (7a) can be moved to the right of the noun *tomodati*, as in (7b) but not to the right of *kara*, as in (7c). The contrast in acceptability between (7b) and (7c) shows that a numeral quantifier cannot be moved out of an argument marked with *kara*, i.e. it can cross the noun, but not the postposition *kara*.

We would not expect a contrast in acceptability between (5b) and (6b), on the one hand, and (7c), on the other hand, if there were no structural difference between phrases occurring with *ga/o* and those appearing with *kara*. The difference in the possibility of NQ floating can be given a structural account; numeral quantifiers can be moved from within the host NP to a position outside if no maximal projection intervenes between them. For the nominative nominal *kodomo-ga* and the accusative nominal *kodomo-o*, the quantifier *huta-ri* is extractable from the NP (and hence can be construed as a floated modifier to the NP), since there is no maximal projection that blocks its extraction, as shown in (8a). By contrast, the *kara*-marked nominal is within a PP, and numeral quantifier floating is not possible from the NP embedded under PP, as shown in (8b), since PP counts as an intervening maximal projection that blocks its extraction.

(8) a.   ...... [$_{NP}$ ~~huta-ri~~ tomodati-ga/-o]   huta-ri   ....

    b.   ...... [$_{PP}$ [$_{NP}$ ~~huta-ri~~   tomodati]-kara]   huta-ri ....
                                            X

The facts of NQ floating can be taken as an indication that nominative *ga* and accusative *o* are case markers that attach to NP arguments, without projecting a phrase, as in (4a), while *kara* serves as a postposition that projects to PP, taking an NP as its complement, thus having the structure [$_{PP}$ [$_{NP}$ N] P], as in (4b).

12.2 From NP to DP

Nominal expressions that are allowed to occur in argument position are labeled as NPs traditionally. Recently, this idea has been called into question, and the so-called **DP hypothesis** has been advanced in generative literature. On the DP hypothesis, what we refer to as a "noun phrase" (in pre-theoretical terms) is construed as a DP (=Determiner Phrase) consisting of the two projections of DP and NP. In the classic NP analysis, *sono hon* 'that book' has the structure in (9a). But the DP hypothesis takes a D head to project to DP for the topmost nominal structure, and the noun phrase *sono hon* has the structure in (9b).

(9)   a.   b.

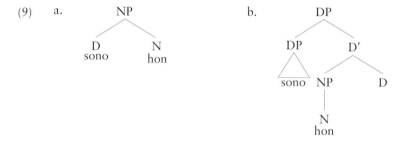

In Japanese, the determiner *sono*, comprised of *so* 'that' and a genitive marker *no*, can be assumed to occupy the specifier position of the DP projected from the invisible head D, while forming another DP inside.

   The DP hypothesis can capture a number of facts regarding nominal constructions. To substantiate the DP hypothesis, observe first that English has complex nominal expressions like *we linguists*, *you fools*, etc., which are combined expressions that can occur in argument positions, as in (10).

(10) [We linguists] take them seriously, don't we?

This fact suggests that the expression *we linguists* works as a unit, i.e. a "noun phrase" (in pre-theoretical terms). In Japanese as well, a complex expression like *watasi-tati gengogakusya*—the Japanese counterpart of *we linguists*—can appear in argument position.

(11) [Watasi-tati gengogakusya]-ga ano hito-o   kirat-te   i-ru.
       I-PL   linguist-NOM   that man-ACC   hate-GER   be-PRS
       'We linguists hate that man.'

On the DP hypothesis, *we linguists* has the structure in (12b). (The symbol ϕ indicates that nothing occupies in that position.)

(12) a.   b.

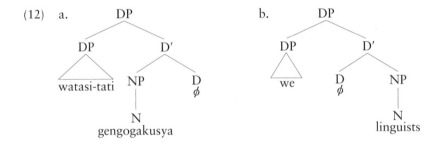

The complex expression *watasi-tati gengogakusya* shares important properties with *we linguists*. With the complex expression *we linguists* in (10), *we* determines the property of the whole expression and does not occur with other determiners (e.g. *we the, *these you, etc.). The same holds true of Japanese, as *watasi-tati sono gengogakusya* [I-PL that linguist] 'we that linguists' is not acceptable. Further, just as the English complex expressions exclude singular pronoun forms (e.g. *I linguist, *he linguist), so Japanese disallows singular pronouns in the complex expressions (e.g. *watasi gengogakusya 'I linguist', *kare gengogakusya 'he linguist'). Moreover, the two component words of the complex expression *watasi-tati gengogakusya* can occur independently.

Given the parallelism between English and Japanese, we can assume that nominal structures have the two projections of DP and NP in Japanese in the same way as English, as dictated by the DP hypothesis. If so, the same type of syntactic structure that is assigned to *we linguists* can be posited for *watasi-tati gengogakusya*, as in (12a). Under this analysis, when the pronoun *watasi-tati* occurs alone, only the DP projection has a lexical item: [$_{DP}$ *watasi-tati* [$_{NP}$]]. When only the noun *gengogakusya* is overt, only the NP contains a lexical item: [$_{DP}$ [$_{NP}$ *gengogakusya*]].

One welcome consequence of the DP hypothesis is that it can offer a ready structural account for the restrictive versus non-restrictive interpretations of relative clauses (or noun modifying clauses).

(13) a. [Ken-ga   kai-ta]   syoosetu
         Ken-NOM   write-PST   novel
         'novels that Ken wrote'
     b. [Ken-ga   kai-ta]   sono   syoosetu
         Ken-NOM   write-PST   that   novel
         'that novel, which Ken wrote'

In (13a), the relative clause (most typically) invokes a restrictive interpretation where the set of novels is limited by the relative clause—the interpretation that, among many novels available, the novels referred to are the ones written by Ken (and not others). In (13b), the relative does not restrict the set of novels denoted by the NP, but adds secondary information to the noun phrase, giving rise to the non-restrictive interpretation that the novels available happen to be ones written by Ken.

On the DP hypothesis, the difference between restrictive and non-restrictive interpretations imposed on the relative clasues in (13) follows from a difference in the position to which the relative clause is adjoined within the DP, as in (14).

(14)
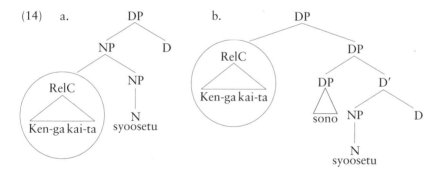

In (14a), the relative clause is adjoined to the NP, and a structure where the relative clause modifies the NP *syoosetu* 'novel' is created. In this structure, the relative clause semantically restricts the set of novels denoted by the NP, thus yielding the restrictive interpretation of the relative clause. In (14b), on the other hand, the relative clause is added to DP rather than to NP. The relative clause adjoined to DP does not restrict the denotation of NP, and hence is taken to provide additional information on the DP *sono syoosetu*, which gives rise to a non-restrictive interpretation.

For Further Research

(A-1) Before the introduction of the DP hypothesis (Abney (1987), Fukui (1995)), noun phrases were considered to be the maximal projection of a noun head. On the DP hypothesis, however, what were previously considered to be noun phrases are regarded as DPs—the maximal projection of D. In Japanese, it might be possible to regard a case particle as occupying a D-head position (Kishimoto (2005)). There are also analyses positing more than two maximal projections (DP, QP/NumP, CaseP, etc.) for noun phrases (see e.g. Watanabe (2006), which posits projections accommodating case markers).

(A-2) Dative case is usually considered as a kind of structural case marker, but it has been observed cross-linguistically that it exhibits properties crosscutting those of a structural case marker and those of a preposition/postposition. In Japanese, *ni* is often considered to be a dative case marker, but it also displays some mixed properties; for instance, some predicates mark their arguments with *ni*, which behaves in a way similar to structural case markers like nominative *ga* and accusative *o*, but the thematic relations it can specify are fairly restricted (e.g. goal or experiencer), displaying behavior akin to a postposition in this respect. In addition, *ni* has many other uses (as a locative marker, copula, conjunction marker, etc.), which makes it difficult to assess when *ni* is categorized as a structural case marker.

(B) Determiners can be divided into two classes. One class of determiners includes demonstratives, and the other class, quantifiers. Possessive expressions may also be included in the class of determiners. However, possessive expressions and the other two classes of determiners show distinct behaviors with respect to *no* replacement.

(i) a. *Watasi-wa   kono ronbun-o   yon-da-ga,   ano-wa
        I-TOP   this   paper-ACC read-PST-CONJ   that-TOP
        yoma-nakat-ta.
        read-NEG-PST
        'I read this paper, but I did not read that.'
     b. *Watasi-wa   san-bon-no   ronbun-o   yon-da-ga,
        I-TOP   three-CL-GEN   paper-ACC   read-PST-CONJ
        ni-hon-no-wa   yoma-nakat-ta.
        two-CL-one-TOP   read-NEG-PST
        'I read three papers, but I did not read two.'
     c. Watasi-wa   Eri-no   ronbun-o   yon-da-ga,   Ken-no-wa
        I-TOP   Eri-GEN   paper-ACC   read-PST-CONJ   Ken-one-TOP

yoma-nakat-ta.

read-NEG-PST

'I read Eri's paper, but I did not read Ken's (one).'

The difference between the examples lies in the choice of prenominal modifier. Why is it that we observe a difference in acceptability between (ia-b), on the one hand, and (ic), on the other hand?

PART IV

Hypotheses on Clause Structures

CHAPTER 13

Unaccusativity [C], [E]

13.1 Intransitive Verbs with Object-like Arguments

Transitive verbs take two arguments, realized as an object and a subject. Intransitive verbs, by contrast, take only one argument, which is invariably realized as a subject: there is no intransitive verb whose single argument is realized as an object rather than a subject. In a sense, this claim is quite reasonable since Japanese does not have an intransitive sentence whose sole argument is marked with accusative case.

(1) a. Kabin-ga   koware-ta.
          vase-NOM   break-PST
          'The vase broke.'
     b. *Kabin-o   koware-ta.
          vase-ACC   break-PST
          'Broke the vase.'

If subjects are marked with nominative case, but not accusative case, as shown in (1), the case-marking facts seem to suggest that intransitive verbs do not take objects. Nevertheless, it would be a bit too hasty to conclude that there cannot be any intransitive verb taking an argument behaving like an object. The idea that some, if not all, intransitive verbs can take object-like arguments might sound absurd, but this is not as crazy as it first appears. In point of fact, a close look at intransitive verbs reveals that some intransitive verbs take single arguments which possess object properties, even though they are marked with nominative case.

To begin, recall that the quantity adverb *takusan* 'many' has the semantic function of specifying the quantity of a direct object (see Chapter 9). In (2), only the object can be the target of modification by *takusan* because of the direct object constraint.

(2) Kodomo-ga   kabin-o   takusan   kowasi-ta.
     child-NOM   vase-ACC   many   break-PST
     'The children broke many vases.'/ NOT 'Many children broke vases.'

One apparent exception to the direct object constraint is found in passive sentences because passive subjects can be modified by the quantity adverb *takusan*.

(3) Kabin-ga   kodomo-niyotte   takusan   kowas-are-ta.
     vase-NOM   child-by   many   break-PASS-PST
     'Many vases were broken by the child.'

The apparent violation of the direct object constraint for the adverbial modification in (3) results from the fact that the passive subject has been promoted from an object via passivization, i.e. the passive subject first appears in object position but is moved to the subject position by DP-movement (or NP-movement).

(4)   [$_{TP}$ kabin [$_{VP}$ kodomo-niyotte ~~kabin~~ kowas-are] -ta]

If the direct object constraint applies at the underlying level, i.e. at the D-structure level, it comes as no surprise that the quantity adverb *takusan* can modify the passive subject in (3), since it starts out from an object position.

   The exceptional behavior of the quantity adverb is found not merely in passive clauses but also in some intransitive clauses. The example in (5) with the intransitive verb *kowareru* 'break' illustrates the point.

(5) Kabin-ga   koko-de   takusan   koware-ta.
     vase-NOM   here-in   many   break-PST
     'Many vases broke here.'

In the intransitive sentence in (5), the quantity adverb *takusan* does specify the quantity of the subject in apparent violation of the direct object constraint. The situation here parallels that of the passive sentence in (3). In the passive clause, the quantity adverb can quantify the passive subject because it first appears in object position. If the direct object constraint applies to (5) as well, it is reasonable to think that the subject of the intransitive verb *kowareru* 'break' starts out in object position, just like the subject of the passive verb *kowas-are-ru* 'be broken', as illustrated in (6).

(6)   [$_{TP}$ kabin [$_{VP}$ koko-de ~~kabin~~ koware] -ta]

Note here that just as the object of the transitive verb *kowasu* 'break' bears a theme role, so too does the subject of the intransitive verb *kowareru*. Thus, from a semantic point of view, it makes sense to posit the derivation in (6) for the intransitive clause.

If a theme role is always assigned to an argument in object position, the derivation yielding the sentence in (1a) proceeds as follows. First, the single argument of the intransitive *kowareru* is generated in the object position and receives a theme role there, as depicted in (7).

(7)   [$_{TP}$ [$_{VP}$ kabin koware$_{<Theme>}$] -ta]

Nevertheless, the intransitive verb is not capable of assigning accusative Case to the argument in object position. Accordingly, the theme argument is moved to the subject position.

(8)   [$_{TP}$ kabin [$_{VP}$ ~~kabin~~ koware] -ta $_{[NOM]}$]

Since T assigns nominative Case to an argument in subject position, the subject of the intransitive verb, which has been moved to TP, is marked with nominative case, even though it originated in the object position. This means that the sole argument of the intransitive verb *kowareru* 'break' undergoes DP-movement in just the same way as the subject of the passive verb *kowas-are-ru* 'be broken'. In passivization, DP-movement to TP is motivated by the verb's losing its ability to assign accusative Case. In the case of intransitive verbs like *kowareru*, DP-movement is induced because the verb inherently lacks the ability to assign accusative Case.

It goes without saying that there are intransitive verbs that take arguments with no object-like properties. For instance, intransitive verbs like *hataraku* 'work' cannot be associated with the quantity adverb *takusan*.

(9)   #Gakusei-ga   koko-de   takusan   hatarai-ta.
       student-NOM   here-in   many   work-PST
       'The students worked a lot here.'/ NOT 'Many students worked here.'

In (9), the quantity adverb *takusan* does not specify the number of students. Rather, the adverb indicates the amount of work done by the students. The subject of the verb *hataraku* 'work' bears an agent role, just like the subject of a transitive verb like *kowasu* 'break', thus suggesting that the subject receives an agent role in its subject position.

(10)   [$_{TP}$ gakusei [$_{VP}$ hatarai$_{<Agent>}$] -ta]

As for Case, T can assign nominative Case to the subject of the intransitive verb *hataraku* in that position.

(11)   [$_{TP}$ gakusei [$_{VP}$ hatarai] -ta $_{[NOM]}$]

The facts pertaining to modification by *takusan* in (9) follow straightforwardly if the subject of *hataraku* 'work' does not appear in object position at any point of the derivation; since this type of subject is in no way associated with the object position, *takusan* cannot specify the quantity of the subject.

The analysis presented here draws on the assumption that an agent role is assigned to a subject position and a theme role, to an object position, regardless of the type of verb involved. This follows from one of the important hypotheses countenanced in generative grammar, i.e. the Uniformity of Theta Assignment Hypothesis (UTAH), which guarantees that the same θ-roles are assigned to the same structural positions (see Chapter 9).

13.2 The Unaccusative Hypothesis

The phenomena observed in the previous section suggest that intransitive verbs can be divided into two classes. The intransitive verb *hataraku* 'work' has a genuine subject argument, while the intransitive verb *kowareru* 'break' has a subject originating from an object position. Verbs belonging to the former class are referred to as **unergative verbs**, and verbs in the latter class, **unaccusative verbs**. These terms sound very difficult at first sight, but the basic idea is straightforward and should be very easy to understand. These two types of intransitive verbs have distinct D-structure configurations, as represented in (12).

(12)   a. [Agent   [Theme   V] T]   (Transitive verb)
       b. [Agent   [V] T]   (Unergative verb)
       c. [[Theme   V] T]   (Unaccusative verb)

The unergative verb has its sole argument originating in the subject position to which the agent role is assigned, as in (12b). The unergative subject does not undergo DP-movement because it appears in the position where nominative Case is assigned. On the other hand, the unaccusative verb has its sole argument generated in object position, where it receives a theme role from the verb; the argument is moved to the subject position to receive nominative Case from T, as in (12c). The agent argument generated in subject position and the theme argument generated in object position are often referred to as **external argument** and **internal argument**, respectively.

Since the subject of an unaccusative verb, unlike the subject of an unergative verb, appears in object position initially, it displays object properties in certain syntactic contexts, despite its surface position. The hypothesis positing the distinct syntactic configurations for the two types of intransitive verbs in (12b) and (12c) is called the **Unaccusative Hypothesis**. Under this hypothesis, some intransitive verbs, i.e. unaccusative verbs, take arguments that, because they are first generated in object position, possess properties shared by the objects of transitive verbs. There are a number of linguistic phenomena that are claimed to distinguish between unergative and unaccusative verbs in Japanese, some of which we will discuss briefly below.

First of all, the so-called *kake*-construction, which includes a kind of deverbal nominal derived by suffixation with -*kake* 'be about to', serves as one such test. This construction picks out the object, but not the subject, of a transitive verb, as shown in (13a).

(13) a. kiri-kake-no   daikon/*ryoori-nin
          cut-about.to-GEN   radish/cooking-person
          'the radish/the cook, about to cut'
      b. siore-kake-no   hana
          wither-about.to-GEN   flower
          'a flower, about to wither'
      c. *hataraki-kake-no   Takao
          work-about.to-GEN   Takao
          'Takao, about to work'

As shown in (13), the subject of an unaccusative verb, as well as the object of a transitive verb, but not the subject of an unergative verb or the subject of a transitive verb, qualifies as the head noun of the construction. Similar facts are observed for resultative predication: a resultative predicate can be predicated of an unaccusative subject, as well as the object of a transitive verb, but an unergative subject cannot be the target of resultative predication.

(14) a. Kodomo-ga   kabin-o   konagona-ni   kowasi-ta.
          child-NOM   vase-ACC   pieces-to   break-PST
          'The children broke vases into pieces.'
      b. Kabin-ga   koko-de   konagona-ni   koware-ta.
          vase-NOM   here-in   pieces-to   break-PST
          'Vases broke into pieces here.'
      c. *Robotto-ga   koko-de   konagona-ni   hatarai-ta.
          robot-NOM   here-in   pieces-to   work-PST
          'Robots worked into pieces here.'

In both *kake*-construction and resultative predication, the target of modification is restricted to direct objects (internal arguments). Since intransitive verbs are partitioned into the two classes of unergative and unaccusative verbs according to whether their single arguments have object properties, both constructions offer tests for **unaccusativity** in Japanese.

Another unaccusative diagnostic is found in the V-*te iru* construction. In (15a), V-*te iru*, which is associated with the verb *hasiru* 'run', gives rise to a progressive interpretation, but for the verb *sinu* 'die' in (15b), V-*te iru* has a resulting-state interpretation.

(15) a. Ken-ga   hasit-te   i-ru.
          Ken-NOM   run-GER   be-PRS
          'Ken is running.'
      b. Musi-ga   sin-de   i-ru.
          insect-NOM   die-GER   be-PRS
          'The insect has been dead.'

The difference in aspectual interpretation reflects the distinction between unergative and unaccusative verbs. A generalization regarding the V-*te iru* construction is that the progressive interpretation is available when the subject is an agent, which is base-generated in subject position, while the resulting-state interpretation is generated if the subject is derived by movement from within VP.

(16) a. [$_{TP}$ AGENT [$_{VP}$ V]-te iru]
      b. [$_{TP}$ THEME [$_{VP}$ THEME V]-te iru]

Since an unaccusative verb taking an internal argument appears in the aspectual construction in (15b), the V-*te iru* form receives a resulting-state interpretation. In the case of an unergative verb, no movement takes place from the internal argument position to the subject position, so a progressive interpretation is obtained in (15a).

Cross-linguistically, quite a number of linguistic phenomena have been found that lead us to postulate that intransitive verbs are divided into two classes. If the distinction is drawn according to whether their sole arguments display subject or object properties, it can be hypothesized that it comes from a difference in the structure of intransitive verbs. The Unaccusative Hypothesis claims that the two classes of intransitive verbs—unergative and unaccusative verbs—have distinct underlying structures, motivated by some semantic factors and confirmed by syntactic tests, even when their surface configurations are unvarying. The unaccusative phenomena offer us insight into the structural organization of intransitive clauses, which is considered to be constant across languages.

For Further Research

(A-1) Numeral quantifier floating provides a different kind of test for unaccusativity. The examples in (i) illustrate that a difference in acceptability emerges between unergative and unaccusative verbs when a numeral quantifier is separated from the noun phrase it quantifies by another argument or an adjunct.

(i)   a. *Kodomo-ga   sensei-ni   huta-ri   hanasi-ta.
         child-NOM   teacher-DAT   two-CL   talk-PST
         'Two children talked to the teacher.'
      b. Kodomo-ga   miti-de   huta-ri   taore-ta.
         child-NOM   road-LOC   two-CL   fall.down-PST
         'Two children fell down on the road.'

A numeral quantifier can appear in a position where an argument appears at the underlying level. If the subject of the unaccusative verb, not the unergative verb, starts out from the object position, the contrast in acceptability between (ia) and (ib) follows straightforwardly (see Miyagawa (1989a, 1989b)).

(A-2) When -te iru is combined with a verb like kowasu 'break', different interpretations are derived between active and passive clauses like (ii).

(ii)   a. Kodomo-ga   omotya-o   kowasi-te   i-ru.
          child-NOM   toy-ACC   break-GER   be-PRS
          'The child is breaking the toy.'
       b. Omotya-ga   kowas-are-te   i-ru.
          toy-NOM   break-PASS-GER   be-PRS
          'The toy has been broken.'

The active clause in (iia) has a progressive meaning, but a resulting-state interpretation is readily obtained for the passive clause in (iib) (see Takezawa (1991)).

   V-te iru has "progressive" and "resulting-state" interpretations as their basic interpretations, but it can have other interpretations, such as "experiential" and "habitual" interpretations. Although the experiential interpretation shows some similarity to the resulting-state interpretation semantically, these two interpretations need to be distinguished.

(iii)   Kodomo-ga   kinoo   hasit-te   i-ru.
        child-NOM   yesterday   run-GER   be-PRS
        'The child has run yesterday.'

The sentence in (iii) has an experiential, but not a resulting-state, interpretation. This can be seen from the fact that the sentence is compatible with the adverb *kinoo*, which can only refer to a past point of time. On the experiential interpretation, the child does not participate in the act of running at the present time.

(B-1) Unergative verbs select agents as their single arguments while unaccusative verbs take theme arguments. Semantically, unergative verbs describe an intentional action, and unaccusative verbs, non-intentional actions. This characterization does not seem to be valid in all cases. The verb *iku* 'go' can describe an intentional action, since an intentional adverb *wazato* 'intentionally' can occur with it.

(iv)   Ken-ga   wazato   gakkoo-ni   ika-nakat-ta.
       Ken-NOM   intentionally   school-to   go-NEG-PST
       'Ken intentionally did not go to school.'

Nevertheless, the subject of the verb *iku* 'go' can be modified by the quantity adverb *takusan* 'many'.

(v)   Kodomo-ga   sono   gakkoo-ni   takusan   it-ta.
      child-NOM   that   school-to   many   go-PST
      'Many children went to that school.'

The data in (iv) and (v) seem to be in conflict with the premise that verbs are unergative if they express intentional meanings, taking an agent subject. How can these apparent conflicts be reconciled?

(B-2) When a transitive or intransitive verb takes an agent subject in the *V-te iru* construction, it gives rise to a progressive interpretation, but when a transitive verb like *itameru* 'hurt' takes an experiencer subject, as in (vi), a resulting-state interpretation is obtained.

(vi)   Ken-ga   asi-o   itame-te   i-ru.
       Ken-NOM   leg-ACC   hurt-GER   be-PRS
      'Ken's leg hurts.'

Why is it that the sentence in (vi) has a resulting-state interpretation rather than a progressive interpretation?

CHAPTER 14

Where Do Subjects Come From? [C], [E]

14.1 The True Origin of Subjects

Subjects have special syntactic status, in that they are located outside VP, while other arguments are included inside VP. A transitive clause formed on the verb *homeru* 'praise' in (1a) has the structure given in (1b), where the subject is located in TP.

(1) a. Ken-ga   Eri-o   home-ta.
          Ken-NOM   Eri-ACC   praise-PST
          'Ken praised Eri.'
    b. [$_{TP}$ Ken-ga [$_{VP}$ Eri-o home] -ta]

In the analysis espoused thus far, the subject of a transitive verb like *homeru* 'praise' is generated in the specifier position of TP, because an agent role is assigned there. An object appears in the complement position of VP because it receives a theme role in that position, as illustrated in (2).

(2) [$_{TP}$ Ken [$_{VP}$ Eri home$_{<Agent, Theme>}$] -ta]

The arguments need to receive θ-roles for their semantic interpretation, but they also need to be Case-marked. When they are Case-marked, they are allowed to appear in a clause structurally. T assigns nominative Case to the subject, and the object receives accusative Case from V.

(3) [$_{TP}$ Ken [$_{VP}$ Eri home $_{[ACC]}$] -ta $_{[NOM]}$]

If we look at the way in which Cases and θ-roles are assigned, it is easy to see that there is a structural asymmetry between Case and θ-role assignment. Specifically, both nominative Case and accusative Case are assigned within the projection of the Case-assigning head (i.e. TP and VP, respectively). With regard to θ-role assignment, however, a V head assigns a theme role to the object within VP, but the same V head assigns an agent role to the subject in TP, which is a projection located above VP. The assignment of the agent role is exceptional in the sense that V assigns its agent role across the VP boundary. There is a general theoretical assumption that grammatical operations are (normally) implemented within the closest, hierarchically lowest possible structural domain, which is often discussed under the notion of **locality**. In the cases at hand, the maximal projection of a licensing head is considered to constitute such a local domain.

The assignment of an agent θ-role to the subject is not a local operation and hence an exception to the notion of locality mentioned above. This brings a great deal of complication into the theory. Of course, simpler explanations are better than those involving complications, and it is theoretically desirable not to have such an exception. There is one straightforward way of resolving this problem. This can be accomplished by generating the subject within VP, making V assign its agent role to the subject in VP, as illustrated in (4).

(4)   [$_{TP}$ [$_{VP}$ Ken Eri home$_{<Agent\ Theme>}$] -ta]

This simple change brings about the consequence that V assigns all θ-roles to arguments within VP, eliminating the asymmetry in θ-role versus Case assignment. If the mechanism of Case assignment remains intact, V assigns accusative Case to the object position in VP, and T assigns nominative Case to the subject position in TP. This being the case, the subject generated within VP needs to move to its subject position for the purpose of receiving nominative Case.

(5)   [$_{TP}$ Ken [$_{VP}$ ~~Ken~~ Eri home $_{[ACC]}$] -ta$_{[NOM]}$]

In this analysis, the subject receives a θ-role in a VP-internal position but moves to TP to receive nominative Case. Hence, the subject ends up in a privileged position outside the VP. By contrast, the object receives both accusative Case and its θ-role in its base position, and thus, no movement of the object is required. This analysis, taking the subject to originate the VP, is called the **VP-Internal Subject Hypothesis**—another important syntactic hypothesis advanced in generative grammar. Under the VP-Internal Subject Hypothesis, a transitive clause involves the derivation illustrated in (6).

(6)

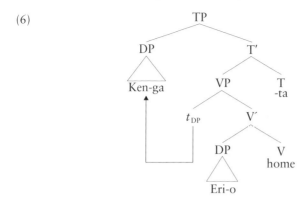

In (6), the subject *Ken* is moved from VP-internal position to TP. The pre-movement site is indicated by t_{DP}. The symbol t_{DP} represents a **trace** created by movement and signifies the position from which the DP has been moved. (The symbol t, which comes from the initial letter of the word *trace*, is used to designate the position from which some element has been displaced (like a footprint left behind when someone walks on sand).) There is also the view that what is left by movement is not a trace but a **copy**, and this theory is called the **copy theory of movement**. For the present purposes, it does not matter which theory is adopted, however.

Under the VP-Internal Subject Hypothesis, Case assignment and θ-role assignment are implemented uniformly with a proximate relation to the head (with a θ-role or Case to assign), i.e. within the projection of the relevant head. This hypothesis naturally accounts for the puzzling fact that it has been difficult to determine what counts as a specifier to VP. X′-theory dictates that not merely noun phrases but also other phrasal categories can have a specifier, but at first sight, this generalization does not seem to apply to VP. This discrepancy finds a solution if a subject generated in the specifier position of VP is moved to the specifier position of TP by DP-movement. Under the VP-Internal Subject Hypothesis, a subject fills the specifier position of VP initially, but is moved out of VP later. Therefore, it looks on the surface as if nothing is allowed to occur as a specifier to VP.

14.2 Empirical Justification

The VP-Internal Subject Hypothesis brings about a number of desirable theoretical consequences, as described above. Interestingly, Japanese provides empirical evidence in support of the VP-Internal Subject Hypothesis. In

Japanese, some types of subjects remain in the base-generated position inside
VP. To make this point, let us consider how subjects are case-marked in
Japanese. The most typical case marking on subjects is nominative case, but it is
also possible with some predicates to mark the subject with the postposition
kara 'from'.

(7) a. Otona-ga   kodomo-ni   hanasi-ta.
         adult-NOM   child-DAT   talk-PST
         'The adult talked to the child.'
     b. Otona-kara   kodomo-ni   hanasi-ta.
         adult-ABL   child-DAT   talk-PST
         'The adult talked to the child.'

In (7a), the DP *otona* 'adult' is marked with nominative case, but the same DP
bears *kara*-marking in (7b). This *kara*-marking is possible because the argument *otona* can be thematically identified as a source, as well as an agent. The
postposition *kara* is used to mark a source, and thus the subject with *kara* can
be considered as representing a **source subject**.

The *ga*- and *kara*-marked arguments in (7) are agents (i.e. initiators of
actions), and both possess the status of subjects syntactically, which can be confirmed by making use of subject diagnostic tests. One such diagnostic is **subject
honorification**. Subject honorification is signaled by a subject-honorific predicate, which most typically appears in the *o-V-ni-naru* form. Subject honorification, as its name suggests, takes a subject as the target of honorification (and,
needless to say, the target of subject honorification must refer to an individual
worthy of deference). Thus, we observe a difference in acceptability between
(8a) and (8b).

(8) a. Itoo-sensei-ga   kodomo-o   o-home-ni-nat-ta.
         Ito-teacher-NOM   child-ACC   HON-praise-DAT-become-PST
         'Prof. Ito praised the child.'
     b. *Kodomo-ga   Itoo-sensei-o   o-home-ni-nat-ta.
         child-NOM   Ito-teacher-ACC   HON-praise-DAT-become-PST
         'The child praised Prof. Ito.'
     c. Kon-kai-wa   Itoo-sensei-kara   o-hanasi-ni-nat-ta.
         this-time-TOP   Ito-teacher-ABL   HON-talk-DAT-become-PST
         'This time, Prof. Ito talked.'

In (8a), the subject is targeted for subject honorification, and the sentence is
legitimate. On the other hand, (8b) is not acceptable, since it is not the subject
but the object, which cannot be targeted for subject honorification, that refers

to a person worthy of respect. Note that the *kara*-marked agent argument in (8c) can be targeted for subject honorification in much the same way as the nominative subject. If the (potential) targets of subject honorification are confined to subjects, it must be the case that the agent argument marked with *kara* in (8c) serves as a subject syntactically, just like the nominative-marked subject in (8a).

Another well-discussed diagnostic for subjecthood is **reflexivization**, which makes use of reflexive forms like *zibun* 'self'. In Japanese, reflexive *zibun* can take a subject, but not an object, as its antecedent, as shown in (9b).

(9) a. Ken_i-ga zibun_i-no heya-de   Mari-ni   hanasi-o   si-ta.
     Ken-NOM   self-GEN   room-LOC   Mari-DAT   talk-ACC   do-PST
     'Ken_i talked to Mari in self_i's room.'
   b. Ken_i-kara-wa zibun_i-no   hanasi-o   si-nakat-ta.
     Ken-ABL-TOP   self-GEN   talk-ACC   do-NEG-PST
     'Ken did not talk about himself.'

The *kara*-marked argument in (9b) can be the antecedent of the reflexive *zibun* in the same way as the nominative argument in (9a), which shows that this argument functions as a subject syntactically.

Subject-oriented adverbs like *sibusibu* 'reluctantly' and *nessin-ni* 'earnestly' provide us with another kind of evidence. If adverbs have subject orientation, they can modify only subjects.

(10) a. Ken-ga   Mari-o   sibusibu   sikat-ta.
     Ken-NOM   Mari-ACC   reluctantly   scold-PST
     'Ken reluctantly scolded Mari.'
   b. Ken-ga   Mari-ni   sibusibu   hanasi-ta.
     Ken-NOM   Mari-DAT   reluctantly   talk-PST
     'Ken talked to Mari reluctantly.'
   c. Ken-kara   Mari-ni   sibusibu   hanasi-ta.
     Ken-ABL   Mari-DAT   reluctantly   talk-PST
     'Ken talked to Mari reluctantly.'

In (10a), the subject, but not the object, can be modified by the adverb *sibusibu*. In (10b), the adverb can modify the *ga*-marked subject, but not the *ni*-marked argument. In (10c), *sibusibu* can be taken as modifying the *kara*-marked argument in the same way as the *ga*-marked subject in (10b). The data illustrate then that the *kara*-marked argument in (10c) serves as a subject syntactically.

Ga- and *kara*-marked subjects occupy distinct constituent positions in clause structure. For present purposes, it is instructive to see how indeterminate pro-

138

nouns are interpreted in (11).

(11) Ken-wa   **dare**-ni   hanasi-**mo**   si-nakat-ta.
     Ken-TOP   anyone-to   talk-Q   do-NEG-PST
     'Ken did not talk to anyone.'

Indeterminate pronouns like *dare* 'anyone' and *nani* 'anything', which are construed with *mo*, are interpreted as **negative polarity items** (NPIs)(like *anyone* in English). Observe here that the sequence of *dare... mo* is legitimate in (11), where *mo* follows the verb. (Note that an NPI sequence can only appear in a negated clause, and thus, the sentence is excluded if the predicate is not negated.) On the other hand, there are cases where indeterminate pronouns cannot be construed with *mo* occurring after the verb.

(12) a. *****Dare**-ga   Eri-ni   hanasi-**mo**   si-nakat-ta.
        anyone-NOM   Eri-DAT   talk-Q   do-NEG-PST
        'Anyone did not talk to Eri.'
     b. **Dare**-kara   Eri-ni   hanasikake-**mo**   si-nakat-ta.
        anyone-ABL   Eri-DAT   talk-Q   do-NEG-PST
        'No one talked to Eri.'

In (12a), the particle *mo* cannot be associated with the indeterminate pronoun *dare* 'anyone' properly, so that the sequence of *dare* and *mo* fails to serve as an NPI. In contrast, in (12b), where the subject is marked with *kara*, the same sequence of *dare* and *mo* can be interpreted as an NPI sequence.

When *mo* is attached to the right of the verb, it attaches to VP, which suggests that it takes scope over VP. If *mo* can be associated only with indeterminate pronouns located within VP (at the S-structure level), the facts of (12) lead to the conclusion that the *kara*-marked subject remains in VP, whereas the nominative subject is moved from within VP to TP, as depicted in (13).

(13) a. [$_{TP}$ Otona-ga   [$_{VP}$ ~~Otona-ga~~   hanasi] -ta]

     b. [$_{TP}$ [$_{VP}$ Otona-kara   hanasi] -ta]

Under the VP-Internal Subject Hypothesis, V assigns an agent role to an argument in the VP-internal subject position, and thus the argument, which is thematically identified as an agent, behaves as a subject.

The fact that the *kara*-marked subject in (12b) functions as an NPI within the VP is naturally expected given the structure of (13b). This is because *kara* is a postposition that projects to PP. Since PP can stand in a clause without receiving

Case from an external Case-assigning head, the *kara*-marked subject need not receive nominative Case from T. It follows from this that the *kara*-subject does not move to TP. On the other hand, the nominative subject cannot remain in the specifier position of VP, but must move to the specifier position of TP to receive nominative Case, which is assigned by T. In this connection, observe that both nominative and *kara*-marked subjects possess subject properties with regard to reflexivization, subject honorification, and subject-oriented adverbs. Since *kara*-subjects are not raised to TP, we can state that arguments appearing in VP-internal subject position, i.e. the specifier position of VP, acquire subject properties.

The facts regarding varying positions of subjects, distinguished according to whether they are marked with nominative *ga* or *kara*, fall out naturally under the VP-Internal Subject Hypothesis. Especially, the facts of *kara*-marked subjects, which do not undergo DP-movement to TP, offer direct empirical evidence that subjects are base-generated in VP-internal position. In addition, given that *kara*-marked subjects are not moved to the specifier position of TP, it follows that the subject diagnostic tests noted above pick out a subject located in the specifier position of VP.

For Further Research

(A-1) Unaccusative predicates like *taoreru* 'fall down' take a nominative subject that starts out in object position but is raised to TP, as confirmed by the fact that *mo* attached to the verb cannot be associated with the subject *dare* 'anyone'.

(i)   a. Ken-ga   taore-ta.
           Ken-NOM   fall-PST
           'Ken fell down.'
    b. *Dare-ga   taore-**mo**   si-nakat-ta.
          anyone-NOM fall-also   do-NEG-PST
          'Anyone did not fall down.'

An unaccusative subject displays subject properties, since it can be targeted for subject honorification and reflexivization, as shown in (ii).

(ii)   a. Kimura-sensei-ga   o-taore-ni-nat-ta.
          Kimura-teacher-NOM   HON-fall-DAT-become-PST
         'Professor Kimura fell down.'
    b. Ken$_i$-ga   zibun$_i$-no   heya-de   taore-ta.
        Ken-NOM   self-GEN   room-in   fall-PST
       'Ken fell down in his own room.'

As discussed in this chapter, *kara*-marked subjects, which are generated in the specifier position of VP without raising to TP, can be targeted for these operations. Given this, it can be reasonably stated that unaccusative subjects obtain subject properties when they appear in the specifier position of VP. The facts show, then, that unaccusative subjects are first generated in the complement position of VP and are raised to TP by way of the specifier position of VP, as illustrated in (iii).

(iii)   [$_{TP}$ SUBJ [$_{VP}$ ~~SUBJ~~ [$_{V'}$ ~~SUBJ~~ V]]]

The successive DP-movement indicated in (iii) may be motivated by a locality requirement that movement must proceed by stopping at the closest landing site.

(A-2) In Japanese, there are several distinct types of honorification, with subject honorification and non-subject honorification being the types most often discussed. Subject honorification can only target subjects. On the other hand, non-subject honorification targets a non-subject argument, as exemplified in (iv).

(iv) Ken-ga   Yamada-sensei-o   uti-made   o-okuri-si-ta.
      Ken-NOM   Yamada-teacher-ACC   home-to   HON-take-do-PST
      'Ken took Professor Yamada to his home.'

Most typically, non-subject honorification takes the form of o-V-suru [HON-V-do]. In (iv), non-subject honorification targets a direct object, which is a non-subject argument. Non-subject honorification can also be anchored to other arguments (in different types of clauses). For the syntactic distribution of non-subject honorification, see Harada (1976) and Hasegawa (2006).

(B) Besides ablative kara 'from', there is another postposition that can appear on subjects, the instrumental (or locative) marker de 'with'. Subjects can be marked with de if they refer to a group of people, as in (va). If the subject marked with de does not refer to a group, unacceptability results, as shown in (vb).

(v)   a. Ken-tati-de   hanasi-ta.
          Ken-PL-INS   talk-PST
          'People in Ken's group talked.'
      b. *Ken-de   hanasi-ta.
          Ken-INS   talk-PST
          'Ken talked.'

The subject status of the de-marked argument in (va) is confirmed by (vi), which shows that this argument can be a target of subject honorification.

(vi) Hara-sensei-tati-de   o-hanasi-ni-nat-ta.
      Hara-teacher-PL-INS   HON-talk-DAT-become-PST
      'People in Professor Hara's group talked.'

De specifies a specific semantic relation, which suggests that it is a postposition. If this is the case, where is the de-marked subject in (va) expected to be located? Does it appear in VP or TP?

CHAPTER 15

Control and Raising [C], [E]

15.1 Invisible Subjects

Japanese allows two verbs to appear side by side in a sentence, making a single morphological verbal complex—a construction that is often claimed to constitute a unique grammatical characteristic of the language, not found in European languages. The verbal complexes are called **compound verbs** (or **V-V compounds**). Some representative examples of the compound verb constructions are given in (1).

(1)   a. Ken-wa   doa-o   sime-wasure-ta.
            Ken-TOP   door-ACC   close-forget-PST
            'Ken forgot to close the door.'
    b. Ken-wa   hon-o   yomi-dasi-ta.
            Ken-TOP   book-ACC   read-start-PST
            'Ken started to read the book.'

In the light of the fact that verbs generally project to VP, it can be hypothesized that in compound verb constructions, the two verb sequences have structures where one VP is embedded under another VP, as represented in (2).

(2)

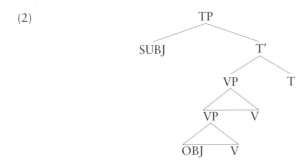

The two compound verb constructions in (1) are comprised of both subject and object owing to the fact that the main verb, i.e. the first verb (*simeru* 'close', *yomu* 'read'), is a transitive predicate.

In the two compound verb constructions in (1), where the verbs are positioned in tandem, the only visible difference lies in the choice of second verb: *wasureru* 'forget' in (1a) and *dasu* 'start' in (1b). At first sight, these two constructions in (1) look as though they possess the same syntactic structures. Contrary to appearances, however, they have distinct structures, which cannot be detected by just looking at how the verbs are superficially arranged. In this regard, it is interesting to observe that a discrepancy in acceptability emerges between the two sentences when the subjects are inanimate.

(3) a. *Ame-ga   huri-wasure-ta.
        rain-NOM   fall-forget-PST
        'It forgot to rain.'
     b. Ame-ga   huri-dasi-ta.
        rain-NOM   fall-start-PST
        'It started to rain.'

Where does the behavioral difference observed in (3) come from? The facts suggest that the two constructions in (1) have distinct syntactic structures, and the key to the answer to the question lies in the nature of the second verb.

In the compound verb construction in (1a), the first verb *yomu* expresses the meaning of 'reading' and the second verb *wasureru* carries the meaning of 'forgetting'. Thus, the first main verb has the argument structure <Agent, Theme>, and the second verb, the argument structure <Experiencer>. (The second verb *wasureru* differs from its full independent verb counterpart *wasureru*, in that the former selects an experiencer argument plus a VP-complement, while the latter is a transitive verb selecting experiencer and theme arguments.) If the agent and experiencer roles are assigned to subjects, the compound verb constructions need to have two subjects. Nevertheless, in (1a), only one subject is overtly realized in the matrix clause. It is reasonable, then, to assume that the lower subject appears as an inaudible pronoun **PRO** (an abbreviation for 'pronominal'). If so, (1a) has a derivation where the three arguments are each assigned their θ-roles, as in (4).

(4)   [TP [VP Ken_i [VP PRO_i hon yomi_{<Agent, Theme>}] -wasure_{<Experiencer>}] -ta]

PRO is necessarily understood as having the same reference as the subject in the matrix clause, a c-commanding and co-indexed DP. Here, the matrix subject is said to **control** PRO. The matrix subject is assigned an experiencer role in the upper VP, but the subject bears nominative case marking, which suggests that it is moved to TP to receive nominative Case. On the other hand, the accusative Case is assigned to the object without movement.

(5) $[_{TP}$ Ken$_i$ $[_{VP}$ ~~Ken~~ $[_{VP}$ PRO$_i$ hon yomi$_{[ACC]}]$ -wasure] -ta$_{[NOM]}]$

It is postulated that unpronounced PRO is a special pronoun that does not have to receive Case, unlike overtly realized arguments, so it can stay within VP. The upper verb *wasureru*, which takes a **control complement** with PRO, as in (4), is called a **control verb**. The compound verb construction with *wasureru* forms a **control construction**, which comprises controlled PRO.

The compound verb construction in (1b) has a different syntactic structure. The second verb *dasu* 'start' only carries an aspectual meaning, and hence, it does not have its own argument structure, which means that it does not select any argument. (Note that the full-fledged verb *dasu* selects agent and theme arguments plus an optional goal, but the dependent second verb *dasu* selects a VP complement only and lacks an argument structure entirely.) The main verb *yomu* 'read' has the argument structure <Agent, Theme>. Thus, in (1b), only the main verb assigns thematic roles to their arguments, as depicted in (6).

(6) $[_{TP}$ $[_{VP}$ $[_{VP}$ Ken hon yomi$_{<Agent, Theme>}]$ -dasi] -ta]

The subject *Ken* appears in the specifier position of the lower VP and is assigned an agent role. This argument is moved to the specifier position of TP to receive nominative Case.

(7) $[_{TP}$ Ken $[_{VP}$ $[_{VP}$ ~~Ken~~ hon yomi$_{[ACC]}]$ -dasi] -ta$_{[NOM]}]$

The second verb *dasu* 'start' does not select a subject but allows the subject of the embedded VP to be raised into the matrix subject position. Thus this type of second verb is called a **raising verb,** and the compound verb construction with the raising verb is a **raising construction.**

The structural differences between the two constructions give rise to the discrepancy in acceptability observed in (3). In (3a), the overtly realized subject is understood as the subject of *wasureru* as well as the subject of the main verb. Since the overtly realized subject of the second verb *wasureru* is assigned an experiencer role, it must be animate in order to satisfy the **animacy requirement** on the experiencer (alongside the selectional restriction imposed by the first main verb). Accordingly, (3a) with an inanimate subject is not acceptable. In (3b), by contrast, the second verb *dasu* 'start' does not select any argument, so any type of subject can appear as long as it satisfies the selectional restriction of the first main verb. Thus, (3b) is acceptable even if it has an inanimate subject.

In Japanese, many compound verbs have complex syntactic structures, but there are also compound verbs without a complex syntactic structure, like *hasiri-komu* [run-go.into] 'run into'. The difference between the two can be checked, for instance, by considering whether **soo suru replacement** can apply to the sequence of the first verb plus the arguments it selects, if any. If compound verbs have complex syntactic structures, *soo suru* replacement can affect the first verbs, leaving the second verbs intact, as shown in (8).

(8) a. Kodomo-ga   doa-o   sime-wasure-tara,   otona-mo
         child-NOM   door-ACC   close-forget-COND   adult-also
         [*soo*   *si*]-wasure-ta.
         so   do-forget-PST
         'When the children forgot to close the door, the adults forgot to do so, too.'
     b. Ken-ga   asobi-dasi-tara,   Mari-mo [*soo* *si*]-dasi-ta.
         Ken-NOM   play-start-COND   Mari-also so   do-start-PST
         'When Ken started to play, Mari started to do so, too.'

Note that *soo suru* replacement can substitute for VP in the way *do so* substitutes for VP in English.

(9)   John made a decision, and Mary *did so* (=made a decision), too.

If a VP constituent is replaced by *soo suru*, it follows that the compound verbs *sime-wasureru* and *asobi-dasu* have complex structures with two VP layers, as in (2). On the other hand, no such replacement is possible in the case of a compound verb like *hasiri-komu*. If *soo suru* replaces only the first verb, unacceptability results, as in (10a), but it is possible to replace the sequence of the two verbs with *soo suru*, as shown in (10b).

(10)   a. *Ken-ga   heya-ni   hasiri-kon-dara,   Mari-mo
          Ken-NOM   room-in   run-go.into-COND   Mari-also
          [*soo*   *si*]-kon-da.
          so   do-go.into-PST
          'When Ken ran into the room, Mari did so, too.'

b. Ken-ga   heya-ni   hasiri-kon-dara,   Mari-mo
   Ken-NOM   room-in   run-go.into-COND   Mari-also
   [*soo si*]-ta.
   so do-PST
   'When Ken ran into the room, Mari did so, too.'

The examples in (10) illustrate then that the two verbs *hasiru* 'run' and *komu* 'go into' appearing in the verbal complex *hasiri-komu*, which stand side by side, do not function as separate verbs. Rather, the compound verb *hasiri-komu* serves as a simple verb syntactically.

Compound verbs like those in (1), which have syntactically complex structures where one VP is embedded under another VP, are called **syntactic compound verbs**. On the other hand, the type of compound verb that functions as a simple verb syntactically, e.g. *hasiri-komu* in (10), is called a **lexical compound verb**.

15.2 Clausal Idioms

Control and raising verbs are also distinguished according to whether a **clausal idiom** like *kankodori-ga naku* 'have few customers (lit: a cuckoo sings)'—an idiom where the subject is included in the idiomatic sequence—can be embedded. When this idiom appears in the compound verb constructions, there emerges a difference in availability of idiomatic interpretation depending on the type of second verb.

(11) a. #Kono   mise-de   kankodori-ga   naki-wasure-ta.
         this   store-at   cuckoo-NOM   sing-forget-PST
         'A cuckoo forgot to sing at this store.'
      b. Kono   mise-de   kankodori-ga   naki-dasi-ta.
         this   store-at   cuckoo-NOM   sing-start-PST
         'This store started to attract fewer and fewer customers.'
         'A cuckoo started to sing at this store.'

In (11a), *kankodori-ga naku* can only be interpreted as having a literal interpretation, as indicated by the sign #. In (11b), the same strings of words can have an idiomatic interpretation alongside the literal interpretation.

What makes the control and raising constructions behave differently? This comes from the fact that idioms can have their idiomatic interpretations only when their components are adjacent (in compliance with the so-called **adjacency condition**). To illustrate this point, consider (12).

(12) Kankodori-wa   [ano mise-de   zibun-ga nai-ta   to]
     cuckoo-TOP   that store-at self-NOM sing-PST that
     omot-ta.
     think-PST
     'The cuckoo thought that she sang at that store.'

In (12), the reflexive *zibun* 'self' can be understood to refer to *kankodori* 'cuckoo'. Even so, no idiomatic interpretation is available for (12). The lack of an idiomatic interpretation in (12) is attributed to the fact that *kankodori* and the rest of the material necessary for idiomatic interpretation are not adjacent to each other, i.e. they do not stand in close vicinity.

   Given that idiom formation requires that the adjacency condition be satisfied, the difference in availability of idiom interpretation for the syntactic compound verb constructions in (11) naturally follows from the structures in (13a) and (13b), which can be posited for (11a) and (11b), respectively.

(13) a. [$_{TP}$ kankodori$_i$-ga [$_{VP}$ ~~kankodori-ga~~ [$_{VP}$ PRO$_i$ naki] -wasure] -ta]

      b. [$_{TP}$ kankodori-ga [$_{VP}$ [$_{VP}$ ~~kankodori-ga~~ naki] -dasi] -ta]

In (13a), the subject *kankodori* is moved from the upper VP to TP, and the lower VP contains PRO. In (13a), *kankodori* and *naku* cannot be contiguous syntactically due to the intervening PRO. Consequently, no idiomatic interpretation is available for (11a). In (13b), the subject is generated in the embedded VP, and is moved up to TP (cf. Chapter 20). In (13b), the adjacency condition for idiom formation is satisfied at the lower VP level (before *kankodori* is moved to TP), so the idiomatic interpretation is available for (11b).

15.3 Auxiliary Verb Constructions

The distinction of control versus raising is found in other constructions as well. **Periphrastic auxiliary verb constructions** like (14), which are formed by combining auxiliary verbs with main verbs in the *te*-form, provide another case in point.

(14) a. Ken-ga   koko-o   hasit-te   i-ru.
          Ken-NOM   here-ACC   run-GER   be-PRS
          'Ken is running here.'

b. Ken-ga   koko-o   hasit-te   oi-ta.
Ken-NOM   here-ACC   run-GER   put-PST
'Ken ran here.'

The structural difference between the two types of constructions can be discerned by considering whether they allow clausal idioms and inanimate subjects to be embedded. Since the V-*te iru* construction in (14a) allows both clausal idioms and inanimate subjects to appear, as in (15), it is classified as a raising construction.

(15) a. Ame-ga   hut-te   i-ru.
         rain-NOM   fall-GER   be-PRS
         'It is raining.'
      b. Kono   mise-de   kankodori-ga   nai-te   i-ta.
         this   store-at   cuckoo-NOM   sing-GER   be-PST
         'This store was attracting fewer and fewer customers.'

By contrast, neither an inanimate subject nor a clausal idiom is allowed in the V-*te oku* construction in (14b), as shown in (16).

(16) a. *Ame-ga   hut-te   oi-ta.
         rain-NOM   fall-GER   put-PST
         'It was raining.'
      b. #Kono   mise-de   kankodori-ga   nai-te   oi-ta.
         this   store-at   cuckoo-NOM   sing-GER   put-PST
         'A cuckoo sang at this store.'

The data suggest that the V-*te iru* construction in (14a) has a raising structure, where the subject of the embedded verb is raised to the matrix TP, while the V-*te oku* construction in (14b) has a control structure, where the subject of the matrix verb controls PRO in the embedded clause, as represented in (17).

(17) a. [TP Ken-ga [VP   [TP   [VP Ken-ga hasit]-te] i] -ta]
      b. [TP Ken_i-ga [VP Ken-ga [TP   [VP PRO_i hasit]-te] oi] -ta]

In Japanese, -*te* can be assumed to project to TP, behaving like an infinitive marker semantically with no tense specification of its own. Since TP headed by -*te* cannot accommodate an overtly realized subject, it is reasonable to assume that the overt subjects of the two constructions appear in the specifier position of the matrix TP, as represented in (17). In (17a), the subject of the embedded predicate *hasiru* 'run' is moved from its original position in the lower VP to TP in the matrix clause through the embedded TP. In (17b), the subject of the embedded verb is realized as PRO, which is controlled by the subject of the control verb *oku* 'put' moved from its original position in the upper VP to TP in the matrix clause.

For Further Research

(A-1) The control constructions discussed in this chapter involve **obligatory control** in the sense that PRO must be controlled by its antecedent. There is also a **non-obligatory control** construction, as exemplified in (i).

(i) [Asa   PRO hayaku oki-ru   koto]-wa ii   koto da.
     morning   early   get.up-PRS that-TOP good that COP
     'It is good to get up early in the morning.'

In (i), PRO means 'people in general'. Since this invisible pronoun has a generic interpretation, it is referred to as **arbitrary PRO**.

(A-2) Auxiliary verb constructions are classified into several distinct types (although there are only a handful of auxiliary verbs, including *iru* 'be', *kuru* 'come', *ageru* 'give', *morau* 'get', *yaru* 'give', and *oku* 'put'). One type of auxiliary verb construction displaying unique syntactic behavior is called the **benefactive construction**.

(ii) a. Ken-ga   Mari-ni   hon-o   yon-de   age-ta.
        Ken-NOM   Mari-DAT   book-ACC   read-GER give-PST
        'Ken read the book to Mari.'
     b. Ken-ga   Mari-ni   hon-o   yon-de   morat-ta.
        Ken-NOM   Mari-DAT   book-ACC   read-GER get-PST
        'Ken got Mary to read the book.'

In the benefactive constructions, a dative argument is added to the base clause. In (iia), the dative argument is a benefactive argument, and the nominative argument is an agent. By contrast, in (iib), the nominative argument is a benefactive argument, and the dative argument is an agent.

(B) Another auxiliary verb construction exhibiting peculiar syntactic behavior is a construction with *aru* 'be'. The peculiar fact is that the auxiliary *aru* consturcion in (iii) has an intransitive form with the theme argument of the base verb marked with nominative case, even though the base verb cannot be intransitive by itself.

(iii) Soko-ni   hon-ga   oi-te   ar-u.
      there-LOC   book-NOM   put-GER   be-PRS
      'The book has been placed there.'

Note that (iii) expresses an agentive meaning, but still, an agent can never be overtly realized. What syntactic structure can be posited for (iii), then?

CHAPTER 16

Head Movement [C], [E]

16.1 The VN-*Suru* Construction and Noun Incorporation

Cross-linguistically, it is often observed that predicative expressions are formed by combining semantically light verbs with nouns carrying substantial meanings. This type of construction is called the **light verb construction**. Japanese, too, has light verb constructions, which are derived by combining the light verb *suru* 'do' with a noun with an argument structure—the so-called **verbal noun** (VN). Most typically, VNs are Sino-Japanese words consisting of two Chinese characters, including *benkyoo* (勉強) 'study', *soozi* (掃除) 'cleaning', *hunka* (噴火) 'eruption', *hensoo* (変装) 'disguise', etc. The Japanese light verb construction can have two variants. The verb *suru* can select a VN as its complement marked with accusative case or it can appear in a compound form.

(1) a. Ken-ga   benkyoo-o   si-ta.
         Ken-NOM   study-ACC   do-PST
         'Ken studied.'
     b. Ken-ga   benkyoo-si-ta.
         Ken-NOM   study-do-PST
         'Ken studied.'

In (1b), the VN-*suru* form is identified as a **compound word**, but the VN-*o suru* form in (1a) is a **periphrastic form** comprising two separate elements, i.e. *benkyoo* 'study' and *suru* 'do'. Both sentences in (1) express the identical logical meaning, and this raises the question of how these two forms are related.

The VN *benkyoo* 'study' in (1a) is an object marked with accusative case, which is selected by the verb *suru*. It is commonly assumed that the compound variant in (1b), where *benkyoo* and *suru* form a complex word, is derived from the periphrastic VN form in (1a). This compound formation is considered to involve a syntactic process that moves a noun head and adjoins it to the predicate, a process that is often referred to as **noun incorporation** and is illustrated in (2).

(2)

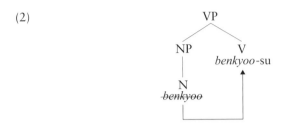

Syntactically speaking, noun incorporation makes a noun head, but not a noun phrase, part of the predicate. Owing to this fact, the two variants of light verb constructions show different syntactic behaviors. As seen in (3), a full phrase *suugaku no benkyoo* 'studying mathematics' cannot be compounded with the verb *suru*, although the same phrase can be marked with accusative case.

(3) a. Ken-ga   [suugaku-no   benkyoo]-o   si-ta.
        Ken-NOM   mathematics-GEN   study-ACC   do-PST
        'Ken studied mathematics.'
     b. *Ken-ga   [suugaku-no   benkyoo]-si-ta.
        Ken-NOM   mathematics-GEN   study-do-PST
        'Ken studied mathematics.'

The type of syntactic movement depicted in (2) is called **head movement** and can move only a head (by the **head movement constraint**). From this, it follows that the verbal noun cannot be combined with a noun phrase containing a genitive phrase in (3b). By contrast, (3a) does not involve noun incorporation (i.e. head movement), and the example, in which a noun phrase occurs as an object of the verb *suru*, is acceptable.

Head movement differs from DP-movement, which moves a phrasal element. The passive clause in (4b), derived from (4a), invokes DP-movement of an object into the subject position.

(4) a. Ken-ga   [Mari-no   kodomo]-o   home-ta.
        Ken-NOM   Mari-GEN   child-ACC   praise-PST
        'Ken praised Mari's child.'
     b. [Mari-no   kodomo]-ga   Ken-ni   home-rare-ta.
        Mari-GEN   child-NOM   Ken-by   praise-PASS-PST
        'Mari's child was praised by Ken.'

Since DP-movement moves a phrase (DP), it is possible in (4b) to have a complex noun phrase containing a genitive phrase in subject position. In contrast, the light verb construction cannot have a phrase form a compound with the verb *suru*, as in (3b).

16.2 Another Kind of Head Movement

The light verb construction with VNs presents a case where the process of head movement is audible. Interestingly, Japanese has another kind of head movement whose effect can be detected only indirectly. Negative predicate formation involves such inaudible head movement, as in (5a).

(5) a. Ken-ga   hon-o   yoma-nakat-ta.
         Ken-NOM   book-ACC   read-NEG-PST
         'Ken did not read books.'
     b. *Ken-ga   hon-o   yoma-naku-**sae**   at-ta.
         Ken-NOM   book-ACC   read-NEG-even   be-PST
         'Ken did not even read books.'

What is notable about the negative clause in (5a) is that the negative *nai* does not allow an adverbial particle like *sae* 'even' to the right of it, as shown in (5b). By contrast, the particle *sae* can be added to the right of verbs, as in (6).

(6) a. Ken-ga   hon-o   kat-ta.
         Ken-NOM   book-ACC   buy-PST
         'Ken bought books.'
     b. Ken-ga   hon-o   kai-**sae**   si-ta.
         Ken-NOM   book-ACC   buy-even   do-PST
         'Ken even bought books.'

The verb and the past morpheme -*ta* are coalesced into one morphological unit (as *kat-ta*) when they are adjacent. Nevertheless, when a particle is inserted between the two elements, they appear separately with the help of the verb *suru* (as *kai-sae si-ta*), as in (6b), which stands in contrast with (5b). The insertion of *suru* to the left of the tense morpheme is comparable to what is observed in an English sentence like (7b).

(7) a. John bought a book.
     b. John *did* not buy a book.

156

When the verb and the tense element are not adjacent, the two elements are spelled out separately. In English, *not* serves as an intervening element, which separates the tense from the verb. In (7b), the inflected verb *do* (i.e. *did*), which indicates the tense, is inserted (by **do-support**) and the main verb appears in the bare form (*buy*).

In English, tense and the verb occupy distinct syntactic positions, and a comparison of (6) and (7) suggests that in Japanese as well, the verb and the tense constitute separate heads syntactically. In Japanese, when a particle is added to the verb, the supportive verb *suru*, which does not carry substantive meaning, is inserted to the left of the tense marker in TP to save a bound morpheme morphologically that would otherwise be stranded (Note that the supportive verb *suru* behaves differently from the light verb *suru* 'do', which gives rise to the light verb constructions where the VN-*suru* form is derived from the periphrastic form VN-*o suru*). The operation of inserting a supportive verb in Japanese is often called ***suru*-support** (the Japanese equivalent of *do*-support in English) and is implemented a last resort strategy to save a stranded bound morpheme (like tense), which cannot occur on its own as a separate word.

The same strategy applies to adjectives. The example in (8b) shows that an adjectival predicate can be separated from the tense by inserting an adverbial particle.

(8) a. Kodomo-ga   kawaikat-ta.
        child-NOM   cute-PST
        'The child was cute.'
     b. Kodomo-ga   kawaiku-**sae**   *at*-ta.
        child-NOM   cute-even   be-PST
        'The child was even cute.'

As seen in (8b), the stranded tense, which is a bound morpheme, is saved morphologically if the verb *aru* 'be' is inserted to the left of it (i.e. *aru*-support). The two saving operations—*suru*- and *aru*-insertions—differ only in the choice of verb: *suru* is used for a verbal clause and *aru* for an adjectival clause. In both cases, the semantically empty verb is used to support a tense element, which is a bound morpheme that needs to be attached to a preceding host.

One important exceptional behavior is observed for the negator *nai*. Note that the negative *nai* inflects just like an adjective. This leads to the expectation that an adverbial particle could stand between the negator and the tense if *aru*-insertion is implemented. This expectation is not fulfilled, however. In (5b), the predicative sequence is formed by adding the supportive verb *aru* 'be' to the left of the tense, which is separated from the negative *nai* by an adverbial particle *sae* 'even'. Even though this is a correct morphological sequence when assigned to an adjectival predicate, the sentence in (5b) is not acceptable.

The unacceptability of (5b) and the acceptability of (8b) is the result of the presence or absence of head movement. First, *suru/aru*-insertion is an operation to add a supportive verb to the left of a stranded morpheme, which results when a particle follows the predicate. This insertion operation can be implemented if the two heads occupy distinct syntactic positions.

(9)

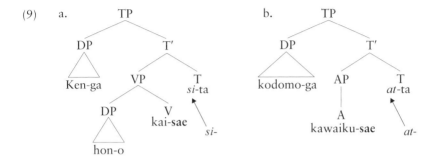

Suru/aru-insertion may take place if there is a syntactic gap where the supportive verb *aru* or *iru* is inserted. In (9a) and (9b), this gap is available, and thus these sentences are well-formed. On the other hand, the ill-formedness of (5b) comes from the fact that the gap that allows the supportive verb to be inserted does not exist, which can be attributed to the negative head's undergoing head movement to the tense. If the negative *nai* is a head that projects to NegP (=Negative Phrase), (5b) has the structure given in (10).

(10)

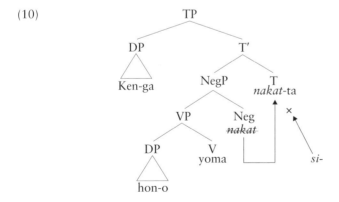

In (10), the negative head and the tense form a complex head as a result of the Neg-head undergoing movement (i.e. **Neg-head movement**). If an adverbial particle *sae* is to be inserted to the right of the negative head, the supportive verb *aru* needs to be added to the left of tense (for morphological support).

Nevertheless, this strategy does not work because the Neg-tense sequence forms a complex word with no syntactic break between them. Thus, both adverbial particle and the supportive verb *aru* are prevented from being inserted, and accordingly, the sentence in (5b), where *sae* is added to the right of the negative *nai*, is unacceptable.

The operations of adding adverbial particles and the supportive verbs *suru/aru* are possible only when the predicative heads do not undergo syntactic head movement to a higher position. Given the facts of supportive verb insertion, it can be stated that main predicates do not undergo head raising in Japanese (like English). Verbs and adjectives form morphological units with tense because the tense is a bound morpheme, but these morphological complexes are not formed by syntactic head movement. On the other hand, the negative *nai* forms a complex head (or complex word) with T syntactically as well as morphologically via Neg-head movement.

In the case of Neg-head raising, the effect of head movement is not visible, but can be assessed by the syntactic behavior of **negative polarity items**. Negative polarity items, such as *Ken-sika* 'only Ken' and *dare-mo* 'anyone', are licensed only when they appear in the scope of negation—the domain over which the negator exerts its influence as a clausal negator. Negative polarity items in Japanese and English behave differently because the two languages show a difference in the extent of negative scope. In English, negative polarity items are allowed to appear in object but not subject position.

(11)   a. She did not praise <u>anyone</u>.
         b. *<u>Anyone</u> did not praise that child.

The scope of a negative head extends up to the maximal projection in which it resides. In English, the scope of negation does not extend over the subject, because the negator *not* appears in NegP.

(12)   [$_{TP}$ SUBJ did [$_{NegP}$ not [$_{VP}$ praise OBJ]]]

                           (scope of negation)

In Japanese, negative polarity items are licensed regardless of whether they appear in subject or object position, as exemplified by (13), where the NPI *sika* is used.

(13) a. Ken-wa   Eri-sika   home-nakat-ta.
         Ken-TOP   Eri-only   praise-NEG-PST
         'Ken praised only Eri.'
      b. Ken-sika   Eri-o   home-nakat-ta.
         Ken-only   Eri-ACC   praise-NEG-PST
         'Only Ken praised Eri.'

The acceptability of the two sentences in (13) shows that in Japanese, unlike English, the subject position falls under the scope of negation. We can postulate that in Japanese, the negative head extends its scope over TP by virtue of Neg-head movement.

(14) [$_{TP}$ SUBJ   [$_{NegP}$ [$_{VP}$ OBJ   home] ~~nakat~~] nakat-ta]

(scope of negation)

The fact that negative polarity items can appear in either subject or object position in negated clauses, as in (13), follows if the negative head undergoes head movement from its original position to T, as illustrated in (14).

For Further Research

(A) Japanese VN constructions have two subtypes, distinguished according to whether they carry agentive or non-agentive meanings. Agentive VN constructions allow their VNs to be marked with accusative case.

(i)   Ken-ga   benkyoo-o   si-ta.
       Ken-NOM   study-ACC   do-PST
       'Ken studied.'

By contrast, acceptability of the non-agentive VN construction deteriorates if the VN is marked with accusative case.

(ii)   ?*Mizu-ga   zyoohatu-o   si-ta.
        water-NOM   evaporation-ACC   do-PST
       'Water evaporated.'

This case-marking constraint is derived from Burzio's Generalization (Burzio 1986), which states that the predicate can assign accusative case only when it selects an external argument (i.e. the agent). The subject *mizu* 'water' in (ii) is not an agent argument, and accordingly, the object cannot be marked with accusative case.

(B) Indeterminate pronouns like *dare* 'anyone' and *nani* 'anything' can be interpreted as universal quantifiers or negative polarity items if they are construed with a c-commanding *mo* (Kuroda (1965), Kishimoto (2001a)). (iii) is excluded because the *mo*, which is attached to the direct object, fails to c-command the indirect object.

(iii)   *Eri-wa   **dare**-ni   hon-**mo**   yoma-nakat-ta.
       Eri-TOP   anyone-DAT   book-Q   read-NEG-PST
       'Eri did not read the book to anyone.'

Nevertheless, there are some exceptions. (iv) presents a case in which *mo* can be linked to an indeterminate pronoun even if the c-command requirement is apparently violated.

(iv)   Eri-wa   **dare**-ni   soodan-**mo**   si-nakat-ta.
       Eri-TOP   anyone-DAT   consult-Q   do-NEG-PST
       'Eri did not consult anyone.'

Example (iv) is acceptable, despite the fact that *mo* is attached to a direct object, just like (iii). What makes the difference between (iii) and (iv)?

CHAPTER 17

Topics on Sentence-Initial Phrases [C], [E]

17.1 Topicalization

In Japanese, the particle *wa* is used as a topic marker. Since Japanese makes frequent use of **topicalization**, it is often claimed that Japanese is a **topic prominent language**. A topic phrase marked with *wa* most typically appears in sentence-initial position, as seen in (1).

(1)   <u>Mari-wa</u>   Ken-to   hanasi-ta.
      Mari-TOP   Ken-with   talk-PST
      'As for Mari, she talked with Ken.'

In (1), the subject *Mari* is marked with the topic marker *wa*. The topic phrase has a **thematic interpretation** (or **topic interpretation**) that can be paraphrased as 'speaking of X'. It is also possible to give a **contrastive interpretation** that can be paraphrased as 'X in contrast to others' by placing stress on the topic marker, as *Mari-wá*.

Topicalization can apply to non-subjects, and *wa*-marked sentence-initial topics are often placed in a sentence-internal position by way of movement. In (2), the topic marker appears with a *to*-marked argument which the verb *hanasu* 'talk' selects. This shows that the sentence-initial topic accompanying *to* 'with' originates from a VP-internal position, which immediately precedes the verb, and hence, topic movement is involved.

(2)   <u>Ken-to-wa</u>   Mari-ga   hanasi-ta.
      Ken-with-TOP   Mari-NOM   talk-PST
      'With Ken, Mari talked.'

The topic phrase in (2) precedes the subject. This fact suggests that there must be a topic position accommodating the topic phrase, which is higher than the position filled by the subject. It can be postulated here that CP offers such a position, since CP is projected above TP.

(3)

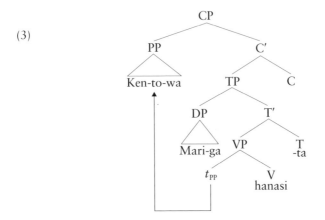

Exactly where the topic phrase is located can be assessed by considering what element the particle *dake* 'only'—placed at the right of tense—can be associated with. To be concrete, let us consider (4).

(4) Ken-to-wa   Mari-ga   hanasi-ta   **dake**   da.
     Ken-with-TOP   Mari-NOM   talk-PST   only   COP
     'It is only that with Ken, Mari talked.'

The sentence (4) can have the interpretation that only Mari talked with Ken, but lacks the interpretation that Mari talked only with Ken. When *dake* appears to the right of the tense element, it is added to TP. Then, the particle *dake* extends its focus domain over TP.

(5) [$_{CP}$ Ken-to-wa$_i$ [$_{TP}$ Mari-ga t_i hanasi-ta] **dake** da]

                            focus domain

In a configuration like (5), TP constitutes the domain within which the focus particle *dake* can take any constituent as the locus of focus semantically—the phenomenon that is often called **association with focus**. In (4), *dake* can be associated with the subject, which suggests that it occurs in a structural position within TP. (4) can have other interpretations, such as one that all Mari did was talk with Ken, which is obtained when the focus of *dake* falls over VP, and one that it is only that Mary talked with Ken (and nothing else happened), which is obtained when focus extends over the entire clause. Nevertheless, the particle *dake* cannot be associated with the topic. This fact follows if the topic is moved into CP via topicalization. Since the topic appearing in CP falls outside the scope of the particle *dake*, as depicted in (5), (4) cannot have the interpretation on which *dake* is associated with the topic.

DP-movement, which is found in passive and raising constructions, targets the specifier position of TP, which constitutes an **argument position** (**A-position**), so that this type of movement is called **A-movement**. In contrast, topicalization targets the specifier position of CP, which constitutes a **non-argument position** (**A′-position** (pronounced 'A-bar position')) since neither Case nor θ-roles are assigned there. This type of movement is called **A′-movement** (pronounced 'A-bar movement'). Generally, a phrase appearing in CP serves as a kind of **operator**, which is a natural language analogue of a logical operator in logic. On the other hand, a copy (or a trace) left by A′-movement is semantically interpreted as a **variable**. In (5), the dislocated topic phrase *Ken-to-wa* serves as an operator binding the variable (i.e. the unpronounced copy in the original position). Owing to the general property that an element A′-moved into the specifier position of CP comes to serve as an operator, A′-movement is also called **operator movement**—movement which creates an operator in CP.

Operator movement (A′-movement) displays properties different from those of DP-movement (A-movement). One difference has to do with the fact that operator movement can be "long distance" in the sense that it can be moved across a number of finite clause boundaries, as exemplified in (6).

(6)   Ken-to-wa$_i$ [Mari-ga   [Eri-ga t_i hanasi-ta   to]
       Ken-with-TOP   Mari-NOM   Eri-NOM   talk-PST   that
       it-ta]   (yooda).
       say-PST   seem
       '(It seems that) with Ken, Mary said that Eri talked.'

Example (6) is a little harder to interpret, but it is acceptable on the intended interpretation. In (6), the sentence-initial topic is identified as a PP selected by the verb *hanasu* 'talk', which suggests that the topic has been moved from the object position in the embedded clause to the sentence-initial position.

In principle, there is no limit on the distance that an operator travels via A′-movement (but memory limitations impose a constraint on processing the movement operation). Nevertheless, there is good reason to believe that **long distance operator movement** cannot take place in one swoop. Rather, movement takes place cyclically by passing through intermediate CPs, as indicated in (7).

(7) [$_{CP}$ Ken-to-wa$_i$ [$_{TP}$ Mari-ga [$_{CP}$ [$_{TP}$ Eri-ga t_i hanasi-ta] to] it-ta]]

The distance that a topicalized phrase travels is strictly limited in such a way that we can easily compute how movement takes place. Since the grammar imposes a locality constraint for the purpose of calculating where a movement starts and where it ends, we need **cyclic movement** to establish a long distance relation. The unacceptability of (8), which involves movement of a topic out of a relative clause, suggests that a topic phrase cannot move too long a distance in one swoop.

(8) *Ken-to-wa$_i$ Mari-ga   [$_{DP}$ [$_{RelC}$ gakkoo-de t_i hanasi-ta]
     Ken-with-TOP Mari-NOM   school-at   talk-PST
     hito]-ni   at-ta.
     man-DAT   meet-PST
     'With Ken, Mari met the man who talked at school.'

The relative clause has a syntactic boundary across which an operator cannot move. In (8), the sentence-initial topic phrase cannot be interpreted as a PP selected by the verb *hanasu* 'talk' since it appears in a position that is structurally too distant from the original position.

(9) *[Topic [$_{DP}$ [$_{RelC}$ ... ~~Topic~~ ...]]]
                         X

The domain from which extraction by movement is blocked is called a **syntactic island**. In (8), an operator can never be moved out of the relative clause legitimately (in a designated cyclic manner) because the relative clause constitutes a syntactic island.

We can find several other instances of A′-movement, such as relativization and clefting (pseudo-clefting). In both examples in (10), the DP *hon* 'book' is understood to serve as the object of the verb *yomu* 'read'.

(10) a. [Ken-ga   yon-da]   hon
         Ken-NOM   read-PST   book
         'the book which Ken read'
      b. [Ken-ga   yon-da]   no-wa   hon   da.
         Ken-NOM   read-PST   that-TOP   book   COP
         'What Ken read was a book.'

Both relativization and pseudo-clefting invoke A′-movement. It is often assumed that in both types of construction, an invisible operator (represented as OP) is moved to its operator position, i.e. CP. In (10), OP is moved from the object position of the verb *yomu* 'read' to CP in the embedded clause, as represented in (11).

(11)   [[$_{CP}$ OP$_i$ [$_{TP}$ .... t_i .... yon-da]] hon$_i$ ...]

Once the DP *hon* 'book' outside the embedded clause is identified as the antecedent of the null operator OP (as indicated by the co-indexation), the DP is semantically linked to the position from which the null operator is moved, and therefore, is understood to be the object of the verb *yomu*.

It is worth noting that topicalized phrases are not required to move to the sentence-initial position. When a *wa*-marked topic appears clause-medially (without movement to the sentence-initial position), it necessarily receives a contrastive rather than a thematic interpretation.

(12)   Mari-ga   Ken-wa   home-ta.
       Mari-NOM   Ken-TOP   praise-PST
       'As for Ken, Mari praised him.'

Notably, when a sentence-internal topic appears inside a relative clause, which constitutes a syntactic island, unacceptability results.

(13)   *Mari-ga   [gakkoo-de Ken-to-wa   hanasi-ta] hito-ni   at-ta.
       Mari-NOM school-at   Ken-with-TOP   talk-PST   man-DAT   meet-PST
       'Mari met the man who talked with Ken at school.'

When *Ken-to* does not accompany the topic maker *wa*, the sentence in (13) is well-formed. The island effect is symptomatic of operator movement. In (13), the topic phrase is located in sentence-medial position. Since the topic is not moved in the syntax (i.e. S-structure), it must be moved to CP at the LF level. This LF movement gives rise to an illegitimate structure which involves extraction out of the relative clause island, and hence (13) is not acceptable.

17.2 Non-Existence of *Wh*-Movement

One remarkable difference between Japanese and English lies in the fact that while English implements **wh-movement**, Japanese does not. English has a grammatical rule whereby *wh*-phrases (*who, what, which, where, how,* and

168

why) are placed at the front of *wh*-question clauses, as exemplified in (14a).

(14) a. What book will you buy?
      b. Anata-wa   nani-o   kat-ta   no?
          you-TOP   what-ACC   buy-PST   Q
          'What did you buy?'

In (14a), the *wh*-phrase *what book* has been moved from the object position to the sentence-initial position. In contrast, Japanese does not have a grammatical rule of *wh*-movement (which places *wh*-words in clause-initial position) and *nani-o* 'what' can remain in the object position preceding the verb (*in situ*).

Incidentally, it is possible in Japanese to move a *wh*-phrase to the sentence-initial position, as in (15a), but this structure is derived not by *wh*-movement but by **scrambling,** which can reorder constituents rather freely.

(15) a. Nani-o$_i$ anata-wa t_i kat-ta   no?
          what-ACC   you-TOP   buy-PST   Q
          'What did you buy?'
      b. Hon-o$_i$ Ken-ga t_i kat-ta.
          book-ACC   Ken-NOM   buy-PST
          'The book, Ken bought.'

In principle, scrambling can apply to any arguments or adjuncts, but not predicates. Since what can be moved to the sentence-initial position is not limited to *wh*-phrases, as shown in (15b), it is fair to say that *nani-o* in (15a) appears in the clause-initial position via scrambling.

Wh-phrases are scope-bearing expressions, i.e. elements that acquire scope. Notably, in English the scope of *wh*-phrases—the level of *wh*-questioning—is determined by their surface position.

(16) a. Who did John say that Mary saw?
      b. John knows who Mary saw.

The sentence in (16a), in which *who* appears in the sentence-initial position, is a direct *wh*-question asking for the identity of the *wh*-phrase. On the other hand, (16b) is an indirect *wh*-question since *who* is placed in the left boundary of the embedded clause.

Exactly the same scope behavior is observed in Japanese *wh*-questions, but in Japanese, the scope of *wh*-phrases is determined by the position of a Q(uestion) element (*ka* or *no*) rather than the position of the *wh*-phrases, as shown in (17).

(17) a. Ken-wa   [Mari-ga   nani-o   tabe-ta   to]   it-ta   **no?**

| | | Ken-TOP | Mari-NOM | what-ACC | eat-PST | that | say-PST | Q |

'What did Ken say that Mari ate?'

b. Ken-wa   [Mari-ga   nani-o   tabe-ta   **ka**]

    Ken-TOP   Mari-NOM   what-ACC   eat-PST   Q

    sit-te   i-ru.

    know-GER   be-PRS

'Ken knows what Mari ate.'

The Japanese sentences in (17) are interpreted in the same way as the English sentences in (16) with regard to the scope of *wh*-phrases: (17a) is a direct *wh*-question, and (17b) is an indirect *wh*-question.

In Japanese, owing to the fact that the scope of *wh*-questions is signaled by the clause-final particle *no* (or *ka*), a *wh*-phrase can be embedded inside a syntactic island from which no constituent can be extracted via *wh*-movement (or operator movement).

(18)   Mari-wa   [gakkoo-de   <u>nani-o</u>   hanasi-ta]   hito-ni

    Mari-TOP   school-at   what-ACC   talk-PST   man-DAT

    at-ta   no?

    meet-PST   Q

    (lit.) 'Mari met the man that talked about what at school?'

Example (18) is well-formed, and is interpreted as a direct *wh*-question, despite the fact that the *wh*-phrase appears inside the relative clause, which constitutes a syntactic island. The fact that (18) does not exhibit any island effect shows that the *wh*-phrase does not undergo movement into its scope position, but rather its scope is determined by a Q element, which is positioned in CP. This suggests that while English has obligatory *wh*-movement at the S-structure level, no *wh*-movement is induced in Japanese (regardless of the level of representation, i.e. S-structure or LF). Instead, Japanese makes recourse to a Q particle, so as to fix the scope of *wh*-phrases—the level of *wh*-questioning.

For Further Research

(A-1) Topicalization sometimes does not induce a strong island effect when a topicalized phrase appears in sentence-initial position.

(i) ??Hawai-wa   Ken-ga   [kyonen   it-ta]   hito-ni   at-ta.
     Hawaii-TOP Ken-NOM last.year go-PST man-DAT meet-PST
     'As for Hawaii, Ken met a man who went (there) last year.'

Apparently, the dubious acceptability of (i), indicated by ??, is due to the possibility for a topic to occur in the topic position by base-generation (see Saito (1985)) (and it might be that the topic is interpreted to be the object of the verb in the relative clause with some kind of aboutness relation). By contrast, when a topic occurs with a postposition, a stronger island effect emerges.

(ii) *Hawai-e-wa   Ken-ga   [kyonen   it-ta]   hito-ni   at-ta.
      Hawaii-to-TOP Ken-NOM last.year go-PST man-DAT meet-PST
      'Speaking of Hawaii, Ken met a man who went (there) last year.'

In (ii), since the embedded verb selects a PP with e 'to', the topic appears in the topic position via S-structure movement, resulting in unacceptability in violation of the relative clause island constraint. Furthermore, when the topic is placed inside the relative clause in the surface string, unacceptability results, as shown in (iii).

(iii) *Ken-ga   [kyonen   Hawai(-e)-wa   it-ta]   hito-ni   at-ta.
       Ken-NOM last.year Hawaii-to-TOP go-PST man-DAT meet-PST
       'Speaking of Hawaii, Ken met a man who went (there) last year.'

The unacceptability of (iii) remains the same regardless of whether the topic remaining in its original position occurs with a postposition or not. In both cases, the sentence is ruled out on the grounds that the topic is moved out of the relative clause at the LF level.

(A-2) When the particles wa and ga appear on subjects, several distinct interpretations are invoked. When ga appears on the subject of action verbs, existential verbs, or adjectives that denote temporary states, it has a neutral-description interpretation; it has an exhaustive-listing interpretation when stress is placed on it (see Kuno (1973a), Shibatani (1978)).

(iv) a. Ken-ga   ki-ta.
          Ken-NOM   come-PST
          'Ken came.'
      b. Ken-gá   ki-ta.
          Ken-NOM   come-PST
          'It was Ken that came.'

In cases where a subject is marked with *wa*, it receives a thematic interpretation, and if a stress is additionally placed, it receives a contrastive interpretation.

(v)   a. Ken-wa   ki-ta.
          Ken-TOP   come-PST
          'Speaking of Ken, he came.'
      b. Ken-wá   ki-ta.
          Ken-TOP   come-PST
          'As for Ken, he came.'

If a topic phrase does not appear in clause-initial position, it necessarily invokes a contrastive interpretation.

(A-3) Japanese allows what looks like a double relativization such as (via), the counterpart of which is not available in English.

(vi) a. [[t_i t_j tabe-ta]   hito$_i$-ga   byooki-ni   nat-te
                    eat-PST   man-NOM   sick-DAT   become-GER
          simat-ta]   onigiri$_j$
          end.up-PST   rice.ball
          'the rice ball which the man who ate (it) got sick'
      b. [t_i onigiri-o   tabe-ta]   hito$_i$-ga   byooki-ni
              rice.ball-ACC   eat-PST   man-NOM   sick-DAT
          nat-te   simat-ta.
          become-GER   end.up-PST
          'The man who ate the rice ball got sick.'

The double relative clause in (via) seems to be derived from (vib) by relativizing the NP *onigiri* 'rice ball' inside the relative clause. It is argued by Kuno (1973a) that the existence of double relative clauses is correlated with the possibility of topicalization. In fact, it is possible to construct a sentence like (vii) from (vib).

(vii)   Sono   onigiri$_j$-wa   [t_i t_j tabe-ta]   hito$_i$-ga   byooki-ni

       that   rice.ball-TOP   eat-PST   man-NOM   sick-DAT

       nat-te   simat-ta.

       become-GER   end.up-PST

       'As for the rice ball, the man who ate (it) got sick.'

(B) In Japanese, *wh*-phrases can be embedded in syntactic islands with the exception of an adjunct *wh*-phrase *naze* 'why'. When *naze* appears in a relative clause, as in (viii), the sentence is unacceptable.

(viii) *Anata-wa   [Ken-ga   naze kai-ta]   ronbun-o   yon-da   no?

       you-TOP   Ken-NOM why write-PST   paper-ACC read-PST Q

       (lit.) 'You read [the paper that Ken wrote why]?'

In Japanese, relative clauses constitute syntactic islands from which no phrase can be extracted. Then, how can we account for the difference in island effects observed between *naze* 'why' and other *wh*-phrases?

PART V

Grammatical Constructions

CHAPTER 18

Complex Predicates [E]

18.1 Complex Predicates and Causativization

In Japanese, verbal predicates are almost always morphologically complex, and even elements that are realized as independent predicates in languages like English often serve as bound elements. Typologically, Japanese is classified as an **agglutinative language**, where many predicative elements occurring after main predicates are bound elements. As a result, we can easily find gigantic **complex predicates**, as seen in (1).

(1) Ken-wa   kodomo-ni   hon-o   yomi-hazime-sase-taku-nakat-ta.
     Ken-TOP   child-DAT   book-ACC   read-begin-CAUS-want-NEG-PST
     'Ken did not want to let the children begin to read the book.'

The underlined complex predicate in (1) includes five predicative elements with the meanings 'read', 'begin', 'cause', 'want', and 'not', but they are realized as the components of a single predicate morphologically. Japanese abounds with such complex predicates. Nevertheless, from a syntactic point of view, the morphological status of complex predicates is a bit misleading because it does not necessarily reflect their syntactic structures. A close inspection of the facts reveals that complex predicates have syntactically analyzable structures, and some of them exhibit a number of unique properties.

Syntactically analyzable complex predicates are found in **causative constructions** formed by agglutinating the causative morpheme *(s)ase* to verbal predicates and adding a **causer** argument to the base clause. Semantically, causative sentences can be either **directive/permissive causatives** (or *let*-causatives), which convey the meaning of 'the **causee** is permitted to do the act described by the main verb', or **manipulative causatives** (or *make*-causatives), carrying the meaning of 'the causee is forced to perform the act or undergo a change of state'. This semantic distinction is manifested in the case marking of the causee argument when the main verb is intransitive.

(2) a. Hahaoya-ga   kodomo-ni   hatarak-ase-ta.
     mother-NOM   child-DAT   work-CAUS-PST
     'Mother let her child work.'

     b. Hahaoya-ga   kodomo-o   hatarak-ase-ta.
     mother-NOM   child-ACC   work-CAUS-PST
     'Mother made her child work.'

In the directive causative (2a), the causee is marked with dative *ni* and in the manipulative causative (2b), it is marked with accusative *o*. The semantic difference between directive and manipulative causation is a bit hard to distinguish when we look at the sentences in isolation, but if the situation in which the causative sentences could be felicitously uttered is taken into account, the distinction between the two becomes clearer. For instance, in a situation where the child is not willing to work, (2a) cannot be legitimately uttered because it implies that the child would like to work. In a different situation where the child is willing to work, it is contradictory to say (2b) because it means that the child is forced to work.

When the main verb is transitive, the semantic distinction of directive/permissive versus manipulative causation is not reflected in the surface case marking. The transitive causative in (3) can be used in both scenarios mentioned above, showing that it can express a permissive as well as an enforcement sense.

(3) Hahaoya-ga   kodomo-ni   hon-o   yom-ase-ta.
     mother-NOM   child-DAT   book-ACC   read-CAUS-PST
     'Mother made/let her child read books.'

In a transitive causative construction, the causee is invariantly marked with dative case regardless of whether it expresses directive/permissive or manipulative causation. This ambiguity results from the fact that when the main verb is transitive, accusative case marking cannot appear on the causee even when manipulative causation is expressed.

(4) *Hahaoya-ga   kodomo-o   hon-o   yom-ase-ta.
     mother-NOM   child-ACC   book-ACC   read-CAUS-PST
     'Mother made her child read books.'

The impossibility of the case-marking pattern in (4) is considered to come from the so-called **double-o constraint**, which requires that a single finite clause not contain two or more *o*-marked arguments. Accordingly, in the causative construction in (3), the causee is marked with dative case even when accusative case is expected (on the manipulative interpretation).

Syntactically, the causative constructions have complex "biclausal" structures in which the causative morpheme *(s)ase* serves as an independent predicate syntactically. This can easily be seen from the fact that in both directive/permissive and manipulative causative constructions, reflexive *zibun* can take either the dative or the nominative argument as its antecedent.

(5)   a. Ken$_i$-ga   Mari$_j$-ni   zibun$_{i/j}$-no heya-de   hatarak-ase-ta.
          Ken-NOM   Mari-DAT   self-GEN   room-in   work-CAUS-PST
          'Ken let Mari work in self's room.'
      b. Ken$_i$-ga   Mari$_j$-o   zibun$_{i/j}$-no heya-de   hatarak-ase-ta.
          Ken-NOM   Mari-ACC   self-GEN   room-in   work-CAUS-PST
          'Ken made Mari work in self's room.'

Since the target of reflexive *zibun* is limited to subjects, the fact suggests that the causee is not an adjunct, but is an argument having the status of subject of the embedded predicate.

The facts of reflexivization remain the same irrespective of whether the causative construction represents a directive/permissive or a manipulative causative. But this does not necessarily indicate that their structures are the same. In fact, the two kinds of causative constructions have distinct syntactic structures. This can be seen by the fact that when the causee argument is inanimate, a difference in acceptability emerges depending on whether it is marked with accusative or dative case.

(6)   a. Kare-wa   hana-o   sak-ase-ta.
          he-TOP   flower-ACC   bloom-CAUS-PST
          'He made the flower bloom.'
      b. *Kare-wa   hana-ni   sak-ase-ta.
          he-TOP   flower-DAT   bloom-CAUS-PST
          'He let the flower bloom.'

The difference is reminiscent of the distinction between control and raising (see Chapter 15). In light of a difference in acceptability between the two sentences in (6), it can be stated that the directive causative construction involves control, and the manipulative causative construction does not, as illustrated in (7).

178

(7)   a. Manipulative:

$$[_{TP}\text{ Causer }[_{VP}\text{ Causer }[_{VP}\text{ Causee } .... \text{ V}]\text{Caus}]\text{ T}]$$

     b. Directive/Permissive:

$$[_{TP}\text{ Causer }[_{VP}\text{ Causer Causee }[_{VP}\text{ PRO } .... \text{ V}]\text{Caus}]\text{ T}]$$

Both types of causative constructions have a structure with two VPs. In the manipulative causative construction, the causative predicate selects the causer, and the causee appears in the embedded VP, i.e. the causative predicate involves simple embedding (**complementation**), as in (7a). Thus, in the manipulative causative in (6a), which has the structure shown in (7a), an inanimate causee is permitted, with no control involved. In the directive/permissive causative construction in (6b), by contrast, the causative selects both causer and causee in addition the embedded VP complement headed by the main verb, and the causee controls PRO in VP, as in (7b). Since PRO cannot have an inanimate controller (i.e. the causee) by the animacy requirement, (6b) is not acceptable.

Under the VP-Internal Subject Hypothesis, two subject positions are available and nominative subjects originating in VP are moved to TP for Case assignment (see Chapter 14). Then this raises the question of whether reflexive *zibun*, which has subject orientiation, is anchored to a subject in TP or in VP. The answer is simple. In the causative constructions, subject-oriented *zibun* can take either the causer or the causee as its antecedent. Since tense is associated with the causative predicate, the causer is moved to Spec-TP and marked with nominative case. The embedded clause does not include tense. Nevertheless, the causee argument can serve as the antecedent of *zibun*. This fact gives us a good indication that *zibun* is anchored to a subject located in VP rather than in TP.

Directive/permissive and manipulative causatives show a difference in passivizability. As seen in (8), direct passivization can apply to manipulative causatives, but not to directive/permissive causatives.

(8)   Ken-ga   (okaasan-niyotte)   hatarak-ase-rare-ta.
       Ken-NOM   mother-by   work-CAUS-PASS-PST
       'Ken was made to work by his mother.'

In (8), only the manipulative interpretation is available. Thus, this causative sentence can be used felicitously only in a context where Ken is hesitant to work. The same holds of transitive causative constructions, for (9a) has only the manipulative interpretation.

(9)   a. Ken-ga   (okaasan-niyotte)   hon-o   yom-ase-rare-ta.
         Ken-NOM   mother-by   book-ACC   read-CAUS-PASS-PST
         'Ken was made to read the book by his mother.'
      b. *Hon-ga   (okaasan-niyotte)   Ken-ni   yom-ase-rare-ta.
         book-NOM   mother-by   Ken-DAT   read-CAUS-PASS-PST
         (lit.) 'The book was made for Ken to read by his mother.'

The causative sentence in (9a) can only be used in a situation where the causee
Ken is not willing to read the book, showing that it is a manipulative causative
construction. Note that the dative-marked causee can be promoted to the subject under direct passivization, but the accusative theme cannot, as shown in
(9).

Japanese causative constructions have the same case-marking patterns as are
found in simple clauses. Notably, the causative construction in (3), which is
formed by adding the causer to the base transitive clause, has the nominative-
dative-accusative case frame, and the same case frame is found in the ditransitive verb construction in (10).

(10)   Hahaoya-ga   Ken-ni   hon-o   atae-ta.
       mother-NOM   Ken-DAT   book-ACC   give-PST
       'Mother gave Ken the book.'

Nevertheless, the causative construction differs from the ditransitive verb construction, in that the former allows either the indirect or the direct object to be
the antecedent of reflexive *zibun*, while the latter does not.

(11)   a. Hahaoya$_i$-ga   kodomo$_j$-ni zibun$_{i/j}$-no hon-o   yom-ase-ta.
         mother-NOM   child-DAT   self-GEN   book-ACC read-CAUS-PST
         (lit.) 'Mother let/made her child read self's book.'
      b. Ken$_i$-ga   Mari$_j$-ni   zibun$_{i/*j}$-no hon-o   age-ta.
         Ken-NOM   Mari-DAT   self-GEN   book-ACC give-PST
         (lit.) 'Ken gave Mari self's book.'

The reflexive *zibun* can be anchored to a subject in a clause, and thus, the data
illustrate that the causative construction has a biclausal structure, while the
ditranstive construction a monoclausal structure. Although the causative construction in (3) bears a surface resemblance to the ditransitive verb construction in (10), these two constructions cannot be treated on a par in syntactic
terms.

18.2 Direct and Indirect Passives

Passive sentences represent another type of complex predicate construction in Japanese. Passives are formed by adding the passive morpheme *(r)are* to the main verb. Japanese has two distinct types of passives: **direct passives** and **indirect passives**. In a direct passive clause like (12b), derived from (12a), its original object is promoted to the subject, with the erstwhile subject being demoted to an adjunct.

(12) a. Sensei-ga   gakusei-o   home-ta.
           teacher-NOM   student-ACC   praise-PST
           'The teacher praised the student.'
      b. Gakusei-ga   (sensei-ni)   home-rare-ta.
           student-NOM   teacher-by   praise-PASS-PST
           'The student was praised by the teacher.'

In direct passive sentences, the agent is optionally realized, because it serves as an adjunct syntactically. When realized, it is marked with *ni* 'by', *kara* 'from', or *niyotte* 'by'.

By contrast, when an indirect passive clause is formed, a new subject that signifies an affected experiencer is added, with a concomitant change of the nominative marking on the original subject to the dative *ni*.

(13) a. Kodomo-ga   nai-ta.
           child-NOM   cry-PST
           'The child cried.'
      b. Ken-ga   kodomo-ni   nak-are-ta.
           Ken-NOM   child-DAT   cry-PASS-PST
           'Ken was adversely affected by the child crying.'

In the indirect passive, the subject is an animate "affectee" argument, which is not derived by promoting an argument, but rather is directly added in subject position. The indirect passive is sometimes referred to as the **adversative passive** owing to the fact that an **adversative meaning** is frequently associated with the clause.

The two types of passive clauses show some behavioral differences. While only the nominative argument can be the antecedent of subject-oriented reflexive *zibun* 'self' in the direct passive clause, either the dative or the nominative argument can serve as the antecedent of *zibun* in the indirect passive clause, as shown in (14).

(14) a. Ken$_i$-ga Mari$_j$-ni zibun$_{i/*j}$-no heya-de home-rare-ta.
          Ken-NOM Mari-by self-GEN room-in praise-PASS-PST
          (lit.) 'Ken was praised by Mari in self's room.'

      b. Ken$_i$-ga Mari$_j$-ni zibun$_{i/j}$-no heya-de nak-are-ta.
          Ken-NOM Mari-DAT self-GEN room-in cry-PASS-PST
          (lit.) 'Ken was adversely affected by Mary's crying in self's room.'

This fact suggests that in indirect passivization, an affectee argument is added, but the dative argument is not demoted to an adjunct.

The distinct behavior of *zibun* found in the two kinds of passive constructions falls into place if they have the structures in (15), which crucially differ as to whether the subject of the main verb is demoted to an adjunct or not.

(15) a. Direct Passive:

          [$_{TP}$ DP-NOM [$_{VP}$ DP-by ~~DP-NOM~~ V-Pass]T]

      b. Indirect Passive:

          [$_{TP}$ DP-NOM [$_{VP}$ ~~DP-NOM~~ [$_{VP}$ DP-DAT V]-Pass]T]

The direct passive construction includes only one subject, marked with nominative case, as illustrated in (15a), and thus, it shows a monoclausal property in that only the nominative subject serves as the antecedent of *zibun*. The biclausal property of the indirect passive construction, which is indicated by the reflexivization facts, comes from the presence of two layers of VP each containing a subject argument. Note that the lower main verb in the indirect passive construction does not include a tense element that projects to TP, so the dative argument of the indirect passive cannot be located in Spec-TP. In this case, the antecedent of reflexive *zibun* is fixed with reference to the argument located in the lower VP-internal subject position.

For Further Research

(A) Japanese has a third type of passive construction, where the passive subject is understood as the possessor of the accusative argument, as in (i).

(i)   Ken-ga   sensei-ni   kodomo-o   home-rare-ta.
      Ken-NOM   teacher-DAT   child-ACC   praise-PASS-PST
      'Ken got his child praised by the teacher.'

A passive clause like (i) is often termed as **possessor passive** (*mochinushi-no ukemi*). Possessor passives may be regarded as falling into the category of indirect passives because the number of arguments is increased by one via passivization.

(B-1) The causative construction is not the only way of expressing the meaning of causation. In some cases, similar causative meanings can be expressed by a transitive verb, as in (iia).

(ii)   a. Ken-ga   Mari-o   butai-no   ue-ni   age-ta.
           Ken-NOM   Mari-ACC   stage-GEN top-LOC go.up-PST
           'Ken raised Mari onto the stage.'
      b. Ken-ga   Mari-o   butai-no   ue-ni   agar-ase-ta.
           Ken-NOM   Mari-ACC   stage-GEN top-LOC go.up-CAUS-PST
           'Ken made Mari go onto the stage.'

At first sight, it looks as if the two sentences in (ii) express the same causative meaning, but their meanings are not identical. What are the differences in meaning that are obtained in the two sentences?

(B-2) The double-*o* constraint that more than one accusative argument is not allowed in a single finite clause is generally in force in Japanese, but we can occasionally find sentences where *o*-marked phrases are stacked, as in (iii).

(iii)   a. Isogasi-i   tokoro-o,   ame-no   naka-o,   anata-wa
           busy-PRS   place-ACC   rain-GEN middle-ACC you-TOP
           nani-o,   bakana   koto-o   si-te   i-ru   Q
           what-ACC   foolish   thing-ACC do-GER   be-PRS   no?
           'Why are you doing such foolish things in the middle of rain, while you are busy?'
      b. Ken-ga   sakamiti-o   zitensya-o   osi-ta.
          Ken-NOM   slope-ACC   bicycle-ACC   push-PST

'Ken pushed his bicycle on the slope.'

c. *Ken-ga   Mari-o   hon-o   yom-ase-ta.

   Ken-NOM   Mari-ACC   book-ACC   read-CAUS-PST

   'Ken made Mari read the book.'

(iiia) is acceptable, although it is a little hard to process with four instances of *o*-marked expressions included in a single clause. (iiib) is less awkward with just two *o*-marked expressions. At least, they are significantly better than (iiic), which is hopelessly bad with the double-*o* constraint violation. Why do the sentences in (iiia-b) behave as if they are exempt from the double-*o* constraint?

CHAPTER 19

Argument Extraction from DP [D], [E]

19.1 Possessor Raising

In generative grammar, predicates are assumed to carry argument structures, which determine the number, as well as the nature of arguments appearing in clauses. Although predicates in most cases determine the number of arguments available for the clauses, there are cases where the clauses contain more arguments than are required by the predicates. For instance, Japanese has **multiple nominative constructions** where more than one nominative argument occurs in a single clause, as in (1).

(1)　Zoo-ga　　　　hana-ga　　　　naga-i.
　　　elephant-NOM　trunk-NOM　　long-PRS
　　　'The elephant has a long trunk.'

The predicate *nagai* 'long' requires only one argument. In (1), the long entity is the elephant's trunk, and thus, the nominative-marked DP *hana* 'trunk' is the **thematic subject** (or the **logical subject**) of the predicate. The leftmost argument, which is also marked by nominative case, is not an argument of the predicate *per se* (i.e. an elephant cannot be a long entity) but is called the **major subject** (conventionally).

　　Semantically, *zoo* 'elephant' is related to *hana* 'trunk' as its possessor, as can be seen from the fact that the multiple nominative sentence in (1) has the same logical meaning as the sentence in (2).

(2)　[Zoo-no　　　　hana]-ga　　　naga-i.
　　　 elephant-GEN　trunk-NOM　　long-PRS
　　　'The elephant's trunk is long.'

Given this fact, it can be hypothesized that the extra, non-thematic argument *zoo* in the nominative case is supplied by the second nominative DP *hana*. Accordingly, we can further postulate that the secondary *ga*-marked argument, i.e. the major subject *zoo-ga* in (1), is derived by virtue of applying the typologically common process of **possessor raising** (or **possessor ascension**) to the genitive argument *zoo-no* in (2), as illustrated in (3).

(3)   [$_{TP}$ Zoo-ga [$_{DP}$ t_{DP} hana]-ga naga-i]

In (3), the possessor argument is extracted from the subject on its right and is rendered as a verbal argument. Note that the extracted possessor argument is allowed to occur as a verbal argument because it is identified as bearing an **aboutness relation** to the rest of the sentence. Since the first argument (i.e. the possessor) is extracted from the argument on the right, the second nominative argument in (1) cannot be elided, as in (4).

(4)   #Zoo-ga   naga-i.
       elephant-NOM   long-PRS
       'The elephant is long.'

In (4), *zoo* 'elephant' is forced to be interpreted as the subject of the predicate in the absence of the thematic subject of the predicate. The sentence is semantically anomalous because *zoo* is not a long animal.

Needless to say, the leftmost nominative argument *zoo* in (1) and the genitive argument *zoo* in (2) have different syntactic statuses, as can be seen from the fact that the former allows an adverb to be inserted on its right, but the latter does not.

(5)   a. Zoo-ga   kanari   hana-ga   naga-i.
          elephant-NOM   fairly   trunk-NOM   long-PRS
          'The elephant has a fairly long trunk.'
       b. *[Zoo-no   kanari   hana]-ga   naga-i.
          elephant-GEN   fairly   trunk-NOM   long-PRS
          'The elephant's trunk is fairly long.'

In (5a), the nominative-marked *zoo* is a verbal argument, so it allows an adverb *kanari* 'fairly', which modifies the predicate, to follow it. In (5b), on the other hand, the genitive-marked *zoo* is included in the nominal projection of the argument *hana* 'trunk', so the insertion of an adverb modifying the predicate is disallowed.

Let us now turn to the question of where the extracted possessors are located.

As the derived nominative argument precedes the thematic subject in (1), it might be thought that it occurs in the CP domain in just the same way as a topic does. Actually, however, unlike a topic phrase, the major subject occurs within TP. To make this point, let us consider the following sentences, where *dake* 'only' is attached to the clause end.

(6) a. Zoo-ga   hana-ga   naga-i   **dake**   da.
         elephant-NOM   trunk-NOM   long-PRS   only   COP
         'It is only that the elephant has a long trunk.'
     b. Zoo-wa   hana-ga   naga-i   **dake**   da.
         elephant-TOP   trunk-NOM   long-PRS   only   COP
         'As for the elephant, it is only that it has a long trunk.'

In (6a), *dake* can be associated with the nominative major subject. Thus, (6a) can mean that <u>only the elephant</u> has a long trunk (and it is also possible for *dake* to be associated with the thematic subject, in which case (6a) has the interpretation that the elephant has <u>only a long trunk</u>). The particle *dake* attached to the end of the tense (T) can be associated with any element inside TP (see Chapter 17). Then, the *ga*-marked major subject must lie within TP, as in (7), for it can be the focus of clause-final *dake*.

(7)

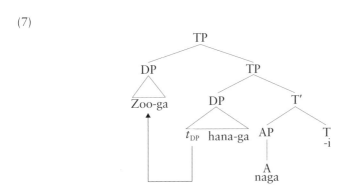

In (7), the major subject appears to the left of the thematic subject by virtue of its **adjunction** to TP. When the major subject is adjoined to TP, two segments of TP are created. Crucially, the adjunction operation does not extract the major subject from the TP domain, and thus, *dake* placed to the right of tense can be associated with the *ga*-marked major subject.

By contrast, in (6b), where the major subject is topicalized, *dake* cannot be associated with the *wa*-marked major subject, and hence it lacks the interpretation that <u>only the elephant</u> has a long trunk. This shows that the topicalized

188

phrase appears in CP, located in a higher position than TP. In other words, when the major subject is marked with *wa*, it undergoes operator movement into the CP domain, as represented in (8).

(8)

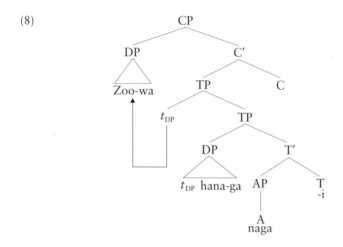

The major subject marked with nominative case is located in TP, and thus the sentence can have the interpretation on which clause-final *dake* is associated with the nominative major subject. But the major subject marked with *wa* is moved to CP by topic-movement (either at S-structure or at LF). Consequently, the topicalized major subject in (6b) falls outside the focusing domain of *dake* and (6b) lacks the interpretation in which *dake* is associated with the major subject.

19.2 Possessor Raising and Possessor Honorification

Possessor raising is not limited to multiple nominative constructions but is observed in other constructions as well. The sentence in (9a) can be assumed to involve possessor raising out of a body-part noun, given that the initial dative argument in (9a) corresponds to the genitive argument in (9b).

(9) a. Mari-ni-wa   sono   kodomo-ga   te-ni   oe-na-i.
        Mari-DAT-TOP   that   child-NOM   hand-LOC   carry-NEG-PRS
        'Mari cannot handle that child.'
     b. Sono   kodomo-ga   [Mari-no   te]-ni   oe-na-i.
        that   child-NOM   Mari-GEN   hand-LOC   carry-NEG-PRS
        'Mari cannot handle that child.'

Since the two sentences in (9) express the same logical meaning, it is reasaonble to postulate that the dative argument in (9b) is rendered as a verbal argument via posssessor raising out of the body part noun *te* 'hand', as illustrated in (10).

(10) [Mari-ni sono kodomo-ga [$_{DP}$ t_{DP} te]-ni oe-na-i]

One piece of evidence in favor of an analysis in which the dative argument is extracted from the possessee argument may be derived from the fact that in (11a), which has the same structure as (9a), possessor honorification is possible.

(11) a. *Sensei*-ni-wa   sono   kodomo-ga   o-te-ni
         teacher-DAT-TOP   that   child-NOM   HON-hand-LOC
         oe-na-i.
         carry-NEG-PRS
         'The teacher cannot handle that child.'
     b. Sono   kodomo-ga   [*sensei*-no   o-te]-ni
        that   child-NOM   teacher-GEN   HON-hand-LOC
        oe-na-i.
        carry-NEG-PRS
        'The teacher cannot handle that child.'

Note that the possessor-honorific marker does not attach to a nominal unless a qualified possessor appears inside it (except when this marker is used for the purpose of "beautification" like *o-hasi* 'chopsticks'). In (11), the possessor honorific marking *o-* appears on the possessee argument, and the possessor may be the target for possessor honorification regardless of where it is overtly realized. This fact follows straightforwardly if the dative possessor in (11b) is extracted from the position where the genitive possessor in (11a) appears.

The unacceptability of (12) further illustrates that possessor honorification targets a possessor inside a possessed nominal.

(12) *Sensei-ga   kabu-ni   o-te-o   dasi-ta.
      teacher-NOM   stock-LOC   HON-hand-ACC   take. out-PST
      'The teacher dabbled on the stock market.'

In (12), *sensei* 'teacher' is the thematic subject of the verb *dasu* 'take out', and hence cannot be generated via possessor raising out of the body-part noun, although the two arguments have a possessive relation semantically. The unacceptability of (12) shows that possessor honorification is not simply sanctioned with a coreferential relation established between the thematic subject of the verb and the understood possessor (without possessor raising). The fact that possessor honorification in (11a) is acceptable, just like that in (11b), gives us a good indication that the possessor is realized as a dative argument via extraction from the possessed noun phrase.

19.3 Verbal Nouns

An extra verbal argument is often created by virtue of raising a possessor from a nominal expression. But there are also cases where "non-possessor" arguments undergo extraction from nominal expressions, and hence this kind of raising operation may more generally be called **argument raising**. The verbal noun (VN) constructions in (13) illustrate that a non-possessor argument can be raised out of a nominal and rendered as a verbal argument, marked in the dative case.

(13) a. Ken-ga   [keikan-no   hensoo]-o   si-ta.
       Ken-NOM   policeman-GEN   disguise-ACC   do-PST
       'Ken disguised himself as a policeman.'
    b. Ken-ga   keikan-ni   hensoo-o   si-ta.
       Ken-NOM   policeman-DAT   disguise-ACC   do-PST
       'Ken disguised himself as a policeman.'

The dative argument in (13b) describing a resultant state corresponds to the genitive argument located inside the verbal noun (VN) in (13a). The logical meaning expressed by the two variants of the VN construction is the same. This fact suggests that the dative-marked *keikan* 'policeman' is not an argument selected by the predicate but is created by raising it out of the VN, as (14) illustrates.

(14)   [Ken-ga keikan-ni [$_{VN}$ t_{DP} hensoo]-o si-ta]

In (13b), the argument derived via extraction from the VN is construed as a verbal arugment, and hence marked with dative case rather than genitive case. Note that when the dative argument is generated as a consequence of argument raising, the host VN *hensoo* 'disguise' cannot be moved across the dative argument by scrambling, as in (15).

(15) *Hensoo-o   Ken-ga   keikan-ni   si-ta.
     disguise-ACC   Ken-NOM   policeman-DAT   do-PST
     'Ken disguised himself as a policeman.'

In cases where the result argument *keikan* is omitted or is included in the VN, it is possible to move the VN to the clause front, as shown in (16).

(16) a. Hensoo-o$_i$ Ken-ga t_i si-ta.
          disguise-ACC   Ken-NOM   do-PST
          'Ken disguised himself.'
      b. [Keikan-no   hensoo]-o$_i$ Ken-ga t_i si-ta.
          policeman-GEN   disguise-ACC   Ken-NOM   do-PST
          'Ken disguised himself as a policeman.'

Obviously, (15) is excluded on the grounds that the dative argument *keikan-ni* 'as a policeman' fails to be identified as a result argument hosted by the VN. This failure occurs because the host VN appears on the left rather than the right of the extracted argument. One syntactic constraint imposed on movement is that a moved element must c-command its copy left by movement. This constraint is violated in (15) because the host VP appears in a higher position than the result argument. On the other hand, the sentences in (16) do not have this problem because the dative result argument, which needs to be generated within the VN, does not appear in the clause.

Note also that the sentence in (17a), where the VN *hensoo* is incorporated into the verb, is acceptable.

(17) a. Ken-ga   keikan-ni   hensoo-si-ta.
          Ken-NOM   policeman-DAT   disguise-do-PST
          'Ken disguised himself as a policeman.'
      b. [....... keikan-ni [t_{DP} t_j] hensoo$_j$-si-ta]

The acceptability of (17a) illustrates that the dative-marked result argument *keikan-ni* can establish a proper syntactic relation with the VN standing on the right of it. The fact shows that even when the host VN forms part of a compound predicate with *suru* by virtue of head movement, as depicted in (17b), it can sanction the occurrence of an extra verbal argument generated via argument raising.

For Further Research

(A) The multiple nominative construction discussed in this chapter can be analyzed as involving possessor raising, but the operation creating an extra nominative argument often is not mentioned as such in the Japanese literature.
Instead, this grammatical process is sometimes called **subjectivization** (e.g.
Kuno (1973a)), mainly due to the fact that nominative marking is made available for a sentence like (ib) as well.

(i) a. Kobe-ni   koosoo-biru-ga   sukuna-i.
        Kobe-LOC   high.rise-building-NOM   few-PRS
        'There are only a few high-rise buildings in Kobe.'
     b. Kobe-ga   koosoo-biru-ga   sukuna-i.
        Kobe-NOM   high.rise-building-NOM   few-PRS
        'It is Kobe that has only a few high-rise buildings.'

Since (ib) has the same logical meaning as (ia), it can be assumed that (ib) is
derived from (ia). In (ib), the locative marker *ni* is changed to *ga*, and as a consequence, a locative argument is rendered as a major subject. This operation cannot be possessor raising, which suggests that subjectivization includes two
distinct operations that change non-nominative case-marking on arguments to
nominative case.

(B-1) In light verb constructions, verbal nouns often allow their genitive arguments to be marked with accusative case as an alternative option, as exemplified in (ii).

(ii) a. Eri-ga   [eigo-no   benkyoo]-o   si-ta.
         Eri-NOM   English-GEN   study-ACC   do-PST
         'Eri studied English.'
      b. Eri-ga   eigo-o   benkyoo-si-ta.
         Eri-NOM   English-ACC   study-do-PST
         'Eri studied English.'

The example in (iib) may be construed as representing another case of argument extraction from the VN *benkyoo*, although the VN itself cannot be
marked with accusative case by virtue of the double-*o* constraint. Argument
extraction is not always possible, however, as shown in (iii).

(iii) a. Eri-ga   [siken-no   benkyoo]-o   si-ta.
           Eri-NOM   exam-GEN   study-ACC   do-PST
           'Eri studied for an exam.'
      b. *Eri-ga   siken-o   benkyoo-si-ta.
           Eri-NOM   exam-ACC   study-do-PST
           'Eri studied for an exam.'

While the light verb construction in (iiia) is acceptable, the VN-*suru* counterpart of this light verb construction given in (iiib) is not acceptable. What conditions the difference in acceptability between (iib) and (iiib)?

(B-2) The light verb construction with the VN *tyoodai-suru* 'get' can have alternation in the case-marking of the source argument, as in (iv).

(iv) a. Ken-wa   Abe-sensei-kara   okotoba-o   tyoodai-si-ta.
          Ken-TOP   Abe-teacher-ABL message-ACC   get-do-PST
          'Ken got a message from Prof. Abe.'
      b. Ken-wa   [Abe-sensei(-kara)-no   okotoba]-o   tyoodai-si-ta.
          Ken-TOP   Abe-teacher(-ABL)-GEN message-ACC get-do-PST
          'Ken got a message from Prof. Abe.'

On the surface, it looks as if (iva) is derived from (ivb) via possessor raising, extracting the ablative argument from within the VN. Nevertheless, (iva) does not occasion a semantic anomaly even if the object of the VN is fronted across the ablative argument.

(v) Ken-wa   okotoba-o   Abe-sensei-kara   tyoodai-si-ta.
    Ken-TOP   message-ACC   Abe-teacher-ABL   get-do-PST
    'Ken got a message from Prof. Abe.'

Why is it that the light verb construction with *tyoodai-suru* 'get' displays apparently conflicting syntactic behaviors?

CHAPTER 20

Non-Canonical Case Marking [D], [E]

20.1 Nominative-Accusative Language

In Japanese, arguments are accompanied by case marking particles—morphological indicators of grammatical relations. From the perspective of morphological typology, Japanese is a **nominative-accusative language**, where the subject, but not the object of a transitive verb, receives the same case marking as the subject of an intransitive verb. The "nominative-accusative" case-marking pattern is found in a transitive clause like (1a).

(1)   a.   Ken-**ga**   kodomo-**o**   sikat-ta.
           Ken-NOM   child-ACC   scold-PST
           'Ken scolded the child.'
     b.   Ken-**ga**   hasit-ta.
           Ken-NOM   run-PST
           'Ken ran.'

This nominative-accusative case marking is by no means the only pattern available for transitive predicates, however. Transitive stative predicates, most typically, potential predicates, show varying case-marking patterns, allowing their subjects to be marked with either dative or nominative case.

(2)   a.   Mari-**ga**   kodomo-**o/-ga**   sikar-e-ru.
           Mari-NOM   child-ACC/-NOM   scold-POTEN-PRS
           'Mari can scold her child.'
     b.   Mari-**ni**   kodomo-**ga/*-o**   sikar-e-ru.
           Mari-DAT   child-NOM/-ACC   scold-POTEN-PRS
           'Mari can scold her child.'

Interestingly, when the subject is marked with nominative case, as in (2a), the object may be marked with accusative or nominative case. When the subject is marked with dative case, as in (2b), the object may be marked with nominative case, but not accusative case. This shows that not all logically possible combinations of case marking are manifested in the stative predicate constructions. The unavailability of accusative case marking on the object in (2b) comes from the **nominative-case constraint**, a constraint specific to Japanese, requiring that a finite clause must have at least one nominative argument.

In the stative predicate constructions, the argument in the initial position is construed as a subject regardless of its case marking. This is confirmed by looking at reflexivization, because the reflexive *zibun* takes a subject as its antecedent.

(3)   Ken$_i$-ga   Mari-o   zibun$_i$-no   heya-de   sikat-ta.
        Ken-NOM   Mari-ACC   self-GEN   room-in   scold-PST
        'Ken scolded Mari in his room.'

In (3), the nominative argument serves as the antecedent of reflexive *zibun*, and hence is identified as a subject. For the potential predicate *sikareru* 'can scold', the experiencer argument qualifies as the antecedent of reflexive *zibun* regardless of its case marking.

(4)   a. Ken$_i$-ga   zibun$_i$-no   kodomo-ga/-o   sikar-e-na-i.
           Ken-NOM   self-GEN   child-NOM/-ACC   scold-POTEN-NEG-PRS
           'Ken cannot scold his own child.'
      b. Ken$_i$-ni   zibun$_i$-no   kodomo-ga   sikar-e-na-i.
           Ken-DAT   self-GEN   child-NOM   scold-POTEN-NEG-PRS
           'Ken cannot scold his own child.'

Reflexive *zibun* has subject orientation, and thus it can be concluded that in the transitive stative predicate constructions, the initial experiencer argument, which may be marked with dative or nominative case, serves as the subject of the clause.

In transitive clauses taking a nominative-accusative case-marking pattern, the nominative arguments are construed as subjects undergoing DP-movement to TP. In **dative-subject constructions**, the subjects are marked with dative rather than nominative case, so the question arises as to whether the subjects are moved to the clausal subject position of TP. The presence or absence of **subject raising** can be assessed by considering where subject honorification applies in the aspectual construction formed on the verb *iru* 'be'. First, observe that when the nominative subject appears in the aspectual construction, subject honorification may apply both in the upper and the lower clauses.

(5)   a. Tanaka-sensei-ga   **o-aruki-ni-nat**-te   i-ru.
          Tanaka-teacher-NOM   HON-walk-DAT-become-GER   be-PRS
          'Prof. Tanaka is walking.'
      b. Tanaka-sensei-ga   arui-te   **irassyar-u.**
          Tanaka-teacher-NOM   walk-GER   be.HON-PRS
          'Prof. Tanaka is walking.'

In the dative-subject construction, it is possible to change both upper and lower predicates into subject-honorific forms.

(6)   a. Tanaka-sensei-ni   Mari-ga   **o-mie-ni-nat**-te
          Tanaka-teacher-DAT   Mari-NOM   HON-see-DAT-become-GER
          i-ru.
          be-PRS
          'Prof. Tanaka can see Mari.'
      b. Tanaka-sensei-ni   Mari-ga   mie-te   **irassyar-u.**
          Tanaka-teacher-DAT   Mari-NOM   see-GER   be.HON-PRS
          'Prof. Tanaka can see Mari.'

When the subject is marked with the ablative *kara* 'from', only the lower predicate can be turned into a subject honorific form.

(7)   a. Tanaka-sensei-kara   Mari-ni   **o-hanasi-ni-nat**-te
          Tanaka-teacher-ABL   Mari-DAT   HON-talk-DAT-become-GER
          i-ru.
          be-PRS
          'Prof. Tanaka is talking to Mari.'
      b. *Tanaka-sensei-kara   Mari-ni   hanasi-te   **irassyar-u.**
          Tanaka-teacher-ABL   Mari-DAT   talk-GER   be.HON-PRS
          'Prof. Tanaka is talking to Mari.'

Subject honorification targets only subjects. The V-*te iru* construction is a type of raising construction where the subject of the main predicate is moved to TP in the upper clause. If this movement takes place, the lower subject of the main predicate is rendered as the subject of the matrix aspectual verb *iru* by moving through the VP in the upper clause. Then the facts of subject honorification in (5), (6) and (7) suggest that the nominative subject and the dative subject are moved to the matrix clause, but the *kara*-marked subject is not, as illustrated in (8).

(8)　　a.　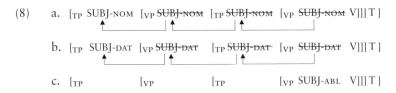

　　　b.

　　　c. [TP　　　[VP　　　[TP　　　[VP SUBJ-ABL　V]]] T]

If subject raising (A-movement) is motivated for Case reasons, the facts of the nominative and the *kara*-marked subjects are naturally expected. The nominative subject moves to TP to receive nominative Case from T. The *kara*-subject does not undergo DP-movement because no Case needs to be assigned by T.

There arises a puzzle in the dative subject construction, however. Under the Case assignment account, since T assigns nominative Case to its specifier position, a nominative object rather than a dative subject is expected to undergo movement to TP in the dative-subject construction. Nevertheless, it is the dative subject that undergoes movement in this construction. The dative-subject construction poses a problem for the theory of Case-driven DP-movement because it looks as if nominative Case, which T assigns to an argument, is not assigned to the argument undergoing DP-movement. The dilemma is that the actual case marking on the moved argument does not match with the case marking expected by the theory of Case assignment. A classic solution to this problem is simply to assume that morphological case marking does not necessarily reflect the type of Case. In the dative subject construction, the subject gets nominative Case from T, but still, it is marked with dative case (for some mysterious reason); accordingly, the traditional Case theory has a distinction between **structural Case** and **morphological case**.

The classic solution to this case puzzle is hardly explanatory, and it appears that there is no easy way out of this dilemma unless the trigger of subject raising is dissociated from Case. In recent years, a different perspective for Case licensing has been introduced, which amounts to saying that the T head is responsible for licensing nominative Case on an argument, but that the licensing can be accomplished by agreement (**Agree**), which can be implemented with a long distance relation. Under this Agree system, subject raising (A-movement) to TP does not depend on Case, but an **EPP feature** on T, which is an abstract grammatical feature, motivates subject raising to TP, instead. (Note that EPP is originally an abbreviation of Extended Projection Principle, which requires that a clause has a subject).

Under the Agree account, the nominative-subject construction has a tense (T) head equipped with the EPP feature [EPP]. (In Japanese, the EPP feature is assigned to a head that participates in nominative Case licensing.) In the nominative subject construction, the T head first licenses nominative Case on the VP-internal subject by Agree (indicated by the dotted double arrow), and then this subject is **attracted** to TP by the EPP feature, as illustrated in (9a).

(9)   a. [$_{TP}$ SUBJ-NOM [$_{VP}$ ~~SUBJ-NOM~~   V] T [EPP]]

      b. [$_{TP}$ [$_{VP}$ SUBJ-ABL   V] T]

The EPP feature is deleted once DP-movement is invoked, and this deletion is necessary for the derivation to be legitimate. The ablative subject construction where the subject is marked with *kara*, on the other hand, has a T head that does not have [EPP], so the subject does not move, as illustrated in (9b). (In (9b), no nominative argument appears, which means that T does not license nominative Case.)

   In the dative subject construction, T licenses nominative Case on the object via Agree, and hence it is marked with nominative case. It is often suggested that dative case *ni* is **inherent Case**, which is linked to a particular θ-role ("experiencer" or "goal"), and that the dative subject (bearing inherent Case) can stand on its own without Agreeing with T or V for Case licensing.

(10)   [$_{TP}$ SUBJ-DAT [$_{VP}$ ~~SUBJ-DAT~~   OBJ-NOM V] T[EPP]]

Since T carries [EPP], it attracts an argument from within VP. In (10), the dative subject appears in a higher structural position than the nominative object, so that the dative subject is attracted to TP.

   From the perspective of Agree, the cause of DP-movement comes from a grammatical factor other than Case, i.e. the EPP feature is responsible for the movement, and T Case-licenses a nominative argument via long distance Agree. The same situation frequently arises, in particular, in languages possessing **quirky subject constructions**. One obvious advantage of this analysis is that it can provide a natural account for the fact that the moved argument does not have to bear nominative case marking.

20.2 Exceptional Case Marking

The analysis taking Agree to be responsible for Case licensing can naturally be extended to the **Exceptional Case Marking (ECM) construction** in (11), where the embedded subject is marked with accusative case, which is made available by (upper) predicates like *iu* 'say' and *omou* 'think'.

(11) Ken-ga   [Mari-o   kawai-i   to]   omot-ta.
      Ken-NOM   Mari-ACC   cute-PRS   that   think-PST
      'Ken thought Mary to be cute.'

The embedded subject in (11) is called an **ECM subject** because accusative case marking is not possible with subjects appearing in simple clauses. The sentence is a little, though not severely, degraded if the embedded predicate *kawaii* is changed to the past form *kawaikat-ta*.

(12) ??Ken-ga   [Mari-o   kawaikat-ta   to]   omot-ta.
      Ken-NOM   Mari-ACC   cute-PST   that   think-PST
      'Ken thought that Mary was cute.'

This fact suggests that in the ECM construction, the embedded predicate is not finite, but behaves like an infinitive verb. Consequently, in (11), the T in the subordinate clause does not license Case for the embedded subject, but the matrix predicate licenses the accusative Case on the embedded subject. This can be verified by the fact that it can be promoted to a subject when passivization applies to the matrix predicate, as in (13).

(13) Mari-ga   minna-ni   [kawai-i   to]   omow-are-te   i-ta.
      Mari-NOM   all-by   pretty-PRS   that   think-PASS-GER be-PST
      'Mari was thought to be pretty by everyone.'

In the ECM construction in (11), the accusative case marking on the embedded subject is naturally expected because the verb *omou* 'think' can take an accusative object, as exemplified in (14).

(14) Ken-wa   Mari-no   koto-o   omowa-nakat-ta.
      Ken-TOP   Mari-GEN   fact-ACC   think-NEG-PST
      'Ken did not think about Mari.'

The verb *omou* 'think' does not take an animate object, for **Mari-o omou* 'think Mari' is not acceptable (unless the verb is used in another sense meaning 'love'). This shows that the ECM subject cannot be an argument of the matrix verb *omou*, although it is Case-licensed by this verb.

Now, for the purpose of pinpointing where the ECM subject is located, observe that when *soo* replacement applies to the embedded clause, the embedded subject cannot be overtly realized, as in (15).

(15) a. Ken-ga   [Mari-o   kawai-i   to]   it-ta.
          Ken-NOM   Mari-ACC   cute-PRS   that   say-PST
          'Ken said Mari was cute.
      b. Eri-mo   (*Mari-o)   soo   it-ta.
          Eri-also   Mari-ACC   so   say-PST
          'Eri also said (Mari) so.'

When (15a) is a linguistic antecedent for (15b), the pronominal *soo* in (15b) is
taken to replace the underlined constituent, i.e. the embedded clause, in (15a).
Thus, the accusative subject, which is included in the embedded clause, cannot
be realized. Note that *soo* does not replace an element located outside a complement clause, as confirmed by (16).

(16) a. Ken-ga   Mari-ni   [kaer-u   to]   it-ta.
          Ken-NOM   Mari-DAT   return-PRS   that   say-PST
          'Ken told Mari to go home.'
      b. Eri-mo   Mari-ni   soo   it-ta.
          Eri-also   Mari-DAT   so   say-PST
          'Eri also told Mari so.'

In (16), *Mari-ni* is an argument of the verb *iu* 'say'. Since *Mari-ni* resides in the
main clause, it can be realized even if *soo* replaces the embedded clause in (16a).
A comparison of the data in (15) and (16) shows that the ECM subject resides
in the embedded clause.

   Under the Case-assignment account, transitive V assigns accusative Case to
an argument in its object position. If this is the only possibility allowed for
accusative Case assignment, the ECM subject needs to move into the object
position of the matrix verb to receive accusative Case.

(17) *[$_{TP}$ ... [$_{VP}$ SUBJ-ACC [$_{CP}$ ~~SUBJ-ACC~~ kawai-i to] it $_{[ACC]}$] -ta]

Nevertheless, the ECM construction does not invoke this DP-movement, as
seen from the facts of *soo* replacement discussed above. If a Case-assignment
account is to be maintained, it is necessary to say that accusative Case may be
assigned to a position other than the object position. Under the theory of Agree,
by contrast, long distance Case licensing is in principle possible, and thus, we
can state that the ECM subject is Case-licensed by long distance Agree with the
matrix verb, as in (18).

(18)   [$_{TP}$ ... [$_{VP}$ [$_{CP}$ SUBJ-ACC   kawai-i   to] it] -ta]

The ECM construction provides another case to lend support to the analysis utilizing (long distance) Agree for Case licensing on arguments.

For Further Research

(A-1) If the theory of Agree is adopted (see Chomsky (1995, 2000, 2001, 2004, 2008)), Case can no longer motivate the raising of subjects into TP. Instead, [EPP] is posited for a feature that triggers subject raising. An EPP analysis was initially motivated by the observation that in English, a finite clause needs a subject, and this requirement is incorporated into the Projection Principle as an extended part, and thus called "Extended Projection Principle" (Chomsky (1981)). (The Projection Principle states that representations at each level (D-, S-, and LF-structure) are projected from the lexicon.) The EPP was later extended to the requirement that T (as well as some other categories) needs a specifier (Chomsky (2000)).

(A-2) Inherent Case is associated with a particular θ-role, as opposed to structural Case, and genitive and dative Cases are representative of inherent Case (Chomsky (1986)).

(A-3) The nominative-case constraint is often considered a general case-marking constraint in Japanese. But it is also known (see Shibatani (1978), Kishimoto (2016)) that there are a number of exceptions to this rule. One such context is found in the ablative (or *kara*-marked) subject construction, discussed in this chapter. This construction, which can be derived by substituting ablative *kara* for nominative case on an agentive-source subject, is acceptable even if it does not include a nominative argument. Another exception is found in a sentence like (i).

(i)   Naze   kare-ni-wa   oyog-e-te   watasi-ni-wa
       why   he-DAT-TOP   swim-POTEN-GER   I-DAT-TOP
       oyog-e-na-i   no?
       swim-POTEN-NEG-PRS   Q
       'Why it is the case that he can swim but I cannot?'

Example (i) with the intransitive potential predicate *oyogeru* 'can swim' has two instances of dative arguments, but does not include any nominative arguments. Although the nominative-case constraint generally applies to intransitive clauses as well, (i) is acceptable when the dative arguments receive a contrastive interpretation.

(B-1) Besides the ECM construction, Japanese has another ECM-like construction in which the accusative argument occurs with *koto* 'fact', and in this construction, *soo* replacement may apply to the embedded clause while leaving the accusative argument intact, as in (iib).

(ii) a. Ken-ga   Mari-no   koto-o   kawai-i   to   it-ta.
          Ken-NOM   Mari-GEN   fact-ACC   cute-PRS   that   say-PST
          'Ken said that Mary was cute.'
      b. Eri-mo   Mari-no   koto-o   *soo*   it-ta.
          Eri-also   Mari-GEN   fact-ACC   so   say-PST
          'Eri as well said so about Mari.'

The fact suggests that (iia) is a "major object" construction, where the accusative argument appears in the matrix clause, selected by the matrix verb. If so, this construction is the Japanese counterpart of a sentence like *John said of Mary that she is smart*. What structure can be assigned to (iia)?

(B-2) *Tough*-constructions headed by *tough*-adjectives like *nikui* 'difficult' and *yasui* 'easy' can have two case-marking patterns, as in (iii).

(iii) a. Ken-ga   okane-o   nakusi-yasu-i.
          Ken-NOM   money-ACC   lose-easy-PRS
          'Ken easily loses his money.'
      b. Ken-ni-wa   kono   zisyo-ga   tukai-yasu-i.
          Ken-DAT-TOP   this   dictionary-NOM   use-easy-PRS
          'It is easy for Ken to use this dictionary.'

A contrast in acceptability shows up between the two kinds of *tough*-constructions when the subjects are inanimate.

(iv) a. Konpyuutaa-ga   netu-o   moti-yasu-i.
          computer-NOM   heat-ACC   hold-easy-PRS
          'The computer easily gets hot.'
      b. *Konpyuutaa-ni-wa   netu-ga   moti-yasu-i.
          computer-DAT-TOP   heat-NOM   hold-easy-PRS
          'It is easy for the computer to get hot.'

The fact suggests that the *tough*-constructions make a distinction between raising and control. What constituent structure do they possess, then?

CHAPTER 21

Focusing on VP [D], [E]

21.1 Focusing in Pseudo-Cleft Constructions

Japanese has a number of complex-clause constructions. Among them, **pseudo-cleft constructions** show some interesting structural properties. They are formed by separating a focused constituent from the rest of a clause and placing it in a position to the right of the predicate. Some representative examples are given in (1).

(1) a. [Ken-ga   kai-ta]   no-wa   [sono   ronbun]   da.
       Ken-NOM   write-PST   that-TOP   that   paper   COP
       'What Ken wrote was that paper.'
    b. [Sono   ronbun-o   kai-ta]   no-wa   [Ken]   da.
       that   paper-ACC   write-PST that-TOP Ken   COP
       'The one who wrote this paper was Ken.'

In both examples in (1), the constituent that precedes *no-wa* constitutes a **presupposition clause**, which represents **old information**—the information which the hearer shares with the speaker. The constituent combined with copula *da* is the **focus**, which represents **new information**—the information new to the hearer. Even though the sentences in (1) have different focused constituents, they have the same logical meaning as (2).

(2) Ken-ga   sono   ronbun-o   kai-ta.
    Ken-NOM   that   paper-ACC   write-PST
    'Ken wrote that paper.'

In light of this fact, we can postulate that both sentences in (1) are derived from a sentence like (2) by applying a syntactic operation of **pseudo-clefting**.

In unmarked cases, a DP or a PP appears in focus position, but it is also possible to place VP in that position if it is followed by the noun *koto* 'that', as in (3a).

(3)　　a. [Ken-ga　　　si-ta]　　　no-wa　　[sono　　ronbun-o　　kaku]
　　　　　　Ken-NOM　　do-PST　　that-TOP　　that　　paper-ACC　　write
　　　　　　koto　　da.
　　　　　　that　　COP
　　　　　　'What Ken did was write that paper.'
　　　　b. *[Sono　　ronbun-o　　si-ta]　　no-wa　　[Ken-ga　　kaku]
　　　　　　that　　paper-ACC　　do-PST　　that-TOP　　Ken-NOM　　write
　　　　　　koto　　da.
　　　　　　that　　COP
　　　　　　(lit.) 'What did that paper was Ken wrote.'

In (3a), the subject appears in the presupposition clause, and a combined constituent of the object and the verb is placed in cleft focus position. (3a) is acceptable since the focused VP includes the verb and the object. By contrast, (3b), where the object is left in the presupposition clause instead of the subject, is an unacceptable pseudo-cleft construction. This suggests that a structure represented in (4) is derived by VP pseudo-clefting, as in(4).

(4)　　[[$_{TP}$ ...SUBJ.... [$_{VP}$　]....]] no wa [$_{VP}$ OBJ V] koto da.

The derivation of pseudo-cleft sentences presumably involves null operator movement in the antecedent clause (see Chapter 17), but for the present purposes, it is sufficient to identify the constituent placed in the focus position, abstracting away from irrelevant details. On the basis of the data in (3), we can state that when VP is placed in focus position, no constituent included inside the VP can be left behind in the presupposition clause.

　　When the pseudo-cleft construction has VP-focusing, the object, but not the subject, can appear in focus position. Note, however, that it is possible to place a locative adjunct either in the presupposition clause or in focus position.

(5)　　a. [Ken-ga　　　si-ta]　　　no-wa　　[kyoositu-de　hon-o　　yomu]
　　　　　　Ken-NOM　　do-PST　　that-TOP　　classroom-in　book-ACC　read
　　　　　　koto　　da.
　　　　　　that　　COP
　　　　　　'What Ken did was read books in the classroom.'

b. [Ken-ga   kyoositu-de   si-ta]   no-wa   [hon-o   yomu]
   Ken-NOM   classroom-in   do-PST   that-TOP   book-ACC   read
   koto   da.
   that   COP
   'What Ken did in the classroom was read books.'

What can this fact tell us about clause structure? Since the locative expression *kyoositu-de* is an adjunct modifying the verb, the constituent including the locative adjunct as well as the one excluding it must be VP. The adjunction operation of the locative PP *kyoositu-de* to VP therefore gives rise to the VP structure given in (6).

(6)

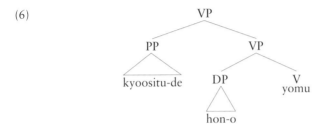

This means that when an adjunct is added to the maximal projection of its modifying element, two segments of the same category label are created. Given the VP-structure in (6), it is naturally expected that two different structures for the sentences in (5) will be derived via VP-clefting.

(7)   a.   b.

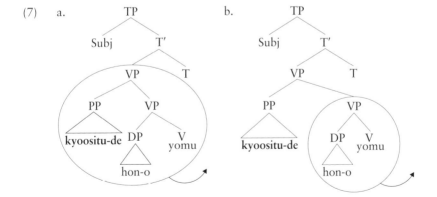

If the upper VP undergoes pseudo-clefting, as in (7a), the locative adjunct is placed in focus position. On the other hand, if the pseudo-clefting operation applies to the lower VP, as in (7b), the VP excluding the locative adjunct appears in focus position.

Let us next consider cases involving subject-oriented adverbs, such as *yoro-konde* 'willingly'. Subject-oriented adverbs, as their name suggests, serve as modifiers to subjects. In pseudo-cleft constructions with VP-focus, these adverbs can be placed either in the presupposition clause or in focus position.

(8) a. [Ken-ga   si-ta]   no-wa   [yorokonde   sigoto-o
          Ken-NOM   do-PST   that-TOP   willingly   task-ACC
          hikiukeru]   koto   da.
          undertake   that   COP
          'What Ken did was undertake a task willingly.'

     b. [Ken-ga   yorokonde   si-ta]   no-wa   [sigoto-o
          Ken-NOM   willingly   do-PST   that-TOP   task-ACC
          hikiukeru]   koto   da.
          undertake   that   COP
          'What Ken did willingly was undertake a task.'

The distribution of the subject-oriented adverb *yorokonde* suggests that it behaves as an adjunct adjoined to VP. The subject that the adverb modifies is overtly realized in the presupposition clause in (8b). Thus, the acceptability of (8b) is naturally expected. By contrast, in (8a), the adverb appears in focus position, even though the subject does not appear in focus position. However, given the VP-internal Subject Hypothesis, it comes as no surprise that (8a), where *yorokonde* appears in the focus position, is acceptable.

Specifically, if the subject first generated in VP is moved to TP, as dictated by the VP-Internal Subject Hypothesis, the adverb modifying the subject can be adjoined to VP, for it can modify a copy (or trace) left by movement in VP.

(9)

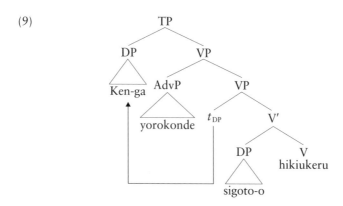

The adjunction of the adverb to VP creates the two layers of VP, either of which can be moved into the focus position. If the upper VP is moved, *yorokonde* appears in the focus position, but if the lower VP is moved, it is left in the antecedent clause.

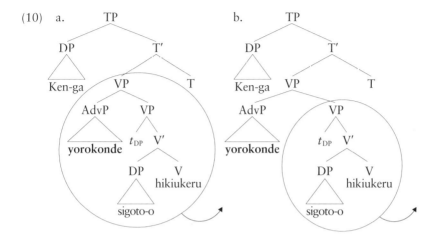

(10) a.

b.

The facts of the subject-oriented adverb in (8) show that VP contains a copy (or trace) of the subject, which provides us with another kind of evidence for the VP-Internal Subject Hypothesis in which subjects in TP originate from VP-internal position.

21.2 Split Verb Projection

Let us now turn to the discussion of how **secondary predicates** behave in pseudo-cleft constructions. Japanese has **depictive predicates**, which fall into the category of adjuncts. They are divided into two types according to whether they modify subjects or objects.

(11) a. Ken-ga   hadasi-de   booru-o   ket-ta.
        Ken-NOM   barefoot   ball-ACC   kick-PST
        'Ken kicked the ball barefoot.'
   b. Ken-ga   nama-de   sakana-o   tabe-ta.
        Ken-NOM   raw   fish-ACC   eat-PST
        'Ken ate fish raw.'

The depictive *hadasi-de* 'barefoot' is predicated of the subject in (11a), and hence is called a **subject-oriented depictive**. On the other hand, *nama-de* 'raw' in (11b) is predicated of the object, and thus, it is identified as an **object-ori-**

ented depictive.

In VP-focus pseudo-cleft constructions, these two types of depictive predicates behave differently. In the first place, the subject-oriented depictive can appear in both presupposition clause and focus component, as shown in (12).

(12) a. [Ken-ga   si-ta]   no-wa   [hadasi-de booru-o   keru]
           Ken-NOM do-PST   that-TOP barefoot   ball-ACC kick
           koto   da.
           that   COP
           'What Ken did was kick the ball barefoot.'
    b. [Ken-ga   hadasi-de si-ta]   no-wa   [booru-o keru]
           Ken-NOM barefoot do-PST   that-TOP ball-ACC kick
           koto   da.
           that   COP
           'What Ken did barefoot was kick the ball.'

The subject-oriented depictive *hadasi-de* modifies the subject, just like a subject-oriented adverb. On the other hand, an object-oriented depictive can be placed in focus position, but not in the antecedent clause, as shown in (13).

(13) a. [Ken-ga   si-ta]   no-wa   [nama-de sakana-o taberu]
           Ken-NOM do-PST   that-TOP raw   fish-ACC   eat
           koto   da.
           that   COP
           'What Ken did was eat fish raw.'
    b. *[Ken-ga   nama-de si-ta]   no-wa   [sakana-o taberu]
           Ken-NOM raw   do-PST   that-TOP fish-ACC   eat
           koto   da.
           that   COP
           'What Ken did raw was eat fish.'

As noted above, adjuncts are modifiers generated by adjunction to the maximal projections they modify, and thus, the facts about the two types of depictives suggest that a verb phrase includes two maximal projections. The subject-oriented depictive *hadasi-de* 'barefoot' is adjoined to VP, which contains the initial copy (or trace) of the subject, and thus, it is allowed to appear either in the antecedent clause or in focus position. On the other hand, the object-oriented depictive *nama-de* 'raw' can only appear in the focus position, indicating that another verbal projection must exist inside VP, to which *nama-de* is adjoined.

If, as the facts of depictive predicates suggest, two verbal projections are present in the verb phrase, it is necessary to assign some category labels to them. For ease of reference, we will put new category labels on the two verbal projections following the recent **Split vP Analysis**. According to this analysis, the upper verbal projection is labeled as vP, and the lower verbal projection, VP. (In this recent analysis, VP is relabeled as vP, which is a bit confusing, though.) Then, the verb phrase with two verbal projections has the structure in (14).

(14)

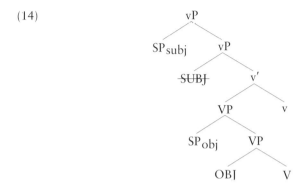

In (14), the subject-oriented depictive is adjoined to vP, forming two layers of vP, while the object-oriented depictive is adjoined to VP, creating two layers of VP. Under the Split vP Analysis, pseudo-clefting, which moves a verb phrase (in pre-theoretical terms), is seen as an operation affecting vP rather than VP.

The distribution of the two kinds of depictives observed in (12) and (13) naturally follows, given the layered structure in (14). The subject-oriented depictive appears in focus position when the upper vP is placed in the focus position, as illustrated in (15a).

(15) a.   b.

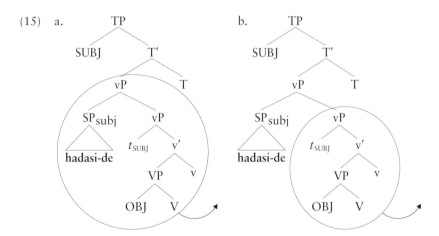

If the lower vP is placed in the focus position, the subject-oriented depictive remains in the antecedent clause, as shown in (15b). The object-oriented depictive *nama-de* 'raw' , which is adjoined to VP, behaves differently.

(16)

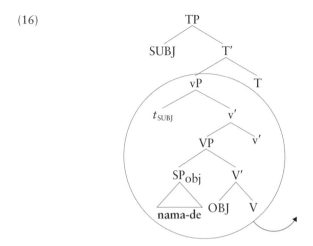

Since the pseudo-clefting operation at issue moves vP, but not VP, into its focus position, the object-oriented depictive can appear only in the focus position. Hence, the observed asymmetry is obtained between the two types of depictive predicates.

There is every reason to assume that a verb phrase (described in pre-theoretical terms) consists of the two projections of vP and VP. Firstly, the split-vP hypothesis is reasonable from a semantic point of view. Note that transitive verbs describe a complex event, consisting of two sub-events—a **causing event** (an action initiated by the agent) and a **caused event** (a change effected on the theme, caused by the agent). Since vP describes an agentive action, which is a causing event, the agentive adverb *yorokonde* 'willingly' can be assumed to involve adjunction to vP. On the other hand, an object-oriented depictive *nama-de* 'raw' describes the state of the caused event, so it is adjoined to the VP. Secondly, the morphological facts of Japanese verbs lend further support to the Split vP Analysis. In Japanese, consonant-stem and vowel-stem verb pairs, such as *kowasu* 'break (trans.)' and *kowareru* 'break (intr.)', can be segmented into two parts (excluding the tense): the base *kowa-* and the suffix *-s/-re*, which indicates the transitivity of verbs. It can be postulated here that the verb base occupies a position corresponding to V, and the transitivity indicator a position corresponding to v syntactically.

For Further Research

(A) The manner adverbs *teinei-ni* 'carefully' and *tate-ni* 'vertically' show divergent syntactic behaviors in vP pseudo-cleft constructions. *Teinei-ni* 'carefully' can appear in the presupposition clause as well as in focus position.

(i)   a. [Ken-ga   si-ta]   no-wa   [teinei-ni   sen-o   hiku]
            Ken-NOM do-PST that-TOP carefully line-ACC draw
            koto   da.
            that   COP
            'What Ken did was draw a line carefully.'
      b. [Ken-ga   teinei-ni   si-ta]   no-wa   [sen-o   hiku] koto da.
            Ken-NOM carefully do-PST that-TOP line-ACC draw that COP
            'What Ken did carefully was draw a line.'

The adverb *tate-ni* 'vertically' can appear in focus position but is not allowed to appear in the presupposition clause.

(ii)   a. [Ken-ga   si-ta]   no-wa   [tate-ni   sen-o   hiku]
            Ken-NOM do-PST that -TOP vertically line-ACC draw
            koto   da.
            that   COP
            'What Ken did was draw a line vertically.'
      b. *[Ken-ga   tate-ni   si-ta]   no-wa   [sen-o   hiku]
            Ken-NOM vertically do-PST that-TOP line-ACC draw
            koto   da.
            that   COP
            'What Ken did vertically was draw a line.'

The facts suggest that the adverb *teinei-ni* involves adjunction to vP, while *tate-ni* involves adjunction to VP. *Teinei-ni* appears in the antecedent clause if the lower vP is moved into a focus position, but it appears in focus position if the upper vP is moved. *Tate-ni* can appear only in focus position because it appears below vP.

(B) Adverbs can be divided into several types, according to where they are located in clause structure. A manner adverb like *naname-ni* 'diagonally' is consonant with a motion verb like *hasiru* 'run'.

(iii)   Eri-ga   naname-ni   hasit-ta.
       Eri-NOM   diagonally   run-PST
      'Eri ran diagonally.'

The adverb *naname-ni* can appear in the focus position, but not in the antecedent clause in a pseudo-cleft construction which places vP in focus position.

(iv)   a. [Eri-ga   si-ta]   no-wa   [naname-ni hasiru] koto da.
          Eri-NOM do-PST   that-TOP diagonally run   that   COP
          'What Eri did was run diagonally.'
    b. *[Eri-ga   naname-ni   si-ta]   no-wa   [hasiru] koto da.
          Eri-NOM diagonally do-PST   that-TOP run   that   COP
          'What Eri did diagonally was run.'

Note that *hasiru* is an unergative verb, which selects an external argument (i.e. agent). What implication does the distribution of the manner adverb have on the structure of an intransitive clause with the unergative verb? What kind of generalization can be drawn from this observation?

Bibliography

Abney, Steven (1987). *The English Noun Phrase and Its Sentential Aspect.* Doctoral dissertation, MIT.

Baker, Mark (1988). *Incorporation: A Theory of Grammatical Function Changing.* Chicago: University of Chicago Press.

Baker, Mark (1997). Thematic roles and syntactic structure. In Liliane Haegeman, (ed.), *Elements of Grammar. Handbook of Generative Syntax*, 73–137. Dordrecht: Kluwer.

Baker, Mark, Kyle Johnson, and Ian Roberts (1989). Passive arguments raised. *Linguistic Inquiry* 20, 219–251.

Bobaljik, Jonathan (1994). What does adjacency do? In Heidi Harley and Colin Philips (eds.), *The Morphology-Syntax Connection, MIT Working Papers in Linguistics* 22, 1–32.

Burzio, Luigi (1986). *Italian Syntax: A Government-Binding Approach.* Dordrecht: Reidel.

Carnie, Andrew (2007). *Syntax: A Generative Introduction.* 2nd ed. Oxford: Blackwell.

Chomsky, Noam (1981). *Lectures on Government and Binding.* Dordrecht: Foris.

Chomsky, Noam (1982). *Some Concepts and Consequences of the Theory of Government and Binding.* Cambridge, MA: MIT Press.

Chomsky, Noam (1986). *Knowledge of Language.* New York: Praeger.

Chomsky, Noam (1995). *The Minimalist Program.* Cambridge, MA: MIT Press.

Chomsky, Noam (2000). Minimalist inquiries: The framework. In Roger Martin, David Michaels, and Juan Uriagereka (eds.), *Step by Step: Essays on Minimalist Syntax in Honor of Howard Lasnik*, 89–155.Cambridge, MA: MIT Press.

Chomsky, Noam (2001). Derivation by phase. In Michael Kenstowicz (ed.), *Ken Hale: A Life in Language*, 1–52. Cambridge, MA: MIT Press.

Chomsky, Noam (2004). Beyond explanatory adequacy. In Adriana Belletti (ed.), *Structures and Beyond: The Cartography of Syntactic Structures: Volume 3*, 104–131. Oxford: Oxford University Press.

Chomsky, Noam (2008). On phases. In Robert Freidin, Carlos P. Otero, and Maria Luisa Zubizarreta (eds.), *Foundational Issues in Linguistic Theory: Essays in Honor of Jean-Roger Vergnaud*, 133–166. Cambridge, MA: MIT Press.

Chomsky, Noam (2013). Problems of projection. *Lingua* 130, 33–49.

Chomsky, Noam (2015). Problems of projection: Extensions. In Elisa Di Domenico, Cornelia Hamann and Simona Matteini (eds.), *Structures, Strategies and Beyond: Studies in Honor of Adriana Belletti*, 3–16. Amsterdam: John Benjamins.

Comrie, Bernard (1989). *Language Universals and Linguistic Universals.* Chicago: University of Chicago Press.

Emonds, Joseph (1976). *A Transformational Approach to English Syntax: Root, Structure-Preserving, and Local Transformations.* New York: Academic Press.

216

Fillmore, Charles (1968). The case for case. In Emmon Bach and Robert T. Harms (eds.), *Universals in Linguistic Theory*, 1–88. New York: Holt, Rinehart, and Winston.

Fukui, Naoki (1995). *Theory of Projection in Syntax*. Stanford: CSLI and Tokyo: Kurosio Publishers.

Haig, John (1996). Subjacency and Japanese grammar: A functional account. *Studies in Language* 201, 53–92.

Harada, S. I. (1976). Honorifics. In Masayoshi Shibatani (ed.), *Syntax and Semantics 5: Japanese Generative Grammar*, 499–561. New York: Academic Press.

Hasegawa, Nobuko (2006). Honorifics. In Martin Everaert and Henk van Riemsdijk (eds.), *The Blackwell Companion to Syntax* 2, 493–543. Oxford: Blackwell.

Himeno, Masako (1999). *Fukugo Dōshi no Kōzō to Imi Yōhō* [Structures, Semantics and Usage of Compound Verbs]. Tokyo: Hituzi Syobo.

Hiraiwa, Ken (2005). *Dimensions of Symmetry in Syntax: Agreement and Clausal Architecture*. Doctoral dissertation, MIT.

Hoshi, Hiroto (1994). Theta-role assignment, passivization, and excorporation. *Journal of East Asian Linguistics* 3, 147–148.

Hoshi, Hiroto (1999). Passives. In Natsuko Tsujimura (ed.), *The Handbook of Japanese Linguistics*, 191–235. Malden, MA: Blackwell.

Howard, Irwin and Agnes Niyekawa-Howard (1976). Passivization. In Masayoshi Shibatani (ed.), *Syntax and Semantics 5: Japanese Generative Grammar*, 201–237. New York: Academic Press.

Inoue, Kazuko (1976). *Henkei Bunpō to Nihongo* [Transformational Grammar and Japanese]. Tokyo: Taishukan.

Inoue, Kazuko (1978). 'Tough sentences' in Japanese. In John Hinds and Irwin Howard (eds.), *Problems in Japanese Syntax and Semantics*, 122–154. Tokyo: Kaitakusha.

Inoue, Kazuko (1998). Sentences without nominative subjects in Japanese. *Grant-in-Aid for COE Research Report (2A): Researching and Verifying an Advanced Theory of Human Language*, 1–34. Kanda University of International Studies.

Ishizuka, Tomoko (2012). *The Passive in Japanese: A Cartographic Minimalist Approach*. Philadelphia: John Benjamins.

Jackendoff, Ray (1972). *Semantic Interpretation in Generative Grammar*. Cambridge, MA: MIT Press.

Jackendoff, Ray (1990). *Semantic Structures*. Cambridge, MA: MIT Press.

Kageyama, Taro (1993). *Bunpō to Gokeisei* [Grammar and Word Formation]. Tokyo: Hituzi Syobo.

Kageyama, Taro (1996). *Dōshi Imiron* [Verb Semantics]. Tokyo: Kurosio Publishers.

Kayne, Richard (1984). *Connectedness and Binary Branching*. Dordrecht: Foris.

Kishimoto (2001a). Binding of indeterminate pronouns and clause structure in Japanese. *Linguistic Inquiry* 32, 597–633.

Kishimoto, Hideki (2001b). The role of lexical meanings in argument encoding: Double object verbs in Japanese. *Gengo Kenkyu* 120, 35–65.

Kishimoto, Hideki (2005). *Tōgo Kōzō to Bunpō Kankei* [Syntactic Structures and Grammatical Relations]. Tokyo: Kurosio Publishers.

Kishimoto, Hideki (2006). Japanese syntactic nominalization and VP-internal syntax. *Lingua* 116, 771–810.

Kishimoto, Hideki (2007). Negative scope and head raising in Japanese. *Lingua* 117, 247–288.

Kishimoto, Hideki (2008). On the variability of negative scope in Japanese. *Journal of Linguistics* 44, 379–435.

Kishimoto, Hideki (2009). Topic prominency in Japanese. *The Linguistic Review* 26, 465–513.

Kishimoto, Hideki (2010). Subjects and constituent structure in Japanese. *Linguistics* 48, 629–670.

Kishimoto, Hideki (2012). Subject honorification and the position of subjects in Japanese. *Journal of East Asian Linguistics* 21, 1–41.

Kishimoto, Hideki (2013). Covert possessor raising in Japanese. *Natural Language & Linguistic Theory* 31, 161–205.

Kishimoto, Hideki (2014). Dative/genitive subjects in Japanese: A comparative perspective. In Mamoru Saito (ed.), *Japanese Syntax in Comparative Perspective*, 228–274. New York: Oxford University Press.

Kishimoto, Hideki (2016). Valency and case alternations in Japanese. In Taro Kageyama and Wesley Jacobsen (eds.), *Transitivity and Valency Alternation: Studies on Japanese and Beyond*, 125–154. Berlin: De Gruyter Mouton.

Kishimoto, Hideki, and Geert Booij (2014). Complex negative adjectives in Japanese: The relation between syntactic and morphological constructions. *Word Structure* 7, 55–87.

Kishimoto, Hideki, Taro Kageyama, and Kan Sasaki (2015). Valency classes in Japanese. In Bernard Comrie and Andrej Malchukov (eds.), *Valency Classes: A Comparative Handbook, Volume 1: Introducing the Framework, and Case Studies from Africa and Eurasia*, 765–805. Berlin: De Gruyter Mouton.

Kishimoto, Hideki, and Satoshi Uehara (2016). Lexical categories. In Taro Kageyama and Hideki Kishimoto (eds.), *The Mouton Handbook of Japanese Lexicon and Word Formation*, 51–92. Berlin: De Gruyter Mouton

Kitagawa, Yoshihisa (1986). *Subjects in Japanese and English*. Doctoral dissertation, University of Massachusetts Amherst.

Kitahara, Yasuo (1981). *Nihongo no Bunpō* [Japanese Grammar]. Tokyo: Chūōkōron-sha.

Koizumi, Masatoshi (1999). *Phrase Structure in Minimalist Syntax*. Tokyo: Hituzi Syobo.

Koizumi, Masatoshi (2008). Nominative object. In Shigeru Miyagawa and Mamoru Saito (eds.), *The Oxford Handbook of Japanese Linguistics*, 141–164. New York: Oxford University Press.

Kuno, Susumu (1973a). *The Structure of the Japanese Language*. Cambridge, MA: MIT Press.

Kuno, Susumu (1973b). *Nihon Bunpō Kenkyū* [A Study of Japanese Grammar]. To-kyo: Taishukan.

Kuno, Susumu (1976). Subject raising. In Masayoshi Shibatani (ed.), *Syntax and Semantics 5: Japanese Generative Grammar*, 17–49. New York: Academic Press.

Kuno, Susumu (1978). *Shin Nihon Bunpō Kenkyū* [A New Study of Japanese Grammar]. Tokyo: Taishukan.

Kuroda, S.-Y. (1965). *Generative Grammatical Studies in the Japanese Language*. Doctoral dissertation, MIT.

Kuroda, S.-Y. (1978). Case-marking, canonical sentence patterns and counter Equi in Japanese (A preliminary survey). In John Hinds and Irwin Howard (eds.), *Problems in Japanese Syntax and Semantics*, 30–51. Tokyo: Kaitakusha.

Kuroda, S.-Y. (1988). Whether we agree or not: A comparative syntax of English and Japanese. In William Poser (ed.), *Papers from the Second International Workshop on Japanese Linguistics*, 103–43. Stanford: CSLI.

Kuroda, S.-Y. (1992). *Japanese Syntax and Semantics: Collected Papers*. Dordrecht: Kluwer.

Levin, Beth (1993). *English Verb Classes and Alternations*. Chicago: University of Chicago Press.

Levin, Beth, and Malka Rappaport Hovav (1995). *Unaccusativity: At the Syntax–Lexical Semantics Interface*. Cambridge, MA: MIT Press.

Levin, Beth, and Malka Rappaport Hovav (2005). *Argument Realization*. Cambridge: Cambridge University Press.

Martin, Samuel E. (1962). *Essential Japanese: An Introduction to the Standard Colloquial Japanese*. Tokyo: Charles E. Tuttle.

Martin, Samuel E. (1975). *A Reference Grammar of Japanese*. New Haven: Yale University Press.

Masuoka, Takashi (1987). *Meidai-no Bunpō: Nihongo Bunpō Josetsu* [The Grammar of Proposition: Prolegomena to Japanese Grammar]. Tokyo: Kurosio Publishers.

Masukoka, Takashi (2000). *Nihongo Bunpō-no Shosō* [Aspects of Japanese Grammar]. Tokyo: Kurosio Publishers.

Matsumoto, Yo (1996). *Complex Predicates in Japanese: A Syntactic and Semantic Study of the Notion 'Word'*. Stanford: CSLI and Tokyo: Kurosio Publishers.

Mikami, Akira (1953). *Gendai Gohō Josetsu* [Prolegomena to Modern Japanese Grammar]. Tokyo: Tōe Shoin.

Miyagawa, Shigeru (1989a). Light verbs and the ergative hypothesis. *Linguistic Inquiry* 20, 659–668.

Miyagawa, Shigeru (1989b). *Syntax and Semantics 22: Structure and Case Marking in Japanese*. San Diego, CA: Academic Press.

Nakau, Minoru (1973). *Sentential Complementation in Japanese*. Tokyo: Kaitakusha.

Newmeyer, Frederick (1999). *Language Form and Language Function*. Cambridge, MA: MIT Press.

Nishigauchi, Taisuke (1990). *Quantification in the Theory of Grammar*. Dordrecht:

Kluwer.

Nishigauchi, Taisuke (1992). Syntax of reciprocals in Japanese. *Journal of East Asian Linguistics* 1, 157–196.

Nitta, Yoshio (1997). *Nihongo Bunpō Kenkyū Josetsu* [Prolegomena to the Study of Japanese Grammar]. Tokyo: Kurosio Publishers.

Perlmutter, David (1978). Impersonal passives and the unaccusative hypothesis. *BLS* 4, 157–189.

Pinker, Steven (1989). *Learnability and Cognition: The Acquisition of Argument Structure*. Cambridge, MA: MIT Press.

Pinker, Steven (1994). *The Language Instinct: How the Mind Creates the Langugage*. New York: William Morrow and Co.

Radford, Andrew (1988). *Transformational Grammar: A First Course*. Cambridge: Cambridge University Press.

Radford, Andrew (1997). *Syntactic Theory and the Structure of English: A Minimalist Approach*. Cambridge: Cambridge University Press.

Radford, Andrew (2009). *Analyzing English Sentences: A Minimalist Approach*. Cambridge: Cambridge University Press.

Saito, Mamoru (1985). *Some Asymmetries in Japanese and Their Theoretical Implications*. Doctoral dissertation, MIT.

Saito, Mamoru, and Hiroto Hoshi (2000). Japanese light verb constructions and the minimalist program. In Roger Martin, David Michaels and Juan Uriagereka (eds.), *Step by Step: Essays on Minimalist Syntax in Honor of Howard Lasnik*, 261–295. Cambridge, MA: MIT Press.

Shibatani, Masayoshi (1976). Causativization. In Masayoshi Shibatani (ed.), *Syntax and Semantics 5: Japanese Generative Grammar*, 239–294. New York: Academic Press.

Shibatani, Masayoshi (1978). *Nihongo-no Bunseki* [An Analysis of Japanese]. Tokyo: Taishukan.

Shibatani, Masayoshi (1990). *The Languages of Japan*. Cambridge: Cambridge University Press.

Simpson, Jane (1983). Resultatives. In Lori Levin, Malka Rappaport, and Annie Zaenen (eds.), *Papers in Lexical Functional Grammar*, 143–157. Indiana University Linguistics Club, Bloomington.

Stowell, Timothy (1981). *Origins of Phrase Structure*. Doctoral dissertation, MIT.

Sugioka, Yoko (1986). *Interaction of Derivational Morphology and Syntax in Japanese and English*. New York: Garland.

Tada, Hiroaki (1992). Nominative objects in Japanese. *Journal of Japanese Linguistics* 14, 91–108.

Takezawa, Koichi (1987). *A Configurational Approach to Case Marking in Japanese*. Doctoral dissertation, University of Washington.

Takezawa, Koichi (1991). Judōbun, nookakubun, bunrifukanōkōbun-to 'te iru'-no kaishaku [Passive sentences, ergative sentences, inalienable possession constructions, and the interpretations of 'te iru']. In Yoshio Nitta (ed.) *Nihongo-no Voisu-*

to Tadōsei [Voice and Transitivity in Japanese], 59–81. Tokyo, Kurosio Publishers.

Takezawa, Koichi, and John Whitman (1998). *Kaku-to Gojun-to Tōgo Kōzō* [Case, Word Order, and Syntactic Structures]. Tokyo: Kenkyūsha.

Takubo, Yukinori (2010). *Nihongo-no Kōzō* [The Structure of Japanese]. Tokyo: Kurosio Publishers.

Tenny, Carol (1994). *Aspectual Roles and the Syntax-Semantics Interface.* Dordrecht: Kluwer.

Teramura, Hideo (1984). *Nihongo-no Shintakusu-to Imi II* [Syntax and Meaning of Japanese II]. Tokyo: Kurosio Publishers.

Tsujimura, Natsuko (1990). Ergativity of nouns and case assignment. *Linguistic Inquiry* 21, 277–287.

Tsujimura, Natsuko (1996). *An Introduction to Japanese Linguistics.* Cambridge, MA: Blackwell.

Van Valin, Robert D. and Randy J. LaPolla (1997). *Syntax: Structure, Meaning and Function.* Cambridge: Cambridge University Press.

Watanabe, Minoru (1971). *Kokugo Kōbun Ron* [On Japanese grammatical constructions]. Tokyo: Hanawa Shobō.

Watanabe, Akira (2006). Functional projections of nominals in Japanese. *Natural Language & Linguistic Theory* 24, 24–306.

Yumoto, Yoko (2005). *Fukugō Dōshi Hasei Dōshi-no Imi-to Tōgo* [The Meaning and the Syntax of Compound and Derivational Verbs]. Tokyo: Hituzi Syobo.

Index

岸本秀樹（きしもと ひでき）

略歴

神戸大学人文学研究科教授
1991年、神戸大学大学院
文化学研究科博士課程修了（学術博士）

Hideki Kishimoto is Professor of
Linguistics at Kobe University,
specializing in lexical semantics,
morphology, and syntax. He is
the author of *Tōgokōzō to Bunpō-Kankei*
[Syntactic Structures and Grammatical
Relations] (Kurosio Publishers, 2005).
He is co-editor of *Handbook of Japanese
Lexicon and Word Formation* (with Taro
Kageyama, De Gruyter Mouton, 2016)
and *Topics in Asian Linguistics* (with
Kunio Nishiyama and Edith Aldridge,
John Benjamins, 2018). He contributed
to *The Oxford Handbook of Japanese
Linguistics* (Oxford University Press,
2008), *Handbook of Japanese Syntax*
(De Gruyter Mouton, 2017), and
*The Cambridge Handbook of Japanese
Linguistics* (Cambridge University
Press, 2018).

Analyzing Japanese Syntax
A Generative Perspective

発行　2020年10月12日 初版1刷
定価　2600円＋税
著者　Ⓒ岸本秀樹
発行者　松本功
ブックデザイン　白井敬尚形成事務所
印刷・製本所　株式会社 ディグ
発行所　株式会社 ひつじ書房
〒112-0011 東京都文京区
千石2-1-2 大和ビル2F
Tel: 03-5319-4916
Fax: 03-5319-4917
郵便振替00120-8-142852
toiawase@hituzi.co.jp
http://www.hituzi.co.jp/
ISBN978-4-89476-988-5